ALWAYS WELCOME

DISCLAIMER: This is a memoir, and, as such, events are presented from the author's point of view. All recollections herein are solely the opinions and impressions of the author.

Copyright © 2018 Welcome W. Wilson Sr.

No part of this book may be reproduced in any form or by any electronic or mechanical means, including information storage and retrieval devices or systems, without prior written permission from the publisher, except that brief passages may be quoted for reviews.

ISBN: 9781793150745

ALWAYS WELCOME

*9 Decades of Great Friends,
Great Times & (Mostly) Great Deals
As a Real Estate Investor*

WELCOME W. WILSON, S R.

My beautiful wife, Joanne Guest Wilson, and I
have been married for over sixty-eight years.
We have been blessed with five remarkable children.
Their support and dedication to the family
has always been extremely strong. I dedicate this book to them.

Joanne Wilson Castleberry is the youngest. A woman of great faith, Joanne is used to getting her way in life by praying for it. It works. Joanne does a tremendous job as a teacher and contributor with her wonderful husband, Howard Castleberry, the rector of Christ Episcopal Church in Nacogdoches, Texas. Joanne graduated from the University of Houston in the Hotel and Restaurant Management school. She and Howard have four fantastic children who accompany their parents on many mission trips to Tanzania, Kenya and Jordan.

Craig Guest Wilson is the chief operating officer of our real estate development company, the Welcome Group. Craig has the wisdom of his godfather, Jack Valenti, who was president of the Motion Picture Association of America for almost forty years. He went to the University of Texas and was president of the DKE Fraternity. Among Craig's many responsibilities are running the Triple W Ranch and looking after four million square feet of industrial facilities that we own. His wife, Lisa Lee Wilson, does a great amount of charitable work in the community. Craig and Lisa have four beautiful daughters and several grandchildren.

Pam Francis Wilson, our middle child, is one of the most creative people I have ever known. She earned her degree in fine arts from the University of Texas, and has become a renowned commercial, editorial, and advertising photographer. Her images regularly appear in *People, Life, Forbes, and Business Week* magazines, along with other notable periodicals, and her picture of Selena was selected for the cover of Time magazine. Her photos have been on the cover of Texas Monthly twice. Pam's loves for animals is outstanding and she has raised many contributions for the SPCA.

Cindi Proler Ray received her cum laude degree from the University of Houston and has contributed greatly with her work on the Baylor College of Medicine Partnership Board and many other charitable institutions. I have had the honor officiating at the marriage of all three of her sons, along with marrying Cindi to Sam Ray at the Museum of Natural Science, Cindi's favorite place. Sam Ray was Chairman of HLSR, and stays involved with the Houston Police Foundation. Cindi has always particularly looked after me and is truly concerned about my health. She has been at my side on every important occasion.

Welcome Wade Wilson, Jr., is our oldest. CEO of the Welcome Group, he is without question the best deal guy whom I have ever known. Welcome seldom misses. Without a doubt, he has inherited what I call "the touch" the ability to make a deal that I first saw in my father. Welcome has contributed greatly to the Houston Food Bank and the Kinkaid School and is currently on the Board of Directors and Chairman of the management committee of the Alamo. He is also Vice Chairman of the University of Houston Board of Regents. His wife, Anita Ford Wilson, has been involved in many charities like the Alzheimer's Association, and they have five wonderful children.

These fine men and women, their children
and grandchildren, are what everything that follows was for.
The strength of being a Wilson has always
come from putting family first.

CONTENTS

Foreword — 9
   Rick Perry, US Secretary of Energy, former Governor of Texas — 9

Welcome to My World — 11
   1 — 15

Growing Up In The Depression And WWII — 15
   Corpus Christi and Brownsville — 15
   2 — 37

From Hungry Student To Happy Husband At The University Of Houston — 37
   Houston — 37
   3 — 59

Anchors Aweigh — 59
   The West Coast and Japan — 59
   4 — 87

The Cold War Warrior — 87
   Houston and Dallas/Fort Worth — 87
   5 — 111

Our First Development — 111
   Jamaica Beach, Galveston — 111
   6 — 129

How To Own A Bank For $600 Cash — 129
   Houston — 129
   7 — 147

The Astrodome — 147
   Houston — 147
   8 — 159

It's Right To Support Civil Rights — 159

Houston — *159*

9 — 169

Thirty Years On River Oaks Boulevard — 169

Houston — *169*

10 — 197

I Owe Everything To Having Good Partners — 197

Houston and Beyond — *197*

11 — 221

Up To My Eyeballs In Politics For Seventy Years — 221

Houston, Austin and Washington DC — *221*

12 — 233

Leading The Cougars — 233

University of Houston — *233*

In Conclusion — 259

Faith And Family — 259

Appendix — 277

Things You May Not Know About Welcome W. Wilson, Sr. — 277

By Cindi Wilson Proler Ray — *277*

Appendix — 285

Welcome's Rules Of Order — 285

HOW TO SUCCEED IN BUSINESS AND LIFE — *285*

Acknowledgements — 291

Foreword

Rick Perry, US Secretary of Energy, former Governor of Texas

Honoring Welcome W. Wilson, Sr.'s many accomplishments is easy. The hard part is deciding which of his countless triumphs to talk about. There was the role he played fighting for his country during the Korean War, as well as his dedicated service working for several US presidents. There is the important work he has done in various roles for his alma mater, the University of Houston, including his efforts to elevate the school to Tier One status. And so many are familiar with his role as an effective and visionary businessman in the Houston area, which has led to valuable development, stronger communities, and countless jobs for Texans.

But perhaps his most important role has been as a loving husband and father, something to which his wife and college sweetheart Joanne can attest. The great state of Texas has a higher population thanks to their descendants and spouses, forty-five people in total.

Now, Welcome has written many of these stories down, and more people will have a chance to get to know this distinguished and import- ant man. Here you will learn about his service under President Dwight Eisenhower, where he reached the civil service rank equivalent to a three- star general. He was just thirty at the time. You will also discover how he came to be appointed to the University of Houston Board of Regents and quickly became chairman, taking the university to new heights.

And one can hardly look around the Greater Houston Area today without seeing evidence of Welcome Wilson's great influence. From the hotels, apartment projects, retail centers, and three office buildings in downtown Houston that he helped develop to the master-planned communities of Jamaica Beach and Tiki Island in Galveston, his presence has left an indelible mark on the area. His work and his impact will be celebrated for many years to come.

Welcome's efforts as an entrepreneur have enriched the community, led to better lives for untold numbers of fellow Texans, and inspired generations of admirers and followers to do greater things.

My hope is that through reading this book, you will come to know Welcome W. Wilson, Sr., as I have—as a brilliant businessman, a loving family man and a proud Houstonian.

Welcome to My World

When I was a young man, I thought it was important to be a big shot. I've learned, sometimes the hard way, that being a good friend, a good husband, a good father, and a good partner is far more worthy. In learning this truth, however, I've led a fascinating life. I've made thousands of friends, developed communities that continue to prosper, survived major setbacks, and made hundreds of successful real-estate deals. I've served my country as a naval officer and a civilian, and I've helped further the agendas of politicians and educators. I've fathered five happy and productive children with my college sweet- heart, Joanne, and I am as crazy about her as ever.

It took some fast-talking, some scrambling, and lots of hard work, but now I've reached the point where I'm not so busy convincing people they need to hear my ideas or working so hard to prove myself. Instead, people come to me: Asking advice and seeking council. Helping these people is rewarding beyond measure. I get invited to give a lot of speeches. My favorite one is titled "How to Be Successful in Real Estate by Avoiding the Mistakes I Made." And I've made many mistakes over the years. For nine decades now, I have found myself thrown over and over into situations where somebody needed to do something fast to make something big happen. And, whether I knew anything about the situation or not, since I was a little boy I have always been willing to step in and give it a try. Many times, if I had known what I was getting into, I would have run the other way; at the time, however, I wasn't worried: I always had great confidence that I could figure out a way to get the job done.

Maybe I've been lucky, but more likely I've been blessed. Things have always had a way of working out. I learned from my parents and the enormous extended family who lived with us during the Depression that showing up with a good attitude and a willingness to work hard goes a long way toward making you successful in whatever situation you may find yourself.

Now, as I look at my beautiful wife, our five kids, sixteen grandchildren, and sixteen great-grandchildren and think about the wonderful life we've built together, I can't imagine my story turning out any other way. But reflecting on the places I've been, the people I've met, and the experiences I've had, I see many pivotal moments where everything could have turned out very differently. My parents, my brother, Jack, and my business partners all had significant impacts on my fortunes, but it is Joanne who has made the most impact on my life.

From the first time I saw her across the table at a college dance, I was determined to work my way into her life. It was the best challenge I ever took. Without Joanne's quiet and determined influence, I would have happily settled for being a big shot, a big frog in a very little pond. I would have missed out on more excitement, more fun, and more big deals than I can begin to describe. And I would not have been able to have the influence that I have had or offer significant support to so many meaningful causes.

I'm the first one to admit I've always thought I had all of the answers. There's an upside and a downside to that attitude. The upside is the confidence to dive in and assume that I can get the job done. The downside is that sometimes I'm wrong. And this is where I have actually been the luckiest; when I have come to one of these significant crossroads where I might have made the wrong decision, someone has always been there to change my mind. I have had several life-changing conversations in my life. Each time I was able to put my ego aside and listen. And many of those conversations were with Joanne.

Yes, I have been Welcome for all but twenty-two days of my life; I have been lucky, and I have been blessed. I have completed many things, and they make me feel both proud and humble. Making friends; building communities; supporting elected officials; working for my alma mater, my city, and my country—it's been quite a ride. Joanne has been by my side for almost seventy years. Without her strong support, her loving companionship, and her willingness to challenge me when necessary, I'd be telling you a very different story.

It's hard not to be confident when your name is Welcome. And confidence is important. But I have learned that it's what you don't know that teaches you the most, and what you don't see that often has the most influence. What you'll see in the following chapters is how energy, focus and a hint of self-promotion can be harnessed to create great success. What you may not see is how many ways Joanne has helped me to turn all my talk into a meaningful walk. I've made a lot of deals and had some powerful partners, but it is my partnership with her that has influenced everything that I consider truly important.

Growing Up In The Depression And WWII

Corpus Christi and Brownsville

WHAT'S IN A NAME

My parents were expecting a girl. When a bouncing twelve-pound boy arrived on March 17, 1928, they were surprised. So surprised, in fact, that for the first three weeks of my life, I didn't have a name. The girl's name my parents had picked, now long forgotten, no longer fit. Because I was born at home, the custom at the time, there was no hospital to require that they name me. Several days went by as my parents discussed what to name the boy. A week went by, and they were still arguing about a name.

Two weeks went by, then three, and they were still arguing. Finally, when I was twenty-two days old, my father arrived home from work with a determined look on his face.

"Why don't we name him Welcome?" he said to my mother. "Why?" she asked.

"So he will know that he is welcome, even though he's not a girl." And that's what they did. My father, who ran a print shop that was part of his family's publishing enterprises, already had the paper stock for the birth announcements ordered. My birth was announced to the world belatedly and with a pink ribbon.

Welcome is a family name now. My oldest son is named Welcome Jr.; his son, Welcome III. But it is still a very uncommon name. In my lifetime, I have run across only seventeen other people named Welcome. One of these was Welcome Wilson of Adak, Alaska. I first learned of his existence during the Korean War when I was stationed in Yokosuka, Japan. I took a letter into the naval post office to mail to my wife, Joanne, back in Houston. The clerk behind the desk looked at my name on the envelope and said, "I thought you were in Adak, Alaska."

Surprised by the existence of another by my name, I assured him that I was not that Welcome Wilson.

Then in the 1950s, I was mistaken for him again. I was at a reception held in my honor by the governor of Oklahoma when a woman came up to me. "I know you, you're from Soper, Oklahoma," she said. "But I thought that you moved to Alaska." I later communicated with Welcome. He was still in Adak and was about twenty years older than I was.

Despite the rarity of my name and the circumstances of receiving it, I did not use it until I was in college. I was Bubba to my family, and known as Wade at school until college, when a chance conversation with bank clerk made me realize what an asset my given name was. As I slid the documents under the window for her to process, he paused and looked up at me. "Welcome," he said. "No one could ever forget that name."

She was right, and I began using it. It took me many years to understand the full power of this name, but I finally realized how important a name is. And how important it is to stick with one name. My companies through the years had gone by many different names, but now we are the Welcome Group. As I have been told around the world, it's a name you don't forget. And in my world, this name, a firm handshake, and my willingness to work have ensured that after those first twenty-two days when I remained nameless, I have always been Welcome.

EARLY DAYS

I was born in San Angelo, Texas. My father, E. E. "Jack" Wilson was from Goldswaithe, Mills County, in Central Texas, which he called West Texas. After he married my mother, Irene Charpiot, he went to work in the oil fields in Orangefield. By the time I came along, he ran the print shop in San Angelo. But his real passion was radio, which was just be- coming popular.

The Wilsons were extroverted people. My father was one of eleven children, and they were all performers—they put on plays, sang, and played the piano. His family had built a radio transmitter in Goldthwaite and opened one of the first radio stations in Texas. Before the Depression, they had expanded to own a network of stations around Texas, and two in Mexico.

My birth announcement had a pink ribbon because the doctor told my parents I would be a girl. (I was a twelve-pound boy.)

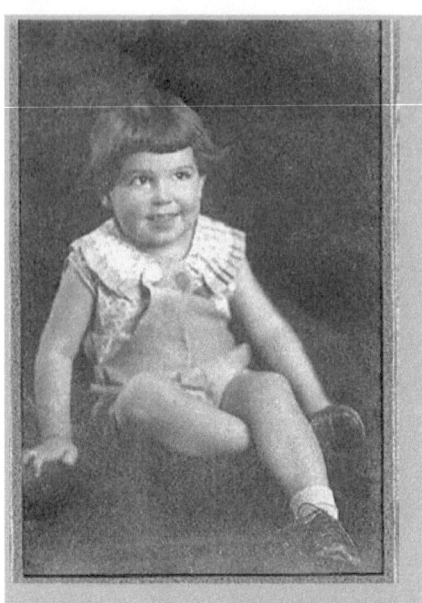

I am three here, in Corpus Christi, Texas, with a Buster Brown haircut, which was very popular during the Great Depression.

In order to extend the range of their broadcasts, my father's family wanted to obtain a station in El Paso. This station could broadcast across the border to a Mexican station with a much stronger frequency, greatly expanding the reach of their broadcast. The Methodist Church in El Paso had just acquired a license for a station, and my father and his brother Ernest went to make a deal with the church.

My father was always the talker and Uncle Ernest was the technical guy. They drove to El Paso and made a pitch to the Elders. My father said that in return for the station, they would manage it for free. The Wilsons would sell advertising, pay the expenses, and keep the profit. In return, four hours of broadcast time each day would be reserved to preach the Gospel.

This was a typical Wilson deal. It was highly favorable to the family, and yet they didn't invest a dime in the station. I learned the skills of the Wilson deal early in my life from watching my father.

They didn't use the term "entrepreneur" in those days, but I suppose it is a good one for the Wilsons. Grandfather Wilson, Dr. E. M.

Wilson, had a degree from Tulane that permitted him to be a doctor, a dentist or a pharmacist. Goldswaithe already had a pharmacist and a doctor, so he became a dentist. In addition to caring for the community's teeth, he also ran a weekly newspaper and the radio station. While making a good deal was an important Wilson family value, it went hand in glove with hard work. Our family has always believed that a man ought to work beginning at age fourteen. When my father turned fourteen, he began to deal in produce. He would go to a farm and buy the produce and sell it at a markup to the markets.

When my father and Uncle Ernest pitched the radio station deal, they were already experienced dealmakers. The board of directors loved the idea, and soon my father moved our family into a room on the tenth floor of the Hotel Paso del Norte, the largest and most ornate hotel in El Paso.

We had two rooms—one for my parents, my older brother Jack, and me, and one for Uncle Ernest, Aunt Jewel and my cousin Frances. Even these two rooms were well out of our family's budget, but we lived there for free, thanks to another Wilson deal. In exchange for space on the hotel's second floor for the station's studios and the two rooms upstairs where the families would live, the new radio station would announce once an hour that their studios were in the Hotel Paso del Norte.

The stock market had crashed in 1929, and there was very little money to go around. We lived in the hotel for a year before moving to a house at the edge of town. I have no memory of El Paso, but I have a copy of an invitation to a recital where Jack and I performed on stage. I am told that, at age three, I went on stage and recited, "When I go out to play, I look so sweet and gay; I have to take my dog along to keep the girls away." Despite hard times and hard work, the Wilsons were finding time to perform. Early on, I was showing signs of being a true Wilson.

The first thing I do remember is traveling from El Paso to Corpus Christi on the train. It was 1932, and my family had just obtained a license for a new radio station. They sold the station in El Paso, got a license for another in Corpus Christi, and started a daily newspaper, The Corpus Christi Chronicle. Leaving El Paso to head toward this new opportunity, Jack and I were in a Pullman car in the lower bunk with my mother. My father was above us in the upper bunk. I had just wo- ken up, and I clearly remember looking out the window and watching the telephone poles zip by. Cattle and horses dotted the landscape as we passed by miles and miles of Texas.

When we arrived in Corpus Christi, we lived in a tourist court on North Beach. The term "motel" had not yet been coined. Tourist courts consisted of individual buildings, each with a bedroom, bath, and tiny kitchen. Typically, there would be no more than fifteen buildings in a complex.

The first photograph that was ever taken of me was taken at our place at the tourist court. My brother and I were sitting-on the front step in our pajamas, with our arms upstretched and yawning. My hair was long over my ears with short bangs, the popular "Buster Brown" hairstyle of the time. My only other memory of those days in the tourist court was that my father bought us a punching bag. I was three, and Jack was five.

In the early 1930s, when you opened a radio station, the first problem was that no one owned a radio. The day our station went live it had only three listeners. A week later there were twelve. With twelve listeners, selling advertising was virtually impossible. But that didn't daunt the Wilsons; in order to draw attention to the new station, Uncle Doc rode the Corpus Christi drawbridge to the top and stood on his head. The newspapers ran pictures, and gradually the radio audience emerged.

The radio station and daily newspaper were a family affair. My grand- father headed the businesses. I never saw Grandfather Wilson wearing anything but a three-piece suit. He even wore it at the beach—but with a hat. All of my grandfather's eleven children worked at either the radio station or the paper. My father was president of the family businesses because he was always the most aggressive Wilson, always willing to put himself on the line to make a pitch. Ernest was the technical brother, and Doc the marketer. The girls worked as secretaries and clerks.

We soon moved from North Beach to another tourist court on Ocean Drive overlooking Corpus Christi Bay. The courts were located about ten miles from town, near where the Corpus Christi Naval Air Station would be built. The owners of the tourist court would come over about once a week with buttermilk ice cream. We thought it tasted terrible; but it was the Depression, and we were grateful for their generosity.

Corpus Christi fared better than many other cities in the Great Depression. A booming town with a new deep-water port, Corpus's population in 1930 was over 27,000 people, close to triple the population just a decade before. The discovery of oil in the county just two years before our arrival helped offset the harshness of the Depression. And for families like ours, it meant more people were able to buy a radio to listen to our new station. While we were still struggling financially, at least we had a product that we could get out to the public. When we had begun broadcasting, nobody thought they needed a radio. As Doc's antics began to convince them that they did, they were able to get a simple set, basically just an earphone and a crystal, for fifty cents. This was within the reach of many people.

We were living in the tourist court on Ocean Drive when Jack turned six years old, and my mother took him down to enroll him in the first grade in private school. The school was advertising on the radio station so, knowing the Wilsons, the tuition was probably a trade-out. I refused to be left behind, so my mother enrolled me in kindergarten at age four.

The kindergarten teacher was distressed that I was named Welcome. Fearing that the other kids would make fun of my name, she insisted that I register as Wade Wilson, my middle name. Thanks to her, I spent my entire school career, through junior college, as Wade Wilson. At home my family called me Bubba, and my brother was called Jackie. I completed kindergarten and first grade at this school; then, when I was six, I entered Menger Elementary School in Corpus Christi in the second grade.

THE ONION ARMS

As the Depression deepened, various family members lost their jobs or businesses around the state. My grandfather bought a giant rooming house in Corpus. It was located across the street from the train station in a less-than-best part of town with a rowdy bar next door. Called the Union Arms, it was a two-story building. The first floor was industrial space and office space, and the second floor had twenty rooms, with one bath for men and one bath for women. As the economic times got worse, one by one, most of the eleven families moved into the rooming house with my grandparents. We were among the lucky families that had two rooms.

I would later discover what a mental strain this communal lifestyle was for the adults, but for us kids it was wonderful. Our family had a way of making everything fun, putting on a show at the slightest excuse. Uncle Doc had gotten his name because he had a traveling medicine show that went all over Texas. He would take his tent to a small town and put on plays—all of my aunts and uncles were the performers. My father frequently played the piano during the intermission. Uncle Ernest only knew one song on the piano, and every intermission he would come in and play the same the song. By the third time he showed up, the audience was singing out the notes to that song.

My father was also a magician. One of the show's attractions had been an electric power generator. In these small farm towns, many people had never seen electricity. People would come from miles around just to see the electric lights. My father had a trick where an audience member would choose a card, and my father would make it magically rise out of the deck. He put a thin thread over the top, so when he poked the card in, the thread saved its place. One time he stumbled, and the cards began to fly out of his deck. "Too much electricity!" he shouted. Taking setbacks in stride was part of being a Wilson, and I soaked up these stories of their adventures.

However tough times were, the show went on, and we made the best of it. At the Union Arms, we even made the train station exciting. When we took family pictures, we would go to the station across the street and act like we were just getting off the train from some fabulous trip. On the vacant lot next to the Union Arms, Uncle Gabe was building a sailboat. We kids would play in it every day. Living with a dozen cousins was a child's dream. My cousin Frances was our leader, and she organized plays and musical presentations.

We ate each meal together as a large family at a mammoth dining table. My grandfather would sit at the head of the table and say the blessing. He mumbled, so nobody ever knew quite what he said. We had onions as the entree at least four days a week. A block away was the city's largest produce house where farmers would sell their vegetables. When a trailer load of vegetables wouldn't sell, the farmers would sim- ply take the sides off the trailer and give them away. Typically, it was the onions that were given away. We had so many onions that we began to call the Union Arms the Onion Arms. The family joke was that the boarding house cook brought his lunch to work every day because he didn't like what we had to eat.

The first floor of the Onion Arms held the offices and presses of the Daily Corpus Christi Chronicle, the newspaper that my grandfather and his sons published. They had founded it as competition to the long-established Corpus Christi Caller Times. As a small child I learned to set type, carefully placing the letters and words of the news stories into their proper places. One name I set frequently in those days was Adolf Hitler. He had recently come into power, and there was great interest in his activities in Europe. No one knew yet if he was good or evil.

In those days before television, whenever a major news story developed, the Chronicle would publish an extra edition. Jack and I would sell the extras on the street. One time when I was about six, the extras warned of German submarines near the Panama Canal. Jack and I grabbed a stack of the papers and headed downtown to sing out, "Extra! Extra!" and spread the news. The extras sold for a nickel each. When we had each made enough to buy a movie ticket and a Coke, we threw the rest away and went into the Capitol Theater to watch a movie.

I wasn't old enough to fully understand the impact of the Great Depression. I understood that as a family we lacked any cash, but we never considered ourselves poor. We always believed that we were rich people who were just temporarily out of money. The reality was that no one had any cash. There were no federal programs for the unemployed, and in order to eat every day, people without work relied on soup kitchens run by charities. In every block in downtown Corpus, there would be two or three beggars on the street. Their typical pitch was for a nickel to get a cup of coffee. A nickel would also buy a hamburger or a pint of milk.

There simply was no cash. Banks went broke, and people lost everything. When the bank shut down, I even lost the five dollars that I had put in a savings account. Without available cash, many transactions became trades. Frequently, when radio stations sold advertising, they would have to take their payments in goods or services. One time we ran ads on the radio for a local fruit stand, with the agreement that the airtime would be paid for with produce. A day after the advertising campaign started, the owner of the fruit stand called up and said to stop the ads. So many Wilsons had shown up for food that he had nothing left to sell. We were back to eating onions.

In the 1960s, Jack, Welcome Jr., and I were driving to Brownsville to go dove hunting. We stopped in Corpus to stay with Uncle Hildred and Aunt Adell who had lived with us back then. Jack and I drove over to the Onion Arms to see if it was still standing. Not only was it still there, but it was also for sale, for ten thousand dollars. Remembering all the wonderful times we had had there, Jack and I decided we should buy it and renovate it as a family heirloom. When we mentioned that to Uncle Hildred, he said, "Boys, those memories may be great for you, but for the adults, it was terrible. I don't want to remember those days."

Of course, I realized. None of them could have made it through those terrible times alone. But banding together, and keeping all our spirits up, they brought us through the Depression helping us believe that we were rich and creating many happy memories.

When the economy started to improve, my father moved us from the Onion Arms to an apartment project on Elizabeth Street. I was in elementary school at the time, and I had a group of friends at the apartments, most of whom were too young to be in school. One day I announced to my younger friends that I was not going to school that day. When my father drove me to school I refused to get out of the car. When he insisted, I lay down on the floorboard and began to kick, screaming that I wasn't going. He drove me home. I proudly walked into the apartment project past my young friends, smiling at my accomplishment.

Inside, my mother took a hairbrush and gave me a spanking. My father did not touch me or say a word. He calmly took me back to the car, past all of my friends, and drove me back to school. I don't remember ever disobeying my parents thereafter.

Whenever I was spanked, which was probably on no more than three occasions, it was always by my mother, never my father. For most of my childhood, my mother was ten times the influence on me that my father was. She was responsible for raising Jack and me. I considered her to be a perfect human being. She didn't smoke and drank very little. She never used a word of profanity my entire life; nor did my father. She taught us to respect black people in the thirties when few in our community did. She told us to always do the right thing. When I think of Irene Wilson, the words that come to mind are responsibility and determination.

GROWING UP AT THE BEACH

When I was about eight, my grandfather, my father, and Uncle Ernest bought five acres on Ocean Drive, overlooking Corpus Christi Bay, one mile out from the city limits at Cole Park. On a corner of the property they built a transmitter station for the radio station. On the other three corners they built small cottages to live in.

Our cottage was on a thirty-foot cliff overlooking the bay. After we moved in, my father immediately began to make changes to our house. It was a tiny, tiny house at first, with just four rooms. We built the additions to the house ourselves. He was the contractor, and Jack and I were the laborers. We even made the building materials ourselves. Concrete blocks had been invented, and my father decided that he could make them better and more cheaply by simply building forms in which to pour concrete around empty oil cans. We drove all over Corpus Christi collecting empty oil cans from filling stations.

It ended up as a two-story, three-bedroom, two-bath house, but the bath on the second floor was never completed. The entire time we lived there, we kept adding on to it, but in my father's opinion, we never did finish it. My father was a creative man, and I don't remember living in a house of my father's that was not under construction.

We had a beach at the bottom of the cliff, and a small stream that went through the property. On the beach, my father built the city's largest merry-go-round. He built sails made out of tin that kept it going by itself, twenty-four hours a day. Lying in bed at night, I could hear the merry-go-round as it spun with the breeze.

He also built a zip line. It was a metal cable that went from the back of the house down to the beach about 200 feet away. He put a pipe on the metal cable that we would grab and zip down to the beach. The pipe would then be thrown back along the cable and caught at the top. If Jack and I had thought the Onion Arms was fun, this was paradise.

My best friend at the time was a boy named Maurice Grossman, who was in my class at Menger Elementary School. Maurice's father had a very large department store called Grossman's. The Grossmans were considered rich, and they lived in a big house about a quarter of a mile farther out on Ocean Drive. Mrs. Grossman would not let us come in the house with shoes on. We had to take them off and walk in stocking feet. One day Jack and I were playing football in the Grossman's side yard. Afterward, Mrs. Grossman told Maurice to please ask us not to spit on the grass. We didn't spend a lot of time at the Grossman's house.

Maurice was with us almost every day, and most evenings he would have dinner with us. My mother complained, because Maurice could not eat with us until he had called his mother to tell her what we were having for dinner. Frequently, we would be having cornbread in a glass of milk, or other modest fare, and my mother was embarrassed that Mrs. Grossman always knew our every meal.

Lunches at school consisted of a pint of milk and a plate of food for fifteen cents. On more than one occasion, my father would drop Jack and me off at school without our lunch money. He would then go to his office, raise thirty cents somehow, and drive back to Menger and give it to us.

When I was seven or eight, I noticed that the table where kids placed their plates when they finished eating was always a huge mess, with food spilling on the floor. I went over and started taking the plates from the students, scraping off the food, stacking the plates neatly, putting the silverware in a container, and putting the milk bottles in the case. I felt like I was performing a good service, so I did it again the next day. The cafeteria manager came over and complimented me on my work. More importantly, she said that if I continued helping with the plates, my lunch would be free.

I was proud to have a job and to be earning something, even if it wasn't cash. Every morning thereafter, when my mother or father gave fifteen cents to my brother, I would say that I didn't need any money because I had "made a deal." That was my first lesson in entrepreneurship: If you see a need and fulfill it, you will be rewarded.

When I was about nine, my mother and father sat Jack and me down and told us, for the first time, that we had a half-brother. His name was Billy Joe Wilson, and he lived in Lampasas, Texas, with his mother and step-father. When my father was about nineteen, he had married a girl in high school, and they had a son. They got divorced three years later. My father was twenty-six years old when he met and married my mother. He always told me that I should wait until I was twenty-six to get married. He believed that kids younger than twenty-six had no business trying to select a spouse.

Billy Joe came to visit us that summer. Since he was a teenager, we could do things with him that we couldn't do on our own. We really enjoyed him, and he visited us several times in the following years. When my father died forty years later, he left a quarter of his net worth to Billy Joe, a share equal to that of my brother, my sister, and me. It reminded me of my father's innate fairness and responsibility, as well as how strongly my father believed that it was important to wait until twenty-six to marry.

THE RUMBLINGS OF WAR

I finished elementary school and went to Wynn Seale Junior High School. It was the late 1930s, and Hitler had ravaged half of Europe. The entire world was watching him, but in America there was little support for entering the war to stop him. We had enough problems of our own. In 1938 and 1939, the school body was called into the junior high auditorium every time Hitler made an important speech. He spoke in German, but an interpreter on the network radio would tell us what he was saying. In each of the speeches, Hitler promised his intentions were only to help German-speaking people in other countries like Austria and Hungary and that he had no further ambitions. A month after his last speech, on September 1, 1939, he invaded Poland and World War II began in earnest. Hitler quickly swept across Europe, conquering France in a matter of a few weeks, and everyone presumed that he was days away from invading England. Instead, he invaded Russia and began to bomb England instead of invading. The Royal Air Force did an excellent job defending London and began to shoot down many of the bombers before they reached the city.

In the evening, my family would sit around the big radio and listen to the news with fascinated interest. I well remember Winston Churchill going on the radio and making the famous speech in which he praised the pilots of the Royal Air Force: "If Great Britain survives a thousand years, never will so much be owed by so many to so few."

With America staying out of the war for the time being, Jack and I and our cousins focused on being kids. In addition to the zip line and merry-go-round at the house, there was a neighborhood fisherman who kept a large skiff, about eighteen feet long, in the water about fifty feet from the beach. We learned how to slip the line off the front end and borrow his boat. One day we were skinny dipping near the drifting boat. Somehow my cousin Billy Smith dropped all of our shorts into the water, where they disappeared. The outgoing tide had taken the boat out to where it was too deep for us to touch bottom. We all climbed in the boat, and Jack and Billy tried to paddle us in with their hands. The tide was strong, pulling us farther out into the deep green water.

I decided to take matters into my own hands and started yelling at the top of my voice for my mother. The boys tried to shut me up. Although we were about three hundred feet from shore, somehow my mother heard me. She came running down to the water's edge and immediate- ly began to wade into the water in her house dress. My mother could barely swim, and the only stroke she knew was the dog-paddle. When the water became too deep for her to wade, she started dog-paddling toward the boat. She grabbed the boat and started paddling back to shore with the help of us boys.

Finally, she pulled us to shallow water. Before coming after us, she had called my father at the radio station, and he had called the police to send an ambulance. By the time we were able to get out of the boat, a crowd of about fifty had gathered on the beach, including the police. Our problem now was that we had no clothes. So, we stood in the waist-deep water until my mother walked back to the house and retrieved more clothes for us. I don't know if we were redder from sunburn on our uncovered skin or embarrassment.

The whole affair was humiliating, but I learned an important lesson that day. My brother and cousin had desperately tried to shut me up when I was yelling, but I refused. It was clear to me that in an emergency, you have to do whatever it takes to solve the problem.

During the Depression, only rich people stayed in hotels. Accordingly, when relatives came to Corpus Christi, they would stay with us, some- times for months. I'm not even sure how many cousins I have; I always say sixty-seven, and I can account for at least fifty. During the summer, the only vacation these cousins got would be to come to Corpus Christi and stay with us for a month or so. With so many cousins, there was company all the time, and it was wonderful.

My mother's mother had died after the youngest baby of her ten, my uncle Marion, was born. When he was a teenager, he came to live with us in Corpus. By the time we lived on Ocean Drive, Marion was in high school and had bought an Indian motorcycle. He worked on a dredge in the Corpus Christi ship channel and was making good money for the 1930s. Later he bought a Chevrolet Coupe. He would take my cousin Frances, three years older than I, to high school in the morning. My cousin Edella and my cousin Lester were my favorites. Edella was a beautiful cheerleader at Humble High School. Lester was tall, handsome, and exciting. He always drove an expensive-looking auto- mobile, which he bought cheap and repaired and repainted. He was always well-dressed, and I admired him. When I was twelve years old, Lester was everything I ever wanted to be. He looked a lot more successful than he actually was, but I was too young to tell the difference. By watching Lester, I learned that appearance makes a huge difference in how others perceive you.

BROWNSVILLE

In the summer of 1940, my father and his brothers sold the radio station in Corpus Christi to Tilford Jones, the nephew and adopted son of Houston entrepreneur Jesse Jones. His partner was Frank Smith. They changed the call letters of the station to KRIS and brought in NBC as the network affiliate. My father acquired a license to open a radio station in Brownsville, Texas, which was without one. That summer we moved to the beach at Boca Chica, twenty miles from Brownsville. Jack and I did not want to move away from all our friends in Corpus Christi, and my father thought if he took us to the beach first we might be more accepting of the idea.

It worked. Many people from Brownsville spent the summer at the Boca Chica beach with their kids. We quickly met many of the teenagers from junior high and high school. By the time summer was over, we were perfectly happy with the idea of living in Brownsville. As summer ended, my father rented a nice house at the edge of town. On the north-bound highway, it was only about a mile from the radio studio. We lived there a couple of years.

MY brother Jack (left) and I, standing in front of the radio station in Brownsville, Texas, where we worked as disc jockeys and newscasters during WWII.

In Brownsville, Jack was the leader of a group of six of us. He was on the football team. I went out for the team but was injured the first week, so I joined the band. In Corpus Christi my father had bought me a set of trap drums, and I had played the drums in a dance band organized by Jack. So, at Brownsville High School, I became a snare drummer in the high school band, directed by J. Walker. It was the best decision I made in high school.

The band was half female, and half of them were gorgeous. The majorettes were all part of the band. One of my good friends, George

McGonigle, was the drum major. We had a fabulous time. We took trips by bus to various towns in the Rio Grande Valley and once to Monterrey, Mexico. I had a girlfriend in the band, and the long bus trips were perfect for hours of kissing and hugging.

Then, on December 7, 1941, the Japanese attacked Pearl Harbor. No one in Brownsville had ever heard of Pearl Harbor, and we all wondered what it would mean. The next day President Franklin Roosevelt went before Congress and made his famous "Day of Infamy" speech. War was declared on Japan—and Germany and Italy as well, since Japan was their ally—and Roosevelt was anxious to get America in the war in Europe before it was too late.

Although I was a sophomore, I was only thirteen. I was excited by the idea that our country was going to war. Jack was an aviation buff, who avidly read any magazine on planes he could find at the drugstore newsstand in town. He was convinced we would win the war in no time with our revolutionary fleet of aircraft. He felt like America had the greatest Army Air Corps in the world. I remember him saying again and again, "We'll lick the Japanese in three months."

The whole country changed overnight. From that day, every American was affected in every part of life. There were drives to collect scrap for the war effort. There was rationing of food, clothing, and supplies. Our entire family received four gallons of gasoline a week for the car. Production of automobiles and appliances and all types of civilian goods stopped as industry converted to the war effort. Retail stores in downtown Brownsville could not stock enough merchandise to sell. Millions of young men were drafted and sent away.

Jack's prediction was wrong. It took four years to beat Japan, and it would've taken another year at least, except for the atom bomb. Once the war started, every teenage boy wanted to be in the service. No one I knew was scared of enlisting. When one of our friends left, we would gather at the train station with banners and drums to see him off. I knew my time was coming.

The effects of the war began to affect my family's radio station, which struggled to find merchants willing to advertise when they already had too little to sell. My father began to lose heart. He had trouble getting up in the morning and going to work. My mother, who had never worked in an office, took over. They went to work together every morning, and she became the company clerk. Watching her jump into this new role, I learned another lesson: always address problems head on, and do whatever it takes to fix the situation.

When I turned fourteen, it was time for me to begin working full time, as my father required. I went to work for my father at the radio

Left to right: me, my mother, Irene; my sister, Beverly; my father, E.E. Jack Wilson, and Jack.

station, and he then became a sizeable influence on me. I saw why he, as the youngest son in the family, was always the leader in their endeavors. He was willing to make a pitch. His three older brothers were happy to let him take the lead, while they carried out staff positions in the enterprises. My mother taught me values, and my father taught me to be aggressive in business.

A year later, I was fifteen, a senior in high school, and still too young for the draft. With the able-bodied young men all enlisted, jobs in America were held by boys under seventeen-and-a-half, men over forty, or women. I worked as a newscaster and disc jockey at the radio station. I was the program director, and we had no network, so I would make up a schedule of what we would play. My dad also let Jack and me do skits on the radio. Jack would write the skits, and my title was "Bubba the Comedian." My father never complained or slowed us down. He thought encouraging his boys was more important than ratings or money. People liked the skits, though, and the disc jockey shows were very popular. I played Tommy Dorsey, Woody Herman, Frank Sinatra—all the best records.

My days in Brownsville were full. Before going to school at 7:45 a.m., I milked two cows, fed the chickens, slopped the hogs, and learned responsibility. There's no such thing as taking a day off when you're milking cows. Rich kids had cars, but we were far from rich, so after the chores were completed, I would walk out to the highway in front of our little farm and hitchhike to high school. After school I would hitchhike to the radio station on the highway, and after my shift I would hitchhike home.

In the evening I would milk the cows again and then would borrow my father's car to go over to my girlfriend's house. Betty Rusteberg, whose father was a prominent potato farmer in Brownsville, was my girlfriend during my junior and senior years in high school, Betty's freshman and sophomore years. It was a wonderful time.

About then, my father sold the radio station to Frank Smith, one of the purchasers of our former Corpus Christi station, and retired. To support the war efforts, he worked as an electrician in a manufacturing plant out by the airport. I remained a newscaster and disc jockey at the station, which was then affiliated with the Blue Network of NBC, later called the American Broadcasting Company, or ABC. My responsibilities were greatly reduced because most of the programming was on the Blue Network, and all I had to do was make station announcements every thirty minutes. My news casting was limited because the network carried all the news about the war. Because it was network radio and I was no longer working for my father, however, my salary was greatly increased, and I felt affluent. I was making $160 a month. Betty would come to the station to visit. We'd be smooching in the station, and I'd run a record that would last for three minutes. Then the record would be skipping, and I'd jump up and run back to put on the next one!

In 1943, by surprise, my mother became pregnant, and in September of that year she gave birth to my baby sister Beverly. My father, invigorated by having a baby girl, never complained about life again.

While my parents focused on the new baby, we teenage boys were all planning for military service. My brother Jack, still infatuated with planes, wanted to be a cadet in the Army Air Corps. My close friend George McGonigle wanted to go to naval officer's school.

When I graduated from high school, I had just turned sixteen, so I enrolled in Brownsville Junior College. The following year, when I was finally seventeen, I registered for the draft. My plan was to be in the Army and talk my way into a public relations job, which would help with my radio career. I was looking forward to the adventure.

I received orders to report to Dallas, Texas, to the Eighth Service Command on September 17, 1945, exactly six months before my eighteenth birthday. I excitedly began to prepare. I felt like I should get into good physical shape before I entered the Army, so I quit the radio station and took a job as a longshoreman at the port of Brownsville, loading lead boats and banana boats.

I was a longshoreman long enough to know that I wanted to get a college education and not be a common laborer. Many of the

My father, E.E. Jack Wilson, with my brother Jack, me, and our mother, Irene Wilson.
This was taken at the train station across the street from where we lived.

longshoremen were Mexican-Americans, and I was taller than most of them. I was always stationed in the very bottom of the banana boat, because they thought it would be easier for me to hand the stalks up to the next level. I spent entire days in total darkness, with fruit flies buzzing around me and, occasionally, tiny snakes crawling on my arms.

During that summer, my father took me on a life-changing trip to Dallas. He wanted me to meet influential people there, like the publisher of the Dallas Morning News, who could help me transfer to a public relations job when I got into the Army. It was a long drive from Brownsville to Dallas and back. Over the three-day period, he and I had a lot of time to talk. This was the first of many the life-changing conversations I would have.

My father told me that in his view, success in business took guts and determination. He did not mean the guts to get into a fight; he meant the guts to make a pitch to a perfect stranger, when what you were pro- posing was likely over your head. Although he had always been known in his family as the brother with the ability to make the best pitch, on that trip he told me that, compared to my mother, he thought he was low in determination. He said I should follow the example of my mother, who had all of the determination in the world.

I can't explain how invigorated that trip and our conversation made me. When I returned to Brownsville, I was so excited about becoming successful in life that I had trouble sleeping at night.

In August of that summer, my friends and I decided to take a vacation by hitchhiking all over Texas before I reported for duty. During World War II, anyone who drove past a man with his thumb out would stop and pick him up. We were in Corpus Christi getting a free meal or two from my family when we heard the news that President Truman had dropped an atom bomb on Hiroshima. No one knew anything about the atom bomb, and no one had the foggiest notion of where it came from. The destruction was devastating and breathtaking. As leaders in the world began to speculate about whether or not it was one of a kind, Harry Truman dropped a second atom bomb on Nagasaki. The war ended a few days later. Disappointed that I had lost the opportunity to serve my country during World War II, I enrolled in a second year at Brownsville Junior College.

A DIFFERENT PATH

When I returned to Brownsville Junior College, a new dean, Neal M. Nelson, had joined the faculty. I enrolled in his speech class, and shortly after the beginning of the semester he called me into his office.

"I don't think you're even aware of the fact that you are a natural leader," he said. He then asked me to recognize that and take advantage of it. I had always assumed that my older brother was the leader. But now Jack was in the service. What Dean Nelson told me changed my whole mindset. Once he pointed them out to me, I began to use my leadership skills. That school year I was president of two out of three of the major clubs on campus, and I was elected president of the student body. I also became the statewide president of the Pan American Student Forum, which had a major involvement with Mexico. My conversation with Dean Nelson was another life-changing moment. I had never thought of myself as a leader, but since that time, wherever I have been, I always assumed that my role was to lead the group.

In my second year in junior college, I decided that every girl in school was after me. I'm not sure why it is, but I've found that girls always flirt with men who are not available. Having decided that I was being held back socially, I broke up with Betty Rusteberg and started dating. It was a terrible time. I found out I was not nearly as popular as I had thought. I dated various girls over the next year, but there were no serious relationships.

In 1946 it came time to plan for a four-year college. Jack had re- turned from the service a few months after the war ended and was at- tending Brownsville Junior College. My father favored us going to the University of Houston, an institution that nobody had ever heard of in Brownsville. His thinking was that by attending school in Houston we could get our feet on the ground in what he thought would be the capital of the business world in years to come. Boy, was he right. Houston had half a million people in the metropolitan area at the time, and today it has six-and-a-half million people.

As always, Dad persuaded us. He drove us to Houston to enroll at the University of Houston. We found housing in a trailer village that consisted of two hundred surplus Army house-trailers bought by the university because there were no dormitories. Only veterans could live there, and we qualified because Jack was a veteran.

I'll never forget what my father told us when he dropped us off in front of trailer #67. "Boys," he said, "I've paid your first semester's tuition, and I've paid the first month's rent on this trailer. Here is fifty dollars each." And then he said, "Whenever you need anything else, just call me up on the telephone. Whatever you need, just call me up… and I'll explain how you can get by without it." That was the last time we relied on our father financially for the rest of our lives. We were on our own, and the whole world was out there—waiting for us to conquer it.

2

From Hungry Student To Happy Husband At The University Of Houston

Houston

In September of 1946, when my father paid the ten dollars rent for Army surplus trailer #67 and dropped us off, the University of Houston was only eighteen years old, the same age I was. It had only been a four-year institution for twelve years. Not only did our father want us to go to the University of Houston because of his belief that Houston, Texas would be the capital of the business world, but he also believed in self-reliance. He wanted us to get jobs to support ourselves through college, and Houston was a city with many opportunities. I had changed my focus from public relations and felt my future was in business. My plan at this point was to get a law degree to help my business career.

SETTLING IN TO UH

The University of Houston had 3,500 students in the spring of 1946. By the September of the year, thanks in large part to the G.I. Bill, enrollment jumped to 10,968 students. Prior to the fall semester, the school ran an ad in the Houston newspapers announcing that registration for classes would take place at 10:30 a.m. that Wednesday in the gymnasium. Ten thousand people showed up and formed a line that went a mile down Calhoun Road.

Jack and I went to the gym and found the huge line, and of course we knew better than to try to break into a line full of a bunch of ex-GIs. Then we saw the assistant registrar, Mrs. J. Perry Honnicutt. When we first arrived at the university, our father had taken us in to meet Assistant President W.W.Kemmerer, because he believed introducing yourself to those in charge was important. We had met Mrs.

Honnicutt that day and befriended her. "Mrs. Honnicutt," we said now, "We want to

Joanne Guest—my future wife—and I on a one-day train trip to Louisiana to attend a UH football game in 1948.

hitchhike to Brownsville to spend the weekend with our family before school starts. But we need to register before leaving. Is there any way you could possibly get us into registration early?" Mrs. Honnicutt liked us, and she turned immediately to a professor who was on his way back to the gymnasium and, in her most official voice, said, "These are the Wilson boys, and they need to get home to Brownsville. Would you take them over to Station One in registration so they can get done and get out of town?"

He agreed, and we followed him over there. Well, Station One was inside the gymnasium, and he was supposed to take us through the back door to get there. Instead he took us to the front door where the ten thousand people were in line. He went up to Walter Kemmerer, the assistant to the president, and later president, who was frantically dealing with the crowd.

"Excuse me, Dr. Kemmerer," he said, "These are the Wilson boys. They're in a hurry to register so they can leave."

"What do you think these other ten thousand people are here to do?" Dr. Kemmerer exploded.

Jack and I realized the professor had blown it, so we said, "Never mind; never mind," and started backing away. We went back over to see Mrs. Honnicutt. She gave better instructions to the next professor, who took us in the back door to Station One. We were registered in fifteen minutes and on our way, hitchhiking to Brownsville. Getting people to help me has been my stock-in-trade, and any success I have had is because of help from kind people like Mrs. Honnicutt.

PAVING OUR OWN WAY

When I graduated from Brownsville Junior College, I felt I needed more experience in sales work. My father had given me the opportunity to sell advertising for the radio station in Brownsville. I called on several businesses, but I never bothered to follow up with any of them. Looking back, I now realize that it was a setup. My father had arranged for them to buy some advertising, but he wanted me to have to work to get it. With no follow through, my efforts resulted in zero sales.

I thought I could get some experience by selling advertising for the University of Houston's student newspaper, The Daily Cougar. I asked Mrs. Honnicutt whom I should talk to, and she arranged for me to meet N. S. Patterson, the head of journalism and supervisor of the newspaper. He referred me to Johnny Goyen, the business manager of the newspaper, the Cougar.

I was startled when I walked into The Cougar office. Johnny sat in the corner at a roll-top desk. The editor and the sports editor, both women, were using some of the foulest language I had ever heard. I believe they thought that was what journalists did.

When I told Johnny, I wanted to sell advertising, he was shocked. No one had ever volunteered to sell advertising before. It was some- thing they had to brow-beat people into doing. When he told me that I would get a twenty-percent commission on any advertising I sold, I thought it was perfect. Not only would I learn how to sell, but also, I would be earning an income as I did it.

The next day, I caught the bus downtown and got off at the corner of Main and McKinney. I walked the two blocks to Milam Street and started walking south between downtown and Elgin. There must have been fifty used-car lots. World War II had eliminated the production of any new cars for four years, and all of the automobile trading was at the used-car lots. I had decided that there was a strong market in selling used cars to University of Houston students.

My objective was to get used to rejection. My father had told me that I had to learn to listen to people saying no and to not let it affect my enthusiasm for selling. I picked the right industry for this learning process. At lot after lot, I would tell the manager about the eight thousand veterans we had on campus and what a great market they were for used cars. The manager would then either tell me no or Hell, no!

After I made about thirty stops, the manager of Little Man Auto agreed, after a lengthy sales pitch, to buy a three-dollar ad in The Cougar. I immediately caught the bus back to the university and reported my first sale to Johnny. He was surprised. Later he told me he didn't think I would ever sell anything

For the next three years, The Cougar was the Wilson brothers' principal source of income. I started as a salesman, later became sales manager and within the year took on Johnny's role as business manager. I made Jack the sales manager, and he was paid a commission. My position paid me a salary of one dollar an hour, the highest paid position for a student on the UH campus. In those early days working for The Cougar, I learned that I loved to work. I would stay at the office until ten at night. There is joy in working.

I hired a secretary, Jean Borchidean, and paid her fifty cents an hour. I was the only student employee on campus who had a secretary. Soon thereafter I became the business manager of the Houstonian yearbook, and Jack became the advertising manager. Again, we earned commissions for our work. The Houstonian was low-hanging fruit because all we had to do was call a major company in Houston, like Reed Rollerbit, and they would quickly agree to buy a two-hundred-dollar ad in the yearbook.

The Cougar was originally housed in a small office in the recreation building, and we were all in one big room. Always being the promoter, I noticed that behind the building was a metal shed three times the size of our office that was being used for storage. I went to the head of the maintenance department and talked him into remodeling it for me so, we could move the newspaper there. I had mentioned the idea to Dr. Kemmerer, so that I could tell the maintenance head that he knew

Rosemary Anderson, my secretary when I was the student business manager of the UH Cougar, and I pose for a yearbook picture.

about the plan. Then I got N. S. Patterson, who ran the journalism department, on board by telling him that the maintenance department supported it. One by one, I built consensus that it was a good idea to have newer, bigger space for The Cougar.

I spent a year on this project. I don't know what maintenance projects did not get done that year, but now we had luxurious offices. One- third of the new space was for the business staff, and the rest held the editorial staff. The newspaper office was the only student office on campus that had people there full-time. As a result, whenever anyone came on campus to hire students for any part-time work, they would come see us. Jack and I would take any job that came in the door. Once, when Pappy's Barbeque opened up downtown, we were hired to dress as chefs in white uniforms and tall hats and stand on Main Street, passing out flyers about Pappy's Barbeque. We each made ten bucks.

Around 1948, a new national product named Brylcreem was introduced in Texas. The merchandising person came to campus and was directed to The Cougar office. He was giving away free samples of Brylcreem, and Jack and I agreed to take some and pass them out.

"How many would you like?" he asked.

"We'll take a hundred," I said, thinking he meant tubes.

But he meant cases. He sent us one hundred cases filled with boxes that each held about fifty tubes of Brylcreem. We had boxes stacked everywhere, and we went through great trouble trying to dispose of them.

One day, a young man who was campaigning for president of the freshman class came into the office. His name was Richard Haynes, and he went by the name Racehorse. Racehorse asked about the boxes of Brylcreem, and I told him the story.

"Could I have a few boxes for my campaign?" he asked me.

"Sure," I said, "We'd be happy to get rid of them." Racehorse took hundreds of tubes and stapled each to a card that read, "Vote for Richard Racehorse Haynes for president of the freshman class!" He passed them out far and wide and was elected in a landslide. Racehorse later became one of Texas's most famous criminal lawyers, winning case after case against all odds, and I've often wondered how much the Brylcreem promotion helped him win that early office.

The Cougar was my principal source of income, but Jack and I also made money by singing in nightclubs and others venues that paid their entertainers. In 1948, the first TV station opened in Houston. It was in a Quonset hut on Post Oak Road. There was one studio, one bathroom for men, and one bathroom for women. The bathrooms also served as dressing rooms. There was no network television at the time in Texas because the coaxial cable had not yet reached the state. Accordingly, all programs were local. And they were all live. They would occasionally run movies by simply pointing a television camera at a small screen on which a sixteen-millimeter film was projected.

Jack and I were hired to perform live commercials for a sports show. He would play the ukulele, and we both would sing. We arrived late for the first performance, but it seemed to go well. The second time we arrived twenty minutes early, arriving during a program called Fashions in Motion. It was a one-hour style show sponsored by Battelstein's Department Store. By arriving early, we learned something startling. The beautiful models had no place to change their dresses quickly, so the minute they stepped off stage and were no longer on camera, they stripped off their dresses down to their underwear. The models then quickly slipped on the next dress and would stand by to go back on TV. I learned that there were many benefits to being punctual!

FRONTIER FIESTA

The Wilson boys were always entrepreneurial. We were always trying to make a buck. Frontier Fiesta, a student-run festival at the University of Houston, had been discontinued during the war and was just getting reestablished. It was a campus-wide endeavor that recreated a western town. There were about twenty facilities, including shows, a general store, and a museum. We built facades out of pine slabs the lumber yards gave away, and the back would be a tent. People went from saloon to saloon to see the shows, about fifteen in all, put on by students. The experience was, and is, incredible—students have to build the entire city, organize the shows, do the promotion, and be in the midway getting people to come in to shows. The first year it was back, even movie star Humphrey Bogart came.

Jack suggested that we publish a program and sell advertising to make some money. I thought it was a great idea. We went to Mac Wetmore, a local publisher, and we proposed to publish this program. Of course, we had no credit. We wanted Mac to work up a price, and then we would return to meet with him again to discuss it. I will never forget Mac's technique when we went back. He was not in his office, but on his almost empty desk sat a contract with a price. Jack and I went in and waited. After a few minutes, we looked and saw the price. Ten minutes later Mac arrived. It turned out that was his routine. He purposely put the contract out so we would get adjusted to the price before he came in. It was $832, all the money in the world as far as we were concerned.

Then he began to sell us on it. "It's simple," he said. "Here's what you do. You go on campus and you get people to pay a dollar to get their signature in the program." Off-set printing had just been invented, so this was a big deal. "You have everybody sign, we'll take a photograph of it, print it with no typesetting, and that is the way you'll raise the money; that plus advertising." It sounded good to us, so we signed the contract.

We went out on campus with a big sandwich board that said, "Get Your Signature in the Frontier Fiesta Program, One Dollar." I can't tell you how hard it was to separate students from one dollar. After all, the highest paid job on campus was for one dollar an hour, which would be more like fifteen dollars today. We only sold about sixty-five signatures. Because nobody knew what Frontier Fiesta was, selling the advertising wasn't very successful either.

We decided we would make up the difference by selling the programs for twenty-five cents each. We sold some, but it's hard to raise $800 twenty-five cents at a time. There were some other collateral expenses, too, so Jack and I were sweating bullets. We had a deal at the time that whenever we had some free time we would stick our heads in the Cavaliers Theatre, one of the Fiesta shows, where they would stop the show to let Jack and I sing our comedy routine. With all modesty, we brought the house down every time we did it. But we were so frantic trying to sell the programs that we could only do it a couple times a night.

The day before Frontier Fiesta ended, I got a call from Dean Williamson. He wanted Jack and me to come into the office. When we got there, Frontier Fiesta's student business manager joined us. The dean told us that when the Frontier Fiesta committee had met, they felt it was unfair for us to make a profit off of the event when everybody else was donating their time. They decided that we ought to turn the profits over to the Frontier Fiesta Association. My head was spinning, because we were drowning. I said, "Well, if that is what you feel is right." I was able to keep a straight face, something I have found to be the most important thing when making a pitch. Agreeing to their terms came with a big advantage. We could now turn every show into a location for selling the programs.

"Here's the way we'll do it," I said, still thinking on my feet. "We'll turn the income directly over to you. You pay the bills and keep the profit." The next day Jack and I went to every show, and gave them 200 copies of the program to sell. We told them to sell it to everyone who came in and turn the money in with their other proceeds; there was no separate accounting necessary. Of course, all the students grabbed the programs, and we could say we sold 200.

We kept records of how many were sold by each venue, although the reality was that they just gave them out without taking payment. The records indicated the printed programs were a mammoth financial success. After the final accounting for all of Frontier Fiesta, the report showed a loss of $812. Jack and I said nothing.

We ended up with two thousand programs left over. We felt like we had to hide them, so we put them in our house trailer. They took up so much space that we had trouble getting around. We loaded them up in my girlfriend's convertible and drove to Galveston to make a bonfire on the beach and burn them. The wind was blowing too hard, though, and we couldn't get them to burn, so we dug a big hole and buried those programs in the sand on the beach.

A month later Jack and I were on the bus, and a guy sitting in front of us was reading a Frontier Fiesta program. "Excuse me, sir," I said. "Where did you get that program?"

"Well, it's the darndest thing," he replied. "I was in Galveston, and there were thousands of them blowing down the beach."

Despite the programs, the Frontier Fiesta experience was good for everybody involved. And it taught the Wilson brothers a great deal, the hard way. It would be thirty years before we would admit to Johnny Goyen what had happened!

FINDING TIME TO PLAY

I had learned from my cousin Lester back in Corpus that if you want to be somebody, you have to dress like somebody. So, even though campus was informal, I always wore a shirt and tie. I was the only student who did. And, despite Houston's heat, it was a long-sleeved shirt. The reason was simple: if you wore a long-sleeved shirt and tie, people thought you were some official. I could go to the head of the line at the cafeteria, or the back of the shelves at the bookstore, because everybody assumed I was somebody. And this perception helped me with all of my jobs.

In addition to my jobs at the university, I also worked for Raymond Pearson Ford Company selling English Fords. There was a long waiting list for regular Fords, so Ford Motor Company started importing English Fords, which were in abundant supply. The English Ford was about half the size of a regular Ford and would carry four passengers at most. The automobile sold for about $1,500, and I was paid a ten-per- cent commission on each sale. It was a bonanza.

Despite all my jobs, and the studying I managed to do in between, I also found time to have fun. In 1946 I had met Odean Spears. We all called her DD. She had a fantastic personality and was absolutely fearless. Her mother and father were separated, and she and her mother lived fairly close to the University of Houston. Her father, a rough- and-tumble successful Texas businessman named O. J. Spears, owned Spears Dairy in Houston. He bought his daughter a brand-new Ford convertible. At that time, one person out of 5,000 had a new car, and it was especially great because her father also provided the gasoline for it. We had a wonderful time in that car. We didn't drink, but Jack and I would take our girls to the movies, then for a bite to eat at 2-Ks by the Sears on Main Street. We explored Galveston, where I was stunned to see the gambling and prostitution that thrived there, and we frequently ventured as far as New Orleans, which was also quite wild, even if we weren't. Jack dated various girls, and we'd always double date. Jack and I did everything together, whatever it was.

Back then, girls would date more than one guy at a time. We'd be busy working many nights, but that didn't mean the girls would sit around waiting for us. When DD started dating a man named Art, who was quite jealous, she broke up with me. Although I had a wonderful time with DD, it was not meant to be. And my newfound freedom, besides giving me more time to work, also prepared me for the most important meeting of my life.

OUR FIRST ENCOUNTER

A beautiful black-haired girl, whose name I no longer remember, invited me to the Sadie Hawkins Day Dance. She thought I was very glamorous, but she didn't know that I couldn't dance worth a hoot. Growing up, I could have taken dancing lessons in eighth grade in Corpus Christi, but that was the year we moved to Brownsville. In Brownsville everyone took dancing in the seventh grade, so I didn't learn how to dance there either. As a kid, I'd avoid anything uncomfortable, so I didn't go out and try to learn to dance. I had no sisters to

In 1947, Joanne Guest, who would later become my wife, posed for the Lamar High School yearbook as a Beauty.

teach me, either. But when this beautiful girl invited me to the dance, I accepted without hesitation.

At the dance, which was held in the college gymnasium, my date and I sat down with another couple at one of the little card tables that were scattered around the dance floor. A candle sat in the middle of each table, but otherwise the gym was dimly lit. I looked across the table and there sat a girl beautiful beyond words, dressed like Daisy Mae.

For anyone who remembers the Lil' Abner comic strip, you know that means she wore a low-cut polka-dot blouse. To quote from a Frank Sinatra song, "And then my heart stood still." I watched this girl across the table, with the candlelight illuminating her beautiful face. She did not say a word the entire evening.

My date and I danced a bit, and she quickly learned that I was a terrible dancer. We dissolved our romance on the spot. On the other hand, if I had told her upfront that I was a lousy dancer, but a great kisser, the pressure would have been off and we would have had a great time. The next morning, I started looking for the beautiful girl across the table, but I didn't know her name. All I could do was walk around campus looking for her.

Finally, in April, six months later, I found her. I was walking down the hall of the recreation building in front of The Cougar office when she walked down the same hall, looking as beautiful as ever. I went over to talk to her, and she didn't remember who I was. She didn't even re- member meeting me. I found out her name was Joanne Guest. She was very shy, and I was determined to get to know her, so I rounded her up and took her into *The Cougar* office.

In the office we were having our regular Friday afternoon party. No alcohol was served, but the entire *Cougar* staff, about thirty students, was there, laughing and raising Cain. Rampant profanity was still a problem in *The Cougar* office, and Joanne wasn't used to this kind of language. She said that she had to go home. I wasn't about to let her get away after a six-month search to find her, so I offered to go with her.

We got into her car, a Packard, and she drove home with me in the front seat. She lived on Branard Street, near River Oaks, in Houston. We sat on a sofa in the living room and talked, and of course I was talking 100 mph. We went into the kitchen, and I kissed her. That was a thrill. I could tell that she thought I was all right.

We were back sitting on her couch when she said "Excuse me," and went into the other room to use the phone. She came back a few minutes later and said, "It's for you." Confused, I asked who it was. She said, "It's my mother." So, I went to take the call.

Opal Guest, who was working downtown, said, "Welcome, Joanne doesn't know how to tell you this, but her date is arriving in about ten minutes to pick her up. If you wouldn't mind excusing yourself, I am sure she would be glad to have you come back another day."

I made like I was leaving but managed to hang around until the guy showed up. He was a cheerleader at Rice University. His name was Sully Sullivan, and he was a nice guy. I gave him my dynamic routine, and I went on my way, filled with excitement about having found Joanne and determined to see her again as soon as possible.

SHE HAD SEVEN DATES A WEEK

After our initial encounter, Joanne and I began to date regularly. I was eager to know as much about her as I could learn, and though she was far quieter than I, as we dated, I began to hear about her childhood.

She was born at St. Joseph Hospital in Houston on October 11, 1930, to parents Opal McCord Guest and James Randolf Guest. Her father owned a Dodge-Plymouth dealership in downtown Houston. When World War II came, the US car companies stopped making autos and made trucks and tanks for the military. Her father then went to work in Freeport for Dow Chemical Company and later switched to promoting boxing matches. At first, he had an arena on Waugh Drive at Buffalo Drive, now called Allen Parkway, in Houston. Later, he moved his boxing enterprises to the City Auditorium downtown, where his fights included world champion Joe Louis in an exhibition match.

Joanne grew up as an only child. She attended St. Anne's Church elementary school, spent one year at St. Agnes Academy, and then went to Lanier Junior High School and Lamar High School. She graduated from Lamar in the spring of 1947 and entered the University of Houston as an art major. She had just been a student there for three months when she attended the Sadie Hawkins dance and changed my life.

Because she had a date seven night a week, and I was perfectly happy to have two of them. I couldn't afford more than that. Although I was only dating her a small percentage of her total time, I felt I was the important person in her life. I was never jealous of the others, because I knew that they were no luckier than I in having anything approaching sex. In those days a proper girl, and Joanne certainly was one, would not consider anything beyond a passionate kiss. And sex before marriage was out of the question.

Joanne and I fell into a routine and had a wonderful time. My brother Jack and I were living in Humble with our parents. They had moved there two years after we left for college. My mother had grown up in Humble, so her family was there, and prospects for business were just better in Houston. Sleeping in a regular bed and having a bathroom and free meals convinced Jack and me to move out of our trailer, even if it meant a commute. We purchased a car together, and we would alternate driving it on dates.

A typical date would be Jack taking his girlfriend Mary Lou, who later would become his wife, and me taking Joanne to an inexpensive dinner. Afterward, we would go to a movie and then get an after-movie snack, often at our favorite hangout, 2-K's. I would drive Jack and Mary Lou to her house and drop them off and then take Joanne to her house. I would stay about forty-five minutes to an hour. Afterward I would drive to Mary Lou's house, pick up Jack, and head home. We would typically arrive after midnight, then get up at 6:30 the next morning to head to class.

This routine took a toll on our sleep, so Jack and I took turns driving home. Whoever was not driving would immediately go to sleep in the front seat. One-night Jack was driving on Little York Road and fell asleep at the wheel. The car drove through the ditch, through the fence, and into a field, where it bogged down among the rows of vegetables.

I was awakened, but when I looked up and saw what the situation was, I immediately put my head back down and went back to sleep. Jack did the same. The next morning a big truck came along the road, and the driver hollered to see if we needed help. We woke up and agreed that we did. He got a long rope and pulled us back to the highway, and we drove on home.

OUR FIRST LIFE-CHANGING CONVERSATION

After about seven months of this routine, Joanne and I were in her car parked in front of the Pig Stand drive-in on Main Street on a crisp November day. We were eating a sandwich, when she said that one of her boyfriends had asked her to marry him for the fifth time. He was a rich kid from River Oaks and a good-looking guy. She had always turned him down, but she had also recently turned eighteen years old. She wasn't about to be unmarried at the age of nineteen.

"So, what are your plans in that regard?" she said.

"It's simple," I replied. "Tell him no. You and I will get married as soon as I turn twenty-six." I explained that my father always said that a man doesn't know what he's doing until he is twenty-six and has no business getting married at a younger age.

She said something to the effect of "good luck with that plan." I realized then that I had to move or she would marry somebody else. And the competition for her hand was fierce: her other dates were tall, handsome guys with new automobiles. Jack and I in our shared a used car weren't what you would consider successful yet. I had convinced Joanne that I was going to be successful, but now it was clear that I would have to act fast if I didn't want to lose her.

THE PROPOSAL

One day in January, a student named Ben Noble, Jr., the son of a diamond merchant, came into The Cougar office and said, "Welcome, it's time you bought Joanne a ring. Tomorrow morning I'm taking you down to my dad's place in the City National Bank building so you can pick it out."

I invited Joanne to go downtown with Ben and me, but I didn't tell her why we were going. When we got there and the salesperson pulled out the engagement rings, she was very surprised—and very pleased— that I was not going to wait until I was twenty-six.

"Welcome, we have to talk to my parents," she said.

I talked to her mother, and her mother thought it was reasonable. Then I talked to her father.

"What are you thinking?" he said. "You're just a couple of kids. You can't possibly think about getting married." I told him that we would not get married until August, and this was January. He relaxed, assuming we would forget all about it by August.

My parents reacted the same way. They said we were too young. When I told them that we were not going to get married until August, eight months distant, they settled down. But, of course, we didn't change our minds.

A few months after our engagement, I decided to join the Catholic church so I could be part of my future wife's religion. I had grown up as a Protestant, but I had lost confidence in my church when the pastor told me that Christ did not drink wine; it was grape juice. Even though I didn't drink wine, I was sure he had made that up. When I told my parents I was going to convert, my mother was very upset. I didn't understand why.

On August 27, 1949, the day I graduated from college, Joanne and I were married in a big formal wedding at St. Anne's church. Joanne was a beautiful bride. My sister, Beverly, who was six, was the flower girl, and Jack was the best man. I wore a tuxedo with a white jacket since it was summer, and the groomsmen were all in white summer jackets, rented. We had High Mass, and one of our friends who had never been to Catholic church said "Welcome, there's no doubt that you're married after all that!"

Joanne Guest and I were married on August 27, 1949, at St. Anne's Church in Houston, Texas, the day I graduated from UH. My brother, Jack, was the best man.

The reception was at her parent's house, just a couple of blocks away. It was a modest affair, with no alcohol. We left for our honeymoon from the reception in a 1942 Plymouth, which I had bought for $200 and Joanne's father had repainted. I had gotten the $200 from an unsecured note at Hampton State Bank, later named River Oaks Bank and Trust. My credit was nonexistent, so I had to ask John Scardino, who owned the printing company where The Cougar was printed, to cosign the note, which he agreed to do. We drove off happily in that fine automobile, with tin cans tied behind it and writing all over the windows. We were headed for Hunt, Texas and our future.

Years later, I was startled to discover why my mother had resisted my Catholic conversion. She told me that she had always respected the Catholic church, but she felt that if I became Catholic, it would deny me the opportunity to become president of the United States. In spite of the great hardships she endured during the Depression, she had remained convinced that no matter the odds, I could become president. It would be more than a decade before John F. Kennedy became the nation's first Catholic president, and, despite my mother's loving faith in my abilities, I was very happy for him to have that honor.

THE GROOM NEEDS A COLLEGE DEGREE

I could hardly be called a scholar when I was at the University of Houston. Since I graduated from Brownsville Junior College with an AA degree, I entered the University of Houston as a junior. Jack entered as a sophomore since he had taken off two years from college while serving in World War II. The first semester I signed up for eighteen hours of courses, an ambitious load. As my work requirements increased, I began to cut back on my course work, until after a couple of years I was going to school half-time. My biggest priority was putting food on the table. Although Jack and I did fine, we never had enough money. My priority was making a living, not making good grades.

After I proposed marriage, I dropped the idea of a Law Degree and it turned out that I lacked sufficient credits to receive a Bachelor's degree. I got permission from Dr. Walter W. Kemmerer, president of the University of Houston whom Jack and I had inauspiciously met when we were trying to avoid the line on registration day, to go to school double- time during both summer semesters. I took eight courses in less than three months. I never studied so hard in my life, and it permitted me to finish enough courses to get a bachelor's degree in business administration and graduate on August 27, 1949. I missed the graduation ceremony because I was at St. Anne's Church getting married.

Dr. Kemmerer not only let me increase my course load in order to graduate and get married, but he also asked me to work for the university. I began visualizing a career in academics. That was a game-changer in my life.

My first job after graduation was assistant director of the School of Nursing, and I talked my way into having an office in the Medical Center. The Medical Center only had three buildings at the time—Hermann Hospital, Baylor College of Medicine, and M. D. Anderson Hospital, which was under construction. My office was in the Hermann Hospital nursing quarters in a converted bathroom on the first floor.

They took out all the stalls and the plumbing, and it made a nice office for my secretary and me.

TOP: My parents, E.E. Jack Wilson and Irene Wilson, at my brother Jack's wedding to Mary Lou Moffit in June 1949.

BOTTOM: My grandfather Dr. E.M. Wilson founded the Christadelphians, a religious
organization. He is seated on the front row with the congregation in Goldthwaite, Texas.

My job consisted of two responsibilities: recruiting students and raising money for scholarships. I went to high schools all around the area and made arrangements with the principals to let me talk with the student body to make a pitch about nursing. Our biggest source of scholarships was Houston Endowment, founded by Jesse Jones. His wife Mary Gibbs Jones had been a nurse, so the Joneses and the endowment looked kindly upon the School of Nursing.

EARLY MARRIED DAYS

After our honeymoon, Joanne and I moved into a brand-new apartment project a block off Kirby Drive near River Oaks. In those days, Kirby Drive was a gravel road going south from Westheimer Road. Because a college friend's father had built the project, we had the opportunity to pick the apartment we wanted before construction was complete. We had a one-bedroom unit.

Joanne's parents were not wealthy, and I had no money at all. Before the wedding we had managed to buy a cedar chest, a king-size bed, a chest of drawers, a dinette set for the kitchen, and a table lamp, which had to sit on the floor in the living room because we had no table. Joanne was a sophomore when we married, and she continued to take courses part-time.

When we married, Joanne did not cook. Every night on the way home from working at the University of Houston, I would stop at a grocery store on Shepherd Drive at Richmond and pick up a package of frozen pork chops and a package of frozen green peas, or something similar. At home she would defrost and cook the meat and heat the vegetable, and we would have dinner at the dinette set. About once a month, the frying pan used for the meat would catch on fire, and I would come in and take over the meal. We didn't care what we were eating at that point; we were just happy as could be in our newlywed routine.

Then on June 25, 1950, the Korean War broke out. I received orders to report to the Navy three days later. Our lives were about to change radically, and neither my newly pregnant wife nor I were very happy about it.

3

Anchors Aweigh
The West Coast and Japan

I reported a day early to the Naval Training Center in San Diego on a Sunday in September of 1950. Dressed in my Louis Roth designer suit and tie, I sat down in front of the Chief Petty Officer in charge of Company 107, soon to be my company, and I began discussing Korean War strategy.

Patience was not one of my virtues. I considered myself an educated, prosperous, and well-informed citizen, who by accident had been summoned to active duty as a lowly seaman apprentice. I was all of twenty-two years old. I had been eager to go to war when I was seventeen, but at twenty-two, I had other plans for my life.

I doubt that many Americans knew or cared much about the two Koreas until war broke out. The Communists ruled the North; the United States supported the South, as did the United Nations. This was at the early stages of what became known as the Cold War, with the constant threat of a wider nuclear war between Russia and China on one side and the US and our allies on the other.

The Chief Petty Officer and I had been chatting for about ten minutes about strategy and politics with me doing most of the talking. I had easily swung into my most dynamic act as an up-and-coming young business person, dominating the soundtrack, until he brought the chatter to a sudden ending. When he cut me off, I had no clue as to how I should respond.

He leaned forward, gripped his desk, and looked at me as if I were from a distant land. "Wilson," he said, "I am going to give you the best advice that you will ever get in the United States Navy. If you take it you will do great; if you do not you are in for years of hell.

"I'm sure you were someone very important as a civilian," he snapped, "but you are in the NAVY now, and you must get with the program. Now I want you to stand up, and I'm warning you never to sit down in my presence again. Get out of here, go back to your bunk, and don't ever come to my office again unless you are called."

His advice turned out to be the best I had ever received. Sheepishly, I went back to my bunk and had a conversation with myself. "Self," I said, "you're a seaman apprentice in the US Navy. You are in boot camp, 2,000 miles from Houston. You can either get with the program and work hard to be successful, or you can fight the system and be miserable." I decided on the spot that I was going to be a Navy man. The next day, when the remainder of the 100 recruits in my company arrived, I was Mister Nice Guy, doing everything to be helpful and accommodating. In boot camp, I was Mister Humble. I never again mentioned my background, education, or status.

When I saw the chief on the parade ground I saluted sharply and said, "Good morning, Chief." Three days later he put me in charge of the company as Recruit Chief Petty Officer. It was the beginning of a productive military career. He taught me an important lesson, and as I moved forward from that conversation, I understood it more fully; talent alone will not ensure success. Nothing is more common than unsuccessful men with talent. Education will not ensure success; the world is full of educated derelicts. Persistence and determined hard work are the keys to success, in the military and in life.

BECOMING A NAVY MAN

As a seventeen-year-old junior college student in Brownsville, I had eagerly awaited my turn to join the Army. While the end of the war changed my plans, it hadn't changed the respect in which I held the military. My impressions, as those of most of my generation, were fueled by the motion picture industry. As Japan swept through the Pacific for most of the war's first year, the studios turned defeat into moral victories, as many of them indeed were. The release of films about the battles for Wake Island and Bataan and Guadalcanal sometimes had to be delayed while the producers waited for the outcome of the action.

I entered the Korean War in 1950 as an enlisted man, but I became an officer in December of 1950. In 1951, I was ordered to Japan.

On one or more levels, this was propaganda in the guise of entertainment, but such movies as The Sands of Iwo Jima, The White Cliffs of Dover, So Proudly We Hail!, and Casablanca became classics. When not cheering for Hollywood's war, entire families collected newspapers, wire coat hangers, rubber bands, and scrap metal as members of what civilians proudly called the home front. Never since have liberals and conservatives, intellectuals and illiterates, rich and poor, young and old come together in such a single, forceful alliance.

Two years after Jack and I moved to Houston to enroll at the University of Houston, the Berlin crisis occurred in Germany. The Soviet Union blocked off all of the Allied forces' access to Berlin where the US, England, and France each controlled a segment of the city. The United States immediately reinstated the draft. I opted for the

Naval Reserve, as it would permit me to attend meetings once a week and continue in college. Jack did the same.

A longtime friend of my father, an official with the Federal Communications Commission, had been a high-ranking officer during World War II in the Naval Security Group, a branch of what would become the National Security Agency. The Naval Security Group was a spooky place, super-secret at the time, but with branches in the three major armed services and the State Department. Each division was charged with monitoring radio transmissions from all over the world, decrypting of these messages, and transmitting the information to Washington DC.

My father's friend urged me to transfer to the Naval Security Group, where he felt I would be in the company of the Navy's best and brightest. I applied and was quickly accepted.

I had attended weekly drills since enlisting in the reserves in 1948, but I now drilled at an armory located in southeast Houston on a street that had no echo of ships or oceans, the Old Spanish Trail (OST). My father's friend was the commanding officer of this reserve unit, and I was promoted from recruit to seaman apprentice, all while working on my college degree and holding down my other jobs.

After graduation, I had applied to become an officer, but my application was denied. When President Truman mobilized the US military, avoiding the need to declare an act of war by labeling the American role in the conflict a "police action," a hotly debated semantic trick, I had received orders. I had been making $300 a month at the University of Houston. Now I was going to be a seaman apprentice at $75 a month. I was able to delay my departure for active duty until September, and over the summer we stored our furniture, shut down the apartment, and Joanne moved home with her parents.

I was to fly to Dallas where I would change planes to head to San Diego. Joanne came with me as far as Dallas. Neither of us had flown on a commercial airline before, and we might have enjoyed it if our emotions had not been so tangled.

The military was a world I had seen only through the romanticized lens of the movies, but, after my initial run-in with the Chief Petty Officer, I began to understand the structure, the pride, and the ways the restrictions provided strength. For me, as for countless other cocky young people, boot camp was a valuable and maturing experience. It was a great leveler. It provided a cross-section of America: there were hayseeds from Arkansas, Jewish intellectuals from New York, Georgia boys with thick southern accents, and tough Pachucos from East Los Angeles, and the same rules applied to all of us. Our success or failure depended on our willingness to live up to those rules.

As the Recruit Chief Petty Officer, I marched at the side of the company and gave them a cadence. I passed on orders from the chief, but the only actual authority I had over the men was to assign which "watch" each would draw. The men alternated one-hour watches, twenty-four hours a day. Although later the watches would be more serious, our watches were to guard our clothesline around the clock. If I needed to punish one of the men, I had the authority to assign him the 3 a.m. watch.

After two or three weeks of isolation, we were granted shore leave and permitted to go to San Diego for the day, with a midnight curfew. Then as now, San Diego was a pretty town, but it was smaller, less shiny, and less modern. The Grant Hotel, overlooking the square, was popular with sailors and Marines. A room cost twenty-five dollars a night. There were no big-league sports teams, no famous zoo—just the huge Navy base, the Marine recruit depot next door, and Tijuana across the border.

One night, my group of friends headed to the part of downtown where strip joints flourished. Since I didn't drink alcohol, it was easy for me to get back to the base on time. Others weren't quite so lucky or punctual. Sometime after midnight, a young Mexican-American staggered into the barracks and brandished a jackknife. If anyone objected to his lateness, or his drunkenness, he snarled, he would be happy to meet that guy in a knife fight. I suggested that he undress and go to bed, a comment not well received.

"Make me," he challenged. "If you think you're big enough!"

I looked at him as one would look at an annoying child. "Which watch would you like if you fail to obey my instructions? 1 a.m.? 2 a.m.? or 3 a.m.?" I asked that same question over and over, until he folded his knife and went to bed.

The day before graduation from boot camp, the 100 men in the company voted on the Honor Award to designate the recruit who worked the hardest, always did the right thing, and was most helpful to others. I was elected, the first time in the history of the training center that a Recruit Chief Petty Officer—not a position designed to win friends—was voted the Honor Man.

BAINBRIDGE ISLAND

On graduation day the band played, the companies paraded past the commanding officer, and I officially became a member of the United States Navy. I received my orders to report to the Naval Security facility at Bainbridge Island, Washington State, a small base located about fifteen miles west of Seattle in the middle of Puget Sound, accessible only by ferry.

I took trains north through Los Angeles and San Francisco, across Oregon, and finally up to Seattle. When I reported to the naval head- quarters on A Street in Seattle, the quartermaster issued additional clothing, and a doctor gave me a medical exam and cleared me to board the ferry to Bainbridge. The school operated by my unit had some 500 enlisted men enrolled. I was a yeoman to the Chief Petty Officer who ran the school. We had two officers at the base, a lieutenant junior grade and a full lieutenant. They were both seldom seen, which made my job more necessary.

A yeoman is the Naval identification for a secretary, in today's vocabulary an administrative assistant. The job was ideal for me; it placed me near the seat of power, and I could easily carry out my functions without further training.

Snow blanketed Bainbridge Island much of the year. I felt like a character in a Russian novel when I went back and forth to Seattle; the ferry would be tossed and turned in the rough waters of Puget Sound, and it was always either raining, foggy, or snowing.

The monotony of the weather was offset only by the abundance of sweet red apples. Apples grew everywhere, along the side streets, in people's yards, front and back. When they began to ripen in the early winter, the owners were pleased to have you come and pick them. I kept a bushel basket of apples next to my upper bunk in the barracks.

Without fully realizing it, in boot camp I had gained eighteen pounds. Before breakfast we had calisthenics—a word not heard much today— and we marched and drilled so hard I thought I could eat all I wanted at meal time. The servers in the mess hall were enlisted men, like me, and most of them pulled the duty for one or two days. Accordingly, as we slid through the line, each swab reached down with a large spoon and hit the plate with a stack of mashed potatoes or macaroni or what- ever the starchy offering was. The food was plentiful, and, given our appetites, it seemed delicious. Every meal came with sodas and an ample dessert, usually pie with ice cream. So, when I waddled aboard the train to leave San Diego, I weighed 218 pounds.

As the winters worsened in Washington State, the nights turned bitterly cold. The snow was so deep that the Navy had to construct a network of wooden slat sidewalks that were about a foot and a half off the ground. These sidewalks connected the school, the barracks, and the chow hall, which was about two blocks away. After a few nights of walking through the snow, slipping and sliding, trying to reach the chow hall in the freezing cold, I started staying in the barracks. My dinner consisted of apples from the bushel basket stored next to my bunk. Six weeks later, the eighteen pounds were gone.

MISSING HOME

In the Navy, as in other branches of the military, you are soon relieved of any obsession with privacy. My bunk was in a cubicle about twelve feet wide with an upper and lower bunk on each side and a table and chair at the end. My three roommates were pleasant enough, but we all had to sit on the lower bunks because of the scarcity of chairs. I chose an upper bunk so that I could be left at peace and not have people sprawling on my bed.

I enjoyed my stint on Bainbridge Island, which exposed me to an environment much different from what I had known in Texas, but I was

My wife, Joanne, poses in front of a Japanese house in Tokyo. She joined me with our son, Welcome Jr., in 1952.

painfully homesick for Joanne and felt guilty about her going through her pregnancy when I was so far away. We wrote each other every single day, and I have kept her letters to this day. I subscribed to the Houston Chronicle so I could keep informed about what was happening on the home front.

The separation occupied my thoughts to the point that I had no sense of time or distance as I had always known them. So I was caught totally off guard one day, after four months or so, when I was walking out of the school building to go to lunch and a seaman standing near the exit immediately snapped to attention and saluted me. He was holding a telegram in his hand.

I was stunned almost speechless until he reminded me that the first seaman to salute a newly named naval officer was entitled to a dollar bill. He explained that the telegram was from Texas Senator Lyndon Johnson and congratulated me on being promoted to officer in the US Navy, an ensign. In the radio shack, of course, they read everyone's mail. With a telegram it was just easier.

My father had known Senator Johnson since salad days as the administrative assistant to Congressman Richard Kleberg of Kingsville. Dick Kleberg was an heir to the King Ranch, and in Congress he represented the Corpus Christi area, where we had lived for many years. After my application to be appointed an officer in the Navy reserves had been declined and I was called into service as a seaman apprentice, my father wrote his old friend, Lyndon Baines Johnson. In the letter he explained what he considered the injustice of his son having a college degree and entering the Navy as an enlisted man. Apparently, the Navy had been persuaded by the senator and advised him of my new rank even before informing me.

My commission arrived a day or so later. I was directed to report to the commanding officer at the Seattle Naval Base, wearing my seaman apprentice uniform, which was very unimpressive attire, complete with bell-bottoms, a button fly, and a long collar down the back that had been designed in the 1800s for seamen who used tar to keep their hair out of the way.

The lovable Yogi Berra, the iconic catcher for the New York Yankees, famously reported to the baseball team wearing this very uniform. When the equipment man stared at him until he grew uncomfortable, Yogi, five-foot-eight and squatty, is rumored to have said, "I guess I don't look much like a ballplayer." The equipment man replied, "You don't look much like a sailor, either." And wearing it, I didn't look much like an officer, either.

After my commanding officer congratulated me, he notified me that I had to be in officer's apparel before sunset. Moreover, he said that he would not permit me, as an officer, to return to the dormitory to collect my personal effects. I would have to send for them instead. He instructed me to go down the street to a uniform store and buy an officer's uniform and hat. This would not be a fashion statement. From age seventeen to ninety, I wore a size forty-four-long suit. The store didn't have my size and instead sold me a forty-three regular. Since I was trim again, close to skinny, the fit didn't look too bad.

The commanding officer, or CO, swore me in and handed over my orders to report to Monterey, California, for Officer Training School. This was an advanced school for people who were already officers, as opposed to those who were candidates to become one. Classes started in January, so I had the opportunity to spend Christmas in Houston with Joanne. The next day, on the advice of the CO, I went to an Army airbase in Seattle to hitch a plane ride back to Houston.

This was a fine system. Servicemen could fly free if they were willing to hop a plane that might not be headed directly to their final destination. The wait was brief. In a couple of hours, I was sitting in the nose of a V-26 attack bomber heading to Oklahoma City. From there I quickly got a ride in the nose of a B-25 to Ellington Field in Houston. The nose of both planes was where the bombardier sat in his goggles and flight suit; I had a great view of the sky but could not see any other part of the plane.

That Christmas was wonderful, and early in January, Joanne and I packed the two-door, 1947 Ford we had gotten to replace the re-paint-ed Plymouth and started the long drive to Monterey. This was the first cross-country trip we had ever made, and we were so glad to be back together, we enjoyed it tremendously.

SUNNY MONTEREY

Our happiness continued in Monterey. Although required to stay on the base in the bachelor officer's quarters, I was allowed to have my wife in town so long as I saw her only between 5 p.m. and 8 p.m. every evening, along with half a day on Saturday and all day on Sunday. The scheduling felt almost clandestine. We found a nice tourist court with an ocean view, one large room with a sofa, and a small kitchenette with a table. We could not have been happier had we been in the Waldorf Astoria. On weekends we drove to Carmel-by-the-Sea or Pebble Beach.

The Naval Training Center had previously been the Del Mar Country Club, which had been confiscated by the government during World War II and used as a Navy training center. Of course, the officers played golf as well. The setting was beautiful beyond words, and the instructors were world class. One of my instructors, whose name I don't recall, was one of the eight surviving pilots of the famous torpedo squadron at Midway that turned back the Japanese fleet.

Although I had been an average student at the University of Houston, I excelled in officer school. There was a simple reason for this transformation: attending class was not optional. From 8 p.m. to 10 p.m. every night, we had to sit at our desks in our rooms, studying. Hall monitors would look in the open door to be sure we were doing exactly that. So, without options, I attended every class and studied every night. Making good grades was a cinch.

I was an assistant platoon leader when we drilled. The training was rigorous, both in the classroom and on the golf-course-turned-field. There were probably 200 men in my class. Most held the rank of ensign, and a few were lieutenants junior grade, including the platoon leader.

At five o'clock every afternoon Joanne picked me up and took me "home." She served dinner in the motel, and we would spend three happy, close to giddy, hours together. Promptly at 8 p.m. she dropped me off at the school, and I returned to my room.

When graduation week arrived three months later, I was called to the office of the commanding officer. He informed me that the faculty had ranked the 200 students in the school, and I had graduated at the top of the class. Being number one is always a thrill, even if you are just pitching pennies at a crack. But I was truly and pleasantly surprised. It had been so easy. You went to class, you studied, and you received high grades. This attitude was part of my new concept, the dedicated Wilson. Before, I had always been going in so many directions at once that I never had the opportunity to see what I could accomplish if I focused all my energy.

CHANGING COURSE

A few days after graduation, I received orders to report to a fleet-tug in San Francisco. A fleet-tug was built like a barge and sailed back and forth to Hawaii, pulling disabled ships. The commanding officer of the school was livid. He was insulted that the person who graduated first in his class would be assigned to a tugboat. He got on the phone, and a few days later I received a change in orders. I was to be sent to one of the historic World War II aircraft carriers, the Hornet, to be a launch officer, dealing with planes that catapulted aloft instead of simply taking off from the deck. I was excited about my new orders and delighted that I had been given ten days to take my wife back to Houston. This was mid-March, and she was expecting our baby at the end of April.

After a few days at home, I went back to Ellington Field and hitched a flight to San Francisco, where I thought I was going to join the Hornet. But in the Navy, you learn about changing course, and, sure enough, while I was in Houston my orders were revised. The Naval Security Group had caught up with me and canceled my aircraft carrier assignment. Instead, I was ordered to report to Yokosuka, Japan, for duty with the NSG detachment based there.

This was a bit of a shock, but I had more immediate concerns. Joanne began having difficulties with the pregnancy, and her doctor warned us that the problem could be life-threatening. He contacted the Red Cross to see if my orders to Japan could be delayed until the baby was born. The Navy consented, and I was reassigned to an office on Market Street in San Francisco. When I reported, it was quickly apparent that I was not expected and had no duties. The officer in charge simply told me to check in each morning at 8 a.m., and then I could spend the rest of the day doing whatever I wanted.

After three days he told me to check in by phone instead of in per- son. One would think that six weeks in San Francisco, with nothing but free time, would be like owning a candy store. But it was frustrating and awful. I missed Joanne terribly. We were nearly 2,000 miles apart, I was worried about her, and by nature I was not equipped to have nothing to do. I slept at the Alameda Naval Air Station in the officers' quarters and spent the first week sightseeing. After that week I had trouble getting out of bed.

The men who cleaned up the officers' quarters got off duty at 4 p.m., so every day around three they would show up and force me to crawl out of bed. I dressed and caught a bus to San Francisco, aimless and ill-suited for solitude. One day I was walking along Powell Street and decided to pop into a bar. I sat down on a barstool and, never having ordered a drink, didn't know what to say when the bartender asked me what I wanted. About that time a customer walked up behind me, and I overheard him order a bourbon and ginger. I quickly said, "I'll have the same." At age twenty-three, I downed my first alcoholic beverage, a bourbon and gin- ger, and it became my drink of choice for the next five years.

Meanwhile, Joanne's doctor decided to induce delivery, a safer procedure, he thought, than waiting. Two weeks before the scheduled delivery date she was admitted to St. Joseph's Hospital in Houston. Two days earlier, I had once again hitched a ride on a military aircraft to be at her side. I remember going out on the fire escape and getting on my knees, praying first that Joanne would be ok and then that the baby would be ok. When our first-born child, Welcome Jr., arrived, it was a monumental moment. We were ecstatic.

When he arrived and everything was fine, it was time for me to go back to duty. I was expecting to go back, and I felt so lucky that I had actually been able to be there when he was born. So, I didn't mind. I knew Joanne was brave. I had great faith in her strength and her ability to take care of him.

A few days after Welcome Jr.'s birth, I hopped a flight back to San Francisco, where I soon boarded an Army transport plane heading to Tokyo. On the transport we sat eight abreast, with an aisle down one side and all of the seats facing backwards. The military was more interested in safety than comfort, and in a plane crash facing backwards was safer.

We stopped briefly at Guam to refuel, crossed the international dateline, and landed in Tokyo early in the morning. I was sent by train to Yokosuka, about thirty miles to the south. Japan was totally different from anything I had ever experienced. The first thing I noticed was that there were zillions of people. A million people were trying to crowd on the train to Yokosuka, and, compared to me, they were all quite short.

When I arrived, I reported to the commanding officer of the communications station, whose name happened to be Captain Wilson. He directed me to the Naval Security Group and explained that he had no idea what was done over there.

Shrouded in secrecy, the NSG employed a staff of about 500 men, including some thirty officers. The task was unchanged from my duty in the reserves: monitor enemy transmissions, break codes, and forward the reports to the National Security Agency (NSA) in Washington DC, by radio teletype. We were sworn to secrecy, but our operations have been declassified and books have been written about the entire operation since then, so I assume I won't be shot for discussing it now.

I was responsible for transmitting a hundred or so daily reports to Washington. As a watch officer, I worked eight hours on, eight hours off for three consecutive "watches," followed by fifty-six hours off. The first shift was from 4 p.m. to midnight; the second was from 8 a.m. to 4 p.m., and the third was from midnight to 8 a.m. In the communications office, a full lieutenant was in charge of each watch, with an additional officer and five or six enlisted men under him.

We encrypted the messages using a machine we called "The Monster." The enlisted men ran Teletype tape through The Monster, which sent the message by radio to those with the highest security clearance. On the top floor of the building, 100 men with earphones sat eavesdropping in eight-hour shifts and typing coded messages from the Russian fleet in the Pacific, the North Korean army, and Chinese radar stations. We operated on the theory that they were each up to various levels of mischief. All of the codes used by the three enemy forces were simplistic. The codes would be changed on the first day of each month, and within three days the National Security Agency in Washington would have broken them and sent instructions on how to decode the messages.

Almost, all of military intelligence, or at least ninety-five percent of it, is routine and boring. Communists were, and probably still are, very bureaucratic and therefore reported everything that happened every single day. At sunset, every captain of every Russian ship in the Pacific sent a report back to Moscow, which included a detailed description of his cargo, a list of the officers on board, their destination, and estimated time of arrival. We knew the names of every officer and, in many cases, the names of their wives and children. We could have mailed them birthday cards.

There was a certain monotony to our routine, but we were also working with various kinds of intrigue in ways that were sometimes mysterious, so it kept us alert. The Chinese constantly complained that US spy planes were flying over mainland China. The Pentagon fiercely denied that any such activity ever occurred. The charge was ridiculous, they said. We wouldn't dare stoop to such a sinister endeavor.

In truth, Navy fighters traveled at top speed for about 300 miles just inside the Chinese coast. The purpose was to cause the radar stations to open up so we could pinpoint them. As each radar station tracked the passing of an American plane, our directional crews would record the exact location of the station. In the event of an invasion of China, our first priority would be to destroy all of the radar stations.

I was a communications officer. Our job was to encode messages and send them back to the NSA. Any communications that came out of our headquarters would come through us. We worked in shifts, listening to Russians, North Koreans, and Chinese. If it was the midnight shift, I was in charge of all the 100 men in the building.

Our officers in the NSG in Japan were an interesting mix. For example, the world-famous chess player Oswald Jacoby was one of the officers assigned to Yokosuka. Oswald was a celebrity among us because he wrote a weekly column on bridge, which was published in 500 news- papers around the globe. His brain worked so fast that he developed a speech impediment—he could not speak as fast as his brain would crank out the words. Every night in the officers' club he challenged me to a game of ping-pong. At the end of his tour of duty, we were about fifty-fifty. I didn't play chess with him, but those who did would say that he complimented them with such remarks as, "You're a good chess player. It took me seven moves to beat you."

Stories like this delighted me because they spoke to competition. I have always been a competitive person. Dwight Eisenhower once said, "You should approach every challenge as if there was a chance of losing at the last minute. This is sports. This is politics. This is business. This is life." Once I became a naval officer, it was no different. In a room full of strangers, I would always try to become the leader.

LIFE IN JAPAN

I lived in a small apartment with two other officers. One was Bud O'Neil from Walnut, California, and the other was a guy from Oklahoma whose name I don't remember. Each apartment was assigned a Japanese house- boy. Ours was named Nakajima. He was a high school student always eager to practice his English. If I slurred my words, or slipped into a Texas accent, he would ask what the words meant. He would follow us around and talk, talk, talk. He was shocked to learn that I didn't know who Helen Traubel was—an American opera star he knew all about.

Our first Christmas in Japan, Nakajima invited Bud and me to come over for Sunday dinner with his family during the holiday season. I accepted the invitation with no hesitation, but Bud said he didn't want to go because the Japanese ate raw fish and other weird dishes. He finally agreed when I told him that we would arrive after dinner and simply visit with the family and perhaps have a dessert.

When the day came, Bud and I timed our trip to show up at 2:30 p.m. at the small village outside of Tokyo where our houseboy lived. I had carefully told Nakajima we would not be there for lunch but would come shortly after the meal. Something was lost in translation. When we arrived at the train station, Nakajima was there and said they had been waiting for us since noon and had not eaten.

When we entered the house, the food looked lovely, if unrecognizable. The Japanese prepared their dishes with a glazing over them, and it was impossible for us to tell what we were eating. The family was very nice, impeccably polite, but spoke little English. Nakajima could not find names we understood for the various foods, so the whole lunch was a mystery. Bud declined to touch any of it, saying that he had already

When the Korean War broke out, I served first in Bainbridge Island, Washington.

eaten. Having a cast-iron stomach, I plunged in and ate everything. Whatever it was I ate, it was all tasty.

Bud was my best friend in Japan, and we went everywhere together. On our fifty-six hours off, Bud and I would take trips to Tokyo, to see Mount Fuji or, in several cases, to Kamakura, the site of the huge 200- foot statue of Buddha, with a nice beach nearby. When we needed a vehicle for such trips, we simply cruised by the transportation barn to see what was available. Jeeps were abundant, but a pickup truck had status because you could keep warm and dry. I schmoozed the transportation chief, and we typically had a pickup truck at our disposal.

Coming back from one trip after dark, we found ourselves lost and bouncing along through the rice fields with no map, no signs, and no streetlights. We came across a farmer walking along the road, and rolled down the window and summoned all of my meager language skills. I spoke a little Japanese but not enough to be confident. I leaned out the window and said, "Yokosuka, doyko deska cue da si," which I hoped meant "Yokosuka, where is it, please?"

He said, loudly, "Huh?"

I repeated my phrase, enunciating each word as carefully as I could. He again said, "Huh?" Speaking even more slowly, I repeated myself a third time, and the farmer responded by saying, in perfect English, "Oh, Yokosuka! It is down the road about eight miles. Keep going the way you are headed." I offered him a ride, but he declined.

Another time Bud and some fellow officers and I were in Tokyo. Occasionally, instead of driving back to Yokosuka after dinner, the men would go to a Geisha house to spend the night. I had heard that it was quite an experience. The girls would put you in a hot tub that was more like a barrel of hot water four feet deep, and then they would scrub your back and massage your arms. On this trip, my fellow officers insisted that we spend the night at the geisha house. I explained to the madam of the house that I wanted to stay in the room without a girl. She carefully explained that such a request was unprecedented. She told me I would have to sleep with a girl because otherwise, the girl assigned to that room would have no place to sleep. A bed in the geisha house with a girl all night cost about $10 or $12. I told the head lady that I would pay double that amount so that there would be money for the girl to go down the street and sleep elsewhere. Shaking her head, she agreed, and my faithfulness was maintained without the slightest shadow of doubt.

From my initial overwhelming impression of masses of Japanese people flooding onto the trains, I was getting very comfortable and familiar with their culture. Indeed, the former foes we had considered fierce and fanatic turned out to be hospitable; in some instances, too much so. Japan, which I had come to learn was a well-educated, cultured, family-oriented, and well-informed culture, was flat on its back. A proud nation had been humbled. I had arrived in Japan shortly after President Truman had fired General Douglas MacArthur. The Japanese thought MacArthur was a god. He wrote their constitution, he created area codes to replace the phone system that had been destroyed by bombs, and he was tremendously respected and liked. He had done so much to help them get back on their feet, and they were flabbergasted when he was no longer in power.

Six years after the war ended with the bombing and devastation of two of their major cities, most of the large factories and plants were gone, and the people struggled to make a living. Many were reduced to menial labor and prostitution. At one point, I had a yardman who had been a brigadier general in the Japanese army. If you had a conscience, you were in no position to judge how the least skilled and the most vulnerable went about it.

Hundreds of small shops lined the streets near the entrance to the naval base, many of them houses of ill-repute. When a seaman walked out of the base, within the first block at least two Japanese girls would approach him and say something along the lines of, "Suck your nozzle, 1,000 yen?" A thousand yen at the time had an exchange rate of about $3.60 in US currency.

For fifteen dollars a month, an enlisted man could afford to keep a full-time girlfriend in a small rooming house near the entrance to the base. The fifteen dollars paid for both her room and her favors. To my amusement, one of my men came to me with a letter he had written to his hometown newspaper, in which he defended the practice. The newspaper had carried an article about the easy availability of sex in Japan. He wanted to convince them that it was all natural and normal, a kind of public service, given the hardships and loneliness of being stationed overseas.

I didn't intend to debate him or argue for the many virtues of celibacy, but I told him he would be foolish to send such a letter because his premise was absolutely wrong. Civilians back home would never understand. He did not send the letter.

Although I took pains to avoid falling prey to the easy sexual market- place that was everywhere in Japan, my own social and cultural education continued. After gaining an appreciation for bourbon in San Francisco, in Japan I learned to drink coffee. I had never swallowed a cup of coffee before, nor desired one. My mother always drilled into me that coffee, alcohol, and cigarettes were for people who possessed no willpower.

But the Navy placed unfamiliar pressures on me. On the day before a midnight shift, dinner would be served at 5:15 p.m. in the officers' club. If I could fall asleep quickly I managed only five hours or less of sleep before I had to wake up and go back to my post for the midnight shift. At two or three in the morning, I felt very drowsy. One day, while making my rounds, rubbing my eyes, some of the men offered me a cup of coffee. I decided to risk it. I filled my mug with about one-third cream, two teaspoons of sugar, and the rest coffee. Your average caffeine patron would have gagged. The combination wasn't great, but I got it down, and it helped me stay awake. If I was going to lose my willpower, a cup of coffee seemed a safe way to do it.

If the rules are clear, I have always found it easy to succeed. In the Navy the rules are always very clear. Although I was only an ensign— the lowest ranked officer—the officer in charge of our communications security group, a full commander named Tom Mackey, who had graduated from the Naval Academy and was now about thirty-nine years old, saw that desire to lead in me.

After a few months I was put in charge of my watch. Although my assistant outranked me, our superiors justified the move by saying it was a training position for my assistant and only temporary. Although there were only half a dozen men in my section during the day watch, during the evening and midnight shifts I was in charge of the entire facility. Every couple of hours I made my rounds to be sure that each man was doing his job and to resolve any small issues. Only in the US Navy would a twenty-three-year-old have the opportunity to supervise 100 people, with most older than he.

As a junior officer, I was expected to go in on my second day off and correct publications, drill the troops for defense battalion, or act as a top-secret messenger to Tokyo. I found drilling the troops interesting. I was the second in command of C-Company, which consisted of about seventy naval enlisted men and two officers. Since I had been part of the marching band in high school and had marched 1,000 miles in boot camp, my marching skills were tops. The purpose of the defense battalion was to fight off an invasion of the base. The expected enemy was the Chinese. We were also vaguely warned about a North Korean invasion or an invasion by a civilian Japanese force from the Japanese Communist Party. We drilled to stay ready.

In addition to standing watch and drilling, at other times I transported top-secret material, some of which could only be handled by an officer. Every day the commander of the Yokosuka Naval Air Base would send a written report to Tokyo for use by the supreme commander. About every two months, the rotation would come around to me. I would strap on an Army .45 pistol, check a jeep out of the motor pool, and pick up my dispatches in a briefcase that was handcuffed to my left wrist.

I would drive about thirty miles to Tokyo, report to the supreme headquarters, have lunch, and drive back. The top-secret messenger was also the delivery boy for the admirals and their wives, transporting such things as peacock eggs being sent from the wife of the Yokosuka commander to the wife of the head naval commander in Tokyo. Frequently, we were also asked to stop by the Tokyo PX to make a strategic purchase. It was always interesting.

The closest I came to combat during the Korean War was in the pool room of the officers' club at Yokosuka Naval Base. I became a skilled pool shooter and ping-pong player. My roommates and I were always first in line in the officers' club for dinner. Afterward, we would go to the pool room, shoot pool or play ping-pong until a few minutes before eight o'clock, and then go to the movie on the base. There were new, first-run movies every night, and they only cost ten cents.

Every week or ten days, a massive aircraft carrier would dock at the Yokosuka Naval Base. Its officers would flood the officers' club, and Bud O'Neil and I would challenge some of them to a game of pool. Bud and I typically won, because there's not much pool being played aboard a rocking ship. During the two- or three-day stay of the aircraft carrier, we would get to know ten or twelve of the flight officers very well. Then the aircraft carrier would weigh anchor and head to Korea. About four weeks later, it would return to Yokosuka and the officers would again come to the club.

Each time, two or three of the officers would be missing because their planes had been shot down over Korea. The new friend that I had played pool with a few weeks before was now dead. The war seemed abstract as long as I was reading about it and looking at written reports, but when people I knew were killed, the war felt up-close and personal.

I attended a Catholic Mass seven day a week at noon. Joanne and Welcome Jr. were 8,000 miles away, and I worried about them. During my time in Japan, I was a most devout and participating Christian. I prayed constantly, and it was very comforting.

In November of 1951, my nose began running and I ran a slight fever. The first three or four times I went to the hospital corpsman, he gave me two APCs, an all-purpose capsule that was basically aspirin, and then sent me home. After about my fourth visit over ten days, they finally let me see a doctor. By this time, I had lost ten pounds. The doctor admitted me to the hospital weighing 187 pounds.

In the US Navy, you are either at work or you are in the hospital. There is no such thing as staying home because you are sick. For that reason, you have to really convince them that you are sick so that they will put you in the hospital. I was so relieved to be going to the hospital because the eight-hours-on, eight-hours-off shifts were making me weaker and weaker. On the second day in the hospital, the doctor came by and gave me a thorough examination. He found my spleen was swollen and that was adequate reason to keep me in the hospital. I was there for three weeks. After about a week, I began to feel better and spent most of my time playing cards and such. However, the protocol was that, at six o'clock every evening, nurses would come to massage the people that were too sick to get out of bed in order to prevent bed sores. Each evening, at six o'clock every man in the hospital, including me, would be in bed groaning so we wouldn't miss the massages. Although the massages only lasted about eight minutes, they were very popular.

Sixty to seventy percent of the officers in the Naval Security Group were lieutenants junior grade—the rank one would obtain after having been an ensign for two years. I was the only ensign in the entire command. We wore khaki uniforms eight months out of the year, but during the winter months we wore our dress blues. Rank with the khaki uniform was simply a gold or silver bar on your collar. Gold bars were worn by ensigns but would typically fade, and it was difficult to tell an ensign from a lieutenant junior grade in the khaki uniform. So when the first winter came, my colleagues were startled by my blue uniform with the single gold stripe on the sleeve, indicating I was a lowly ensign. They couldn't believe that this over-bearing Texan was an ensign. I was razzed a lot during that first winter.

Joanne and Welcome Jr. were still living with her parents on Branard Street in Houston. Joanne's mother was thrilled to have a baby in the house and dominated the baby's supervision. Joanne was the only per- son willing to discipline him, and the baby began to cry whenever my wife picked him up. It was intolerable. Joanne decided that it was urgent that she join me in Japan, or she might lose her son forever.

She wrote me frequently, begging me to figure out a way to get her to Japan. Finally, the Navy approved dependents joining officers there, if it was done at no expense to the Navy. I immediately applied and received approval. In the meantime, Congress intervened, and the Navy established a program that allowed wives and children to travel at the Navy's expense aboard Navy troop carriers. In May of 1952, Joanne, who had only been on a plane once before in her life boarded a plane with our thirteen-month-old son and flew to San Francisco. There, they boarded a troop transport full of Army personnel and sailed for Japan.

WELCOME JR. IN JAPAN

When I learned that my wife and son would be able to come to Japan, there was no base-housing available. I went to a city near Yokosuka and rented a house. The house was lovely, although there was little furniture, as is the custom in Japan. You slept on mats on the floor. The house had a *benjo* but no bathroom. In other words, there was a urinal that simply drained to the dirt underneath the house and then there was a hole in the floor for defecating. Underneath the hole was a bucket, and each day "honey carts" picked up the buckets. I knew that arrangement wouldn't satisfy my wife, so I went to the trouble of having a flush toilet installed, including a small septic tank.

By the time my family arrived, however, base-housing, which was better and cheaper, had become available at a nearby Army base. So, I forfeited my deposit, abandoned my toilet, and terminated the lease. I couldn't believe it when the couple who owned the house paid to have the toilet removed because they thought it was wasteful. In those days, human waste was used for fertilizer on the farms, most of which were no larger than a residential lot in America. The Japanese wasted nothing; they even planted vegetables on the shoulders of the roads.

I'll never forget Joanne and Welcome Jr.'s arrival in Tokyo in May of 1952. I could see them on the guardrail of the ship as it came into dock. I gathered them up, got their luggage, and we proceeded to the Army Post Exchange (PX) in the Ginza retail shopping district in

Tokyo. The Army had taken over a major department store and converted it into a PX, where military men and families could buy anything they needed at bargain prices (cigarettes were a nickel a pack). It also had a major restaurant on the second floor where we went for lunch.

During the lunch, I observed that my thirteen-month old son had not been taught any manners. He played with his food, and he would pick up things and throw them on the floor. I thought to myself, "My wife has taught him nothing." Obviously, I had no experience with thirteen-month-olds, and I quickly learned that all thirteen-month-olds play with and throw their food. I had a lot to learn.

The first time Joanne left me to babysit, Bud was visiting me. Welcome Jr. was in a highchair and began to cry, so I gave him some grape juice. He liked it a lot. For the next half hour or so, I kept giving him grape juice to keep him quiet. Suddenly, there was a grape-colored explosion in his highchair. Purple poop was all over the kitchen floor. I cleaned it up quickly before my wife returned. Bud was startled. He had a son, too, but because he was born while Bud was in Japan, Bud had never been around a baby.

GOING HOME

To obtain permission to bring my wife and son to Japan in May of 1952, I had agreed to extend my tour of duty by one year. In early August, the officer in charge informed me that the Navy had mishandled the paper- work, and if I wanted I could return to America immediately instead of staying the additional year. He made it clear that the choice was mine, and the Navy would not think less of me if I chose to leave. Joanne, bless her, wanted to stay, but I felt life was passing me by, and I needed to be back at the University of Houston, advancing my career.

That decision was among my dumbest, certainly to that point. What difference would nine months make in my so-called career? In Japan, we had the opportunity to travel as a family, free, to the Philippines, Hong Kong, and all the islands of Japan. We could have become fluent in Japanese. We could have attended the classic opera in Tokyo, as well as musical comedies. We had a Japanese maid, and our sixteen-month- old son could have learned the language as well.

But I was adamant. Before the month was over, we were on a troop carrier on our way back to the United States. There were 8,000 men aboard the ship, so time on deck was limited. We spent most of our time in our cabin or in the mess hall. After one stop in Adak, Alaska, home of the other Welcome Wilson, we arrived in Seattle near the end of August. From there we caught a plane to Houston. Our Japanese adventure was over.

We settled easily into the life we had known so well as students and young marrieds. Before I left for the service, we had rented our apartment for $75 a month. When we returned, we rented another for about six months, until we were able to buy a little house with three bedrooms and one bathroom. It cost $10,000. Since I didn't qualify for the loan, on a larger house at $12,500.

Joanne, as an only child, had no experience with babies when Welcome Jr. was born. She was only twenty years old, but she was a natural. She recognized that her mother's spoiling Welcome Jr. was not good for him, and she had taken steps to change the situation. Now that we were back in the States, she began reading books on raising children. She must have read fifty. All of the books emphasized the importance of the early years. My wife dedicated herself to the idea that we must do everything exactly right.

Welcome Jr. was not to be an only child for long. When Joanne had arrived in Japan, we had not had sex for thirteen months. I took her to my newly assigned house on the Army base in Yokohama, Japan, about twenty-five miles south of Tokyo. Needless to say, we were excited to be reunited, and it was a memorable night. Nine months later, back in Houston, our beautiful daughter Cynthia Joanne was born. We have always enjoyed saying she was "made in Japan." Twenty months later, we were blessed with the arrival of Pamela. The next twelve years of Joanne's life were spent raising our first three kids.

BACK TO CIVILIAN LIFE

I returned to work for the University of Houston, with the title of assistant professor. I taught no classes, but Dr. Kemmerer, who ran the university at that time, thought that every member of the staff should have a faculty rank.

I remained in the Navy reserves and attended weekly meetings with a new commanding officer. Jack was also in the unit as an instructor to the enlisted men. I continued in the reserves until 1958, when I held a Federal Civil Service position equal to that of a three-star general.

Joanne and I with Welcome Jr. in front of our apartment on the Army base in Yokohama, Japan.

Recalling what had happened to the lieutenants and lieutenant commanders who stayed in the reserves after WWII, only to revert back to their previous, lower ranks when called back to active duty, I found myself hoping for peace so that I could resign my commission with dignity. I was only thirty, and certain to be called if the Cold War turned hot, as most expected.

In the 1950s, we were confident that sooner or later we would be at war with both Russia and China. Peace looked promising in 1958, so I quietly resigned my commission as a full lieutenant, hoping that, if war came again, I could leverage my service status to a higher military rank (I had been notified about a promotion to Lt. Commander, but I did not accept it). Between 1952 and 1958, Jack and I took two weeks off each summer for active duty training. We would take Joanne and Mary Lou and travel to Key West, Florida, San Diego, New Orleans, and other exotic places—mostly at the Navy's expense. Those two weeks were great.

My military career, which began when I enlisted in the reserves in 1948, ended when I resigned my commission ten years later. Serving in the Navy turned out to be one of the greatest experiences of my life. I felt necessary, patriotic, eager, and willing to do whatever my country asked. I entertained no thoughts of being a hero—I just wanted to be productive.

My feelings echoed, in a smaller way, what General George Patton said in his speech to the Third Army on the eve of D-Day, which included the classic message: "...when you are sitting by the fireplace with your grandson on your knee and he asks you what you did in the great World War II, you won't have to cough, shift him to the other knee and say, 'Well, your Granddaddy shoveled shit in Louisiana.''

Pardon his language, but, after all, he was Patton.

A friend of mine who was chief executive officer of Sears, the department store, always said, "Success in life is simple. You must be prepared, and then you show up."

The Navy taught me how to do both.

4

The Cold War Warrior
Houston and Dallas/Fort Worth

Politics have played an important role in my life, and my interest began early. In 1946, as the student business manager of The Cougar, my principal responsibility was selling advertising. A Houston mayor's race was going on in which the superintendent of schools, Holger Jeppesen, was running against Oscar Holcombe. Oscar had already been mayor three times and had come back to run again.

I was new to Houston, so I knew neither candidate. I telephoned Ed Kaplan at the Houston Press. Ed was running the Jeppesen campaign, and I made an appointment to stop by the Press and talk to him about advertising in The Cougar. I convinced him that the 8,000 veterans at the University of Houston were all old enough to vote and that UH was a rich source for voters.

Ed bought a full-page ad (we didn't sell many of those). I encouraged my friends of voting age to vote Jeppesen, but I have no idea if any did. I was nineteen and too young to vote at the time. I watched the results roll in, and Jeppesen lost in a landslide. That same election, the ballot included a city charter change. Houston had a city manager-type of government, and Oscar Holcombe ran on a campaign to convert to a strong mayor form of government. The charter amendment simply struck through the city manager's name wherever it appeared and wrote in the mayor. So after that election, the mayor of Houston became the most powerful mayor in the United States, because he or she was not only the presiding officer over the legislative body— the city council— but also the chief executive officer of the city.

The next major election was in 1952. I was a Democrat, like nine- ty-nine percent of all Texans. But the Democratic governor of Texas, Allan Shivers, became head of the Democrats for Eisenhower and made

The Commanding General of the 4th Army in San Antonio stands with me in front of my headquarters in Denton, Texas.

it legitimate for me, as a Democrat, to vote for the Republican presidential candidate Dwight D. "Ike" Eisenhower. Eisenhower was one of the most effective presidents the US ever had, but I'm not sure he would be elected today. Eisenhower had a wonderful smile, and any photograph made him look great. However, in an interview situation, he stumbled around. If they had had presidential candidate debates in those days, he would have done terribly. Very few people had a television, though, including Joanne and me. I was persuaded to vote for Ike because of his sterling record in World War II, his wonderful smile, and the million "I like Ike" buttons that everyone wore.

That same year, Judge Roy Hofheinz, the former county judge of Harris County, was elected mayor of Houston. Jack Valenti, a good friend from UH who would also end up being a business partner of mine, not only handled Hofheinz's advertising, but was a close friend of his. Three months after he took office in January of 1953, Hofheinz appointed R. E. "Bob" Smith as director of civil defense for the City of Houston. It was to be a dollar a year job, which was no problem for Bob, because he was a very successful businessman and one of the largest landowners in Harris County. Although Bob was over forty years my senior, he would become an important mentor and dear friend to me in the coming years.

At this juncture, Bob had just hired me to be his assistant in the oil business and, instead of sending me to Snyder, Texas, to be a roughneck and learn oil, he sent me to City Hall to run the civil defense department.

That was the beginning of a three-year stint at City Hall where I developed a close relationship with Hofheinz, was appointed an assistant to the mayor, and became deeply involved in his reelection campaigns. I was given the title of assistant to the mayor because I needed an important title for when Hofheinz would send me to make a speech on his behalf. His top assistant, Gould Beech, would tell me the specific points to make depending on the audience. Whether I was speaking to a large African American church or a small business group, I was provided with the aspects of the mayor's agenda most pertinent to that audience. I was twenty-five years old, and it was a wonderful opportunity for me to learn about the variety of constituents that lived in the city as well as to improve my speaking skills.

Two years later when Hofheinz ran for reelection, I was deeply involved in his campaign. He ran against a city councilman named Louie Welch, who later was elected mayor of Houston and served for many years. Louie was only about five feet, six inches tall, and, since I was six- foot two, I would always stand next to Louie on the platform to make him look small. Years later, Louie and I became great friends, and we would laugh about him trying to get away from me on the platform.

Hofheinz was easily reelected, and I became even more embedded in his political family. His second term began with a major conflict on the city council. His manner tended to be overbearing, and the councilmen resented his putdowns at the council table. Soon every council meeting became a major argument, and little was done. Hofheinz personally considered the councilmembers to be dumb and some to even be crooks. People began to ask themselves, "How can one man be right, and eight be wrong?"

Over Hofheinz's objections, the council passed an ordinance firing Gould Beech. Hofheinz gave me the task to go out and get 20,000 sig- natures to overturn the ordinance. I set up tables on Main and Fannin Streets, gathered signatures, and overturned the ordinance.

By summer, there was open warfare at the council table. The city council held hearings on changing the charter to remove much of the power of the mayor. They proposed eighteen amendments, each of which would make some minor change in the charter. Hofheinz countered by announcing that he would have his own charter hearings with a group of citizens who would propose their own changes. Bob Smith formed the United Citizens Association for the purpose of proposing charter changes and a slate of candidates for both mayor the eight council positions—in other words, a slate that would defeat the encumbrance. I was appointed executive director of the United Citizens Association with the day-to-day responsibility. Bob was chairman, but I basically took my instructions from Hofheinz.

The result was Amendment Nineteen, which made several sweeping changes that are still in effect today. The most notable change provided that an election would be called at the end of that odd-numbered year (1955) to elect all city offices. Instead of the mayor and councilman being elected in even-numbered years, like the president and congressmen, the mayor's races would be held in odd-numbered years along with the Houston school board races. The rationale was that the city races did not get adequate attention if the governors, presidents, and congressmen were also on the ballot in an even-numbered year. Hofheinz's objective was simply to throw out all of the city council members and elect some who were friendlier.

We had to get 20,000 signatures in order to have a special election, and I was assigned to the task again. We succeeded easily in getting the signatures and winning the election to get the charter changed because the public was ready for a change at city hall. All eighteen of the councilmen's charter amendments failed, and our charter amendment number nineteen passed with a whopping majority. We mistakenly thought that was a good sign for us.

The election for new city offices was held in November of 1955, and, as executive director of the United Citizens Association, I was very involved. The newspapers and other civic leaders came out against Hofheinz, so he went on the attack. He would buy a thirty-minute slot on television and make lengthy speeches about how the "fat cats" like Jesse Jones, Gus Wortham, and others were trying to run the city.

I was not very optimistic, but Hofheinz kept insisting that we were winning. On Election Day, we were all at the campaign headquarters on Fannin Street when the first results came in. Hofheinz immediately wanted to know the results of a particular box in Houston's East End. The results were brought to him. I'll never forget that moment. After looking at the results from that one box, he turned to his wife and said, "Dene, we have lost the election by two and a half to one."

That's exactly the way it turned out. Hofheinz received about thirty percent of the vote. Of the slate of city council officers that the United Citizens supported, six were defeated outright, but two ended up in the runoffs—neither one prevailed. Hofheinz was defeated, and Oscar Holcombe became mayor for his eleventh term. Oscar would typically serve for two or four years, then decline to run, and then come back later and run again. Mayor Holcombe asked me to stay on as director of civil defense until he could find a replacement. I agreed, but since I was officially on Bob Smith's payroll, I made sure he concurred. Bob did, and I served about four months in the Holcombe administration, until President Eisenhower appointed me the five-state director of the Federal Civil Defense Administration.

I was just twenty-seven years old, and I had been involved in the very center of the city's political life during exciting times. Now I had the opportunity to move the federal level. My confidence was high, and I was ready for this new challenge.

GETTING INVOLVED ON A FEDERAL LEVEL

As a federal official, I was not involved in election campaigns. However, I was deeply involved with political office holders. My five states were Texas, New Mexico, Oklahoma, Arkansas, and Louisiana, and my responsibilities included working closely with their governors, senators, congressmen, and other elected officials. I knew all five governors extremely well.

My agency had responsibilities for preparations for World War III, but we also had a small division that handled natural disasters in America. My responsibility was to coordinate the federal response in the event of a natural disaster. In other words, I was to direct the regional offices of the federal agencies and assist the state and local governments in a disaster situation. I also handled disaster relief funds from my headquarters in the Dallas/Fort Worth area. That division was later split out and is now called Federal Emergency Management Agency, or FEMA.

My involvement with congressmen and senators was principally related to the disaster funds. When a city wanted money from my headquarters, they would contact their congressman or US senator, who would then contact me. There were ten US senators from my five states, including Lyndon Johnson from Texas and Russell Long from Louisiana. The five states had dozens of congressmen, and I knew each and every one. The southwestern part of the United States is the most natural disaster-prone area of the country. In one year alone, we had seventeen major floods, five tornados, and two hurricanes. In those days, all of the power in Congress was held by senators and congressmen from Texas and the South. The reason was simple: in the South we tended to reelect our senators and congressmen, whereas the Northeast, Midwest, and West Coast were always throwing them out after a few years.

I'll never forget when I met Governor Earl Long of Louisiana. I was visiting with him in the governor's office in Baton Rouge, and he had one foot up on his desk, which didn't have a single piece of paper on it. He wore the old-fashioned high-top shoes that hooked at the top.

After we talked a few minutes, a man came in the back door and walked over to the governor, carrying some legal-looking papers. It turned out he was the attorney general of Louisiana. He said, "Governor, we have some extradition papers for you to sign."

"What was his crime?" the governor asked.

The attorney general explained that the accused had purchased an automobile from a used-car dealer in Beaumont, Texas, and then drove to Lake Charles, Louisiana, where he lived, never making a payment or returning the car.

The governor stared at the papers on his desk. He was not wearing glasses, so I knew that he could not read a word. Suddenly he picked up the papers and tore them in half and said, "I can't imagine anybody being able to take advantage of a used-car dealer." The attorney general laughed and walked out the back door.

The other governors were colorful characters, too. Governor Edwin Mechem of New Mexico was an ex-agent of the FBI. Whenever I went to New Mexico, we would fly around the state in a private plane that he flew himself. He was a tall, strapping guy, and we had a great relationship. The governor of Oklahoma was J. Howard Edmonson. Howard was only thirty-two years old and governor of a major state in America. Since I was only twenty-eight when I met him, we got along just fine. Early on, he gave a reception for me in the governor's mansion in Oklahoma City, which is where I was mistaken for the Welcome Wilson who lived in Adak, Alaska.

The governor of Arkansas was Orval Faubus. Governor Faubus was best known as the governor who called out the Arkansas National Guard in the very early days of the civil rights movement to prevent the Little Rock school system from being integrated. President Eisenhower federalized the troops, and instead of blocking the students they escorted the students to class. Faubus and I later became friends, and he took me on what was probably the coldest, most miserable hunt of my life.

The governor of Texas was Price Daniel. Although the civil defense program in Texas was not very vigorous, they had the right idea. Instead of having a separate civil defense department, the state civil defense director was simply an assistant to the governor. His job was to coordinate various state agencies in the event of either a natural disaster or an enemy attack.

It was Price Daniel who got me hooked on chewing cigars. I was with the governor in his office at the capital. I had stopped smoking ci- gars about three years earlier, and I noticed that he had an unlit cheroot that he held in the side of his mouth. I asked him about it, and he said that he had smoked cigarettes but had given them up, finding the cigar to be comfortable but harmless. I thought that made sense, so I took up the terrible habit of chewing cigars. Call it what you like, but really it is simply chewing tobacco. Ten years later when the insurance company special rated me because I had nicotine in my blood, I finally gave it up.

My interaction with congressmen was typified by an occasion with Congressman Hale Boggs of New Orleans, who was the father of Cokie Roberts and a long-time commentator on National Public Radio. Hale was a friend and later Majority Leader House of Representatives. A massive hurricane had hit Grand Isle, Louisiana, in Hale's district. As an island off the coast of Louisiana, Grand Isle relied solely on tourism. The hurricane had stripped all the beaches of sand. Tourists disappeared. Hale thought that the federal government should provide the funds for Grand Isle to dredge sand out of the Gulf of Mexico and pump it onto the beaches.

The federal disaster aid program was designed to rebuild government facilities. Typically, roads and bridges were the most affected, but occasionally buildings would be rebuilt. The idea of granting money to restore beaches was unprecedented. The beaches were publicly owned, and I reached the conclusion that the beaches were, in fact, a government facility.

I approved the request, but sent it to my Washington headquarters for their concurrence. They declined. I flew to Washington and met with the director of civil defense mobilization to make my case. He was unwilling to overturn the wishes of his natural disaster department heads. After a three-month battle, I was finally able to get the national office's approval to provide the funds for Grand Isle. It saved the town.

Sam Rayburn, who was Speaker of the US House of Representatives, visited my office twice when I was the five-state director. I also worked with Lyndon Johnson on many occasions when he was majority leader of the senate and a Texas senator. In early 1960, Johnson came to Denton, Texas, Dallas and Ft. Worth area, which was the location of my federal headquarters and where I presided as president of the Denton Chamber of Commerce. I had always known that LBJ resembled my father. I was startled when Lady Bird Johnson arrived and I saw that she looked like my mother. I introduced Senator Johnson at a big rally in Denton.

As a civil service employee, I did not directly participate in the presidential race of 1960. While I was a still a federal official, Lyndon Johnson decided to run for president. His principal opponent was John F. Kennedy, the two-year senator from Massachusetts. Everyone underestimated Kennedy. As a junior senator from Massachusetts, no one thought he had a chance. But the Kennedy family was determined. They had organizations in every state. At the end of the day, at the Democratic National Convention in the summer of 1960, JFK was nominated. His first act was to ask LBJ to be his running mate. LBJ accepted.

I met JFK about thirty days later when he came to my hotel room in Washington DC. That makes me sound more important than I was, so let me explain. Adair Gossett was the civil defense director of New Mexico, one of my states. In September of 1960, Adair and I flew to Washington and took a suite at the Congressional Hotel near the capital. We invited the New Mexico congressional delegation, two representatives and two senators, to come to the suite for cocktails.

At the last minute we got the idea of calling the Kennedy campaign headquarters and inviting the nominee to come as well. He accepted. For the next hour or so, the future president of the United States was in our hotel suite visiting. It was my first time to meet him, and he was the most charismatic man I have ever met in my life. He had the warmest and most genuine smile that you could imagine. There seemed to be a buzz around him, and he was extremely likable.

When I was twenty-five, I served as executive assistant to my best friend, R.E. "Bob" Smith, who was sixty-five. We worked out at the health club together five days a week.

ANOTHER LIFE-CHANGING CONVERSATION

Eleven years after our wedding, I thought life was good. From my perspective as a child of the Depression, I thought Joanne and I and the three kids were set in the Dallas/Fort Worth area. I was the five- state head of civil defense, a high-ranking official in the Eisenhower Administration. The year before, I had been promoted to the rank of equivalent to three-star admiral in the civil service of the United States. I made a speech every few weeks, and my remarks would be carried on the front page of the local newspaper, along with my picture. When I would fly into a military installation, no one lower ranking than a full colonel was required to meet my plane, according to protocol. I had a high-ranking staff of about 100 people, and was directing the construction of the underground alternate national headquarters for the federal government was under construction by me at the edge of town.

I sat down with Joanne and told her that I thought I should make a career with the federal government, so we could continue to live a good life. She immediately explained that she did not marry me to be the wife of a federal employee. She agreed that we had a good life, and she was grateful for it, but she wanted her children to have all the things that she and I had never had growing up. She wanted them to have private school educations. She wanted to have a beautiful home for our family in River Oaks in Houston. She wanted to be a patron on the art scene in Houston as well. Sharing these dreams, she reminded me of my original plan to return to private business and pursue the financial gains that would likely to follow.

I always knew Joanne was strong. She had navigated her first pregnancy alone while I was in the Navy. She had been willing to pack up Welcome Jr. as a baby and move to Japan to ensure that he was brought up with proper discipline. She had worked diligently to educate herself on the best parenting practices available and keep our growing family happy and healthy while I was immersed in my work. Now she was strong enough to tell me the truth. She and I had shared a vision for our life together, and I was letting the temptations of fame and security lure me away from it. I could see that she was not nearly as thrilled as I was about the life that we were living. This was a game-changing conversation for me.

Since Kennedy had just been elected, and our national director had resigned, I wanted to take a shot at becoming the new national director of the Office of Civil and Defense Mobilization in the Executive Office of the President. I promised Joanne that if I did succeed, I would serve two or three years, resign, and return to business as planned. If I did not succeed, then I would resign immediately.

She accepted that proposal with patience and grace. When I was not appointed national director, I resigned my position in the summer of 1961 with the intention of becoming president of the Jamaica Beach Corporation (I was already the Chairman of the Board), a partnership I had formed earlier with my brother, Jack, and our University of Houston friends Jack Valenti, Johnny Goyen, and Bill Sherrill.

RETURNING TO POLITICS IN HOUSTON

Leaving federal service to return to the business world did not lessen my interest in politics, however. A few months after I returned to Houston, Johnny Goyen was running for reelection for city-councilman at-large. Cash was in short supply. Johnny suggested that I raise campaign funds

With my best friend and mentor, R.E. "Bob" Smith,
at the Bob Smith ranch in Richmond, Texas.

for him and be paid a twenty percent commission of what I raised. It was easy money. All I had to do was call up every contractor who did business with the City of Houston and ask for a political contribution for Johnny. I quickly raised about $50,000 and was able to get paid $10,000 myself.

Lewis Cutrer was mayor of Houston. Lewis and I were good friends, and after I moved back to Houston we became even closer. I became his "go-to" guy, meaning that whenever anyone wanted something from the mayor they would telephone me. I also raised money for his reelection campaigns, and he trusted me with his most sensitive assignments. For example, when JFK came to Houston to announce the Manned Spacecraft Center development in Houston, the mayor put me in charge of the event. When JFK came to Houston the night before he was assassinated, the mayor put me in charge of the arrival at the airport and the motorcade to downtown Houston. I also took on many less important assignments, such as parade chairman for the returning astronaut Gus Grissom and chairman of the host committee for the American Municipal Association's convention.

Cutrer was a problem-solving mayor, but that doesn't always get you reelected. In order to solve the long-term problem of a shortage of water for the city of Houston, Mayor Cutrer proposed that the city buy a large tract of land in Livingston, Texas, and capture water from the San Jacinto River and pipe it to Houston. He proposed to pay for it with a very modest increase in the water rate, to $16 a month. The rate was to go into effect on a certain date, which meant that every meter in Houston must be read in order to establish the usage after the rate increase occurred.

For many years, the water meter readers in Houston had been goofing off. Instead of going and reading the meters, they would simply go to the nearest topless bar and estimate what everyone's reading was to avoid the trouble of actually reading the meters. That meant that there were thousands of Houston citizens who owed money for back water-usage. Just before the election, they were all hit with a water bill of $100 or more when they were used to getting water bills of four or five dollars a month. People were outraged, and, although Cutrer's plan only raised the water bill an average of four dollars to sixteen dollars a month, he was thrown out of office at the 1963 election.

Mayor Cutrer asked me to organize a trip to Washington DC, to vis- it several federal officials about Houston matters. Bob Smith was also to

When he was running for president in 1960, Lyndon Johnson came to the site of my new headquarters in Denton, Texas, when they were under construction.

GALLERY

LEFT: Joanne and I at the Tiki Island Marina in Galveston. Circa 1966

BOTTOM LEFT: Joanne and I at the reopening of Gilley's Club in Pasadena, Texas. Joanne is on a bucking saddle. Circa 1970

BOTTOM RIGHT: I am in front of the ranch house at the Triple W Ranch. The infinity swimming pool can be seen on the left. Circa 2012

LEFT: This picture of me was taken around 2000.

MIDDLE LEFT: I posed at the San Jacinto Monument for my daughter, Pam Francis Wilson, photographer, for the cover of *Houston Home and Garden Magazine*.

MIDDLE RIGHT: Joanne and I around 2005.

RIGHT: I received Honorary Doctor's Degree at the University of Houston graduation from UH President Renu Khator, 2013.

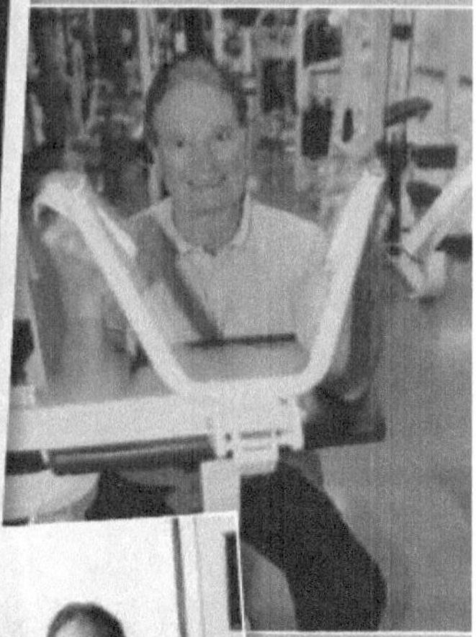

ALWAYS WELCOME

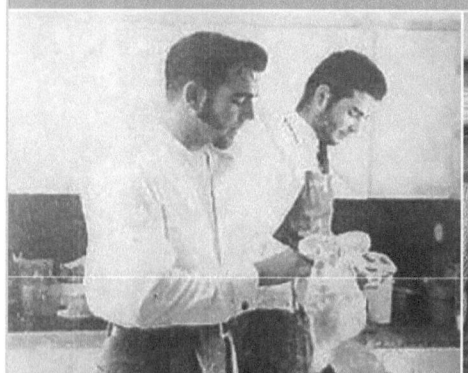

TOP LEFT: Vice President of the United States, Hubert Humphrey with me in Houston when he was running for President against Richard Nixon. Circa 1968

TOP RIGHT: Working out at the Houstonian Health Club. Circa 1995

In my downtown office. Circa 1983

BOTTOM LEFT: My brother Jack and I washing dishes at out parents home in Humble, Texas. We had grown beards for the UH Frontier Fiesta beard contest. Circa 1948

BOTTOM RIGHT: With my brother and sister, Beverly Smith, on the Saltgrass Trail Ride. Circa 1990

The Cold War Warrior

TOP LEFT: I carried the first mobile phone on the Saltgrass Trail Ride (notice the size of the phone). Circa 1995

TOP RIGHT: In the early 1980s, I shot pheasants in England.

BOTTOM LEFT: My photo in the Brownsville High School Sr yearbook. Circa 1944

BOTTOM MIDDLE: My photo in the yearbook at the University of Houston. Circa 1949

BOTTOM RIGHT: In front of the Bachelor Officer quarters at the naval base in Yokosuka, Japan. I am wearing my only civilian suit. Circa 1951

ALWAYS WELCOME

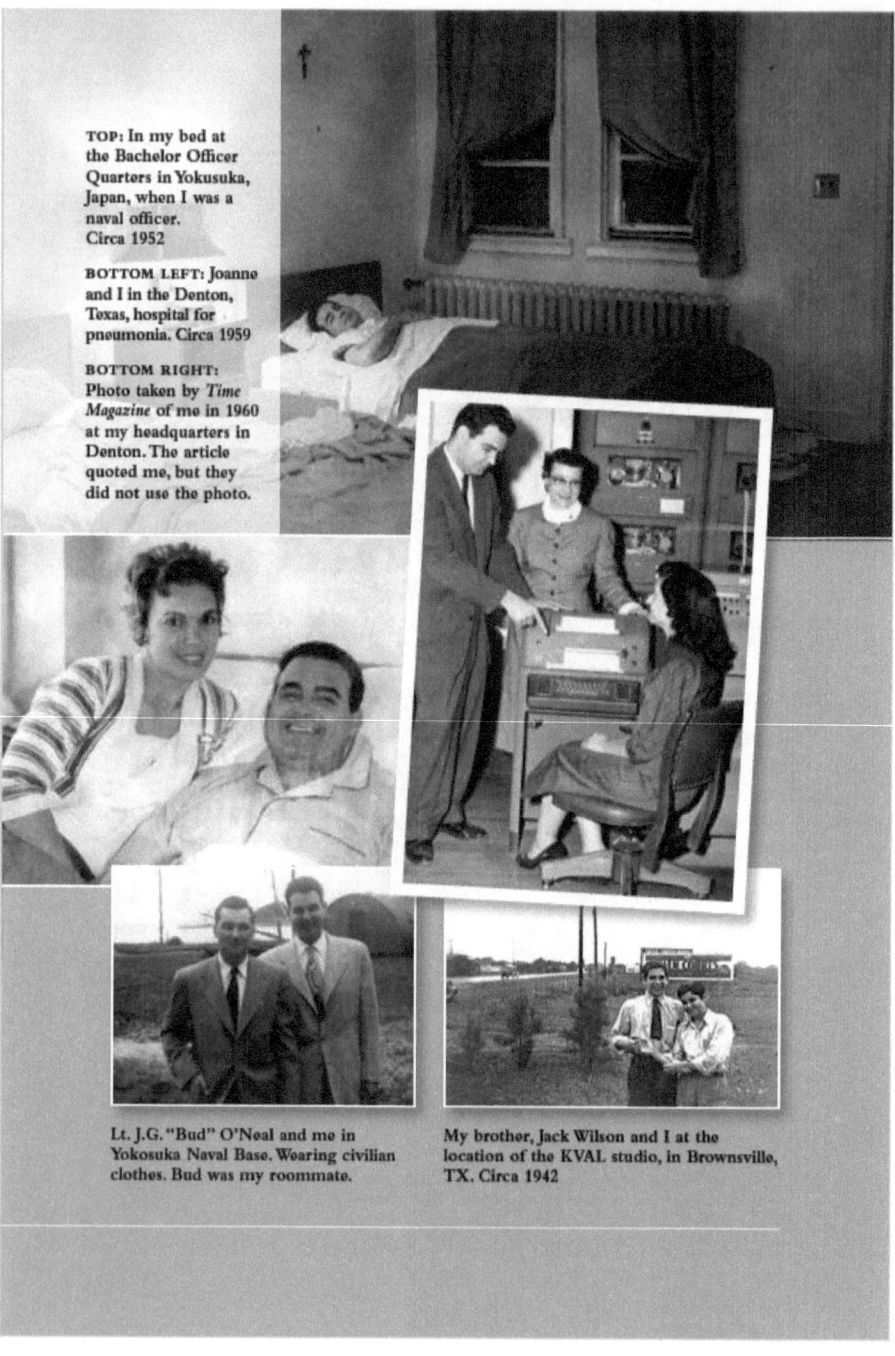

TOP: In my bed at the Bachelor Officer Quarters in Yokusuka, Japan, when I was a naval officer. Circa 1952

BOTTOM LEFT: Joanne and I in the Denton, Texas, hospital for pneumonia. Circa 1959

BOTTOM RIGHT: Photo taken by *Time Magazine* of me in 1960 at my headquarters in Denton. The article quoted me, but they did not use the photo.

Lt. J.G. "Bud" O'Neal and me in Yokosuka Naval Base. Wearing civilian clothes. Bud was my roommate.

My brother, Jack Wilson and I at the location of the KVAL studio, in Brownsville, TX. Circa 1942

LEFT: I am pictured here as a Senior in high school, at age 15. Circa 1943

BOTTOM LEFT: My brother Jack and I in a photo booth at the beach in Corpus Christi, TX. Circa 1939

BOTTOM RIGHT: I was at my girlfriend's farm (Betty Rusteberg) in Brownsville, Texas. Circa 1943

I am in the middle with black sombrero, posing for a publicity picture for Charro Days in Brownsville, TX. Circa 1944

TOP LEFT: Brother Jack Wilson, left, Father E.E. Jack Wilson, me and cousin Lester Ralph at our home in Brownsville, Texas. Beards are for Charro Days. Circa 1945

TOP RIGHT: Circa 1962

LEFT: Joanne and I in the kitchen of our home on Woodhaven in Denton, TX.

BOTTOM LEFT: Joanne and I at our Jamaica Beach house (notice the sideburns). Circa 1970

BOTTOM RIGHT: The pool at our home on River Oaks Blvd. Circa 1990

The Cold War Warrior

TOP LEFT: I am standing behind UH President Renu Khator and Regent Chairman Nelda Blair in Washington DC to lobby Congress for the University of Houston.

TOP RIGHT: Circa 2005

MIDDLE LEFT: Scuba diving at the Flower Garden Reef on James Lyon' yacht. I am in the middle.

MIDDLE RIGHT: My partner Johnny Goyen and I holding up fish (borrowed) in front of the Jamaica Beach sign at the sales office. Circa 1962

BOTTOM RIGHT: On a yacht with, RE "Bob" Smith, fishing for red snapper at an offshore drilling rig out of Galveston, Texas.

be on the trip. With all the friends I had made as the five-state director, it was a piece of cake. I called Congressman Albert Thomas and asked him to set up meetings with Secretary of Defense Robert McNamara and Speaker of the House Sam Rayburn. Because Albert was a senior member of appropriations, they all responded.

In Washington, I squired Bob and the mayor around to the highest officials in town. I called John Connally, who was serving as Secretary of the Navy. I had met Connally in Fort Worth when he was head of Sid Richardson's estate. A friend had introduced us, telling me that Connally was interested in running for governor of Texas. Now, I knew that he was getting ready to announce his campaign for the 1962 race, so I asked him to see Bob and Mayor Cutrer. He instantly agreed. In politics and in life, if you know the right people anything is possible. I was much involved in the election campaign for John Connally. He took office in January of 1963, and in November of that year, when Lee Harvey Oswald shot the president, Connally, riding in the automobile with the Kennedys, was shot, too.

President Kennedy's tragic death thrust LBJ into the presidency. At LBJ's insistence, Jack Valenti flew from Dallas to Washington with him, lived in the White House for six weeks without luggage, and became an assistant to the president. Jack Valenti's company, Weekly & Valenti, had handled advertising for every campaign, and Jack had married Mary Margaret Wiley, LBJ's assistant. This proximity to the White House led to many opportunities for our group of friends from the university. Bill Sherrill was appointed a director of the Federal Deposit Insurance Corporation (FDIC) and eventually to the board of Governors of the Federal Reserve System, and I was appointed Special Ambassador to Nicaragua in 1966.

My experience with Nicaragua was eye-opening. When Joanne and I arrived on an official visit in 1967, we went to the swearing in of President Anastasio Somoza DeBayle and his wife, Hope, an American he met at West Point. She was from Florida. He told the country that she was from Nicaragua, but in reality, she was of multi-national descent. If you're a dictator, you can say anything you want to. We had been there a few days and the time came for the ceremony. His father had been the dictator, his brother had preceded him, and now him.

After the ceremony, we met in the presidential palace before about 500 people. The ambassadors from each country would come up and present their credentials and greet the new president.

As I approached him, he whispered, "Welcome, for God's sake, give me *un abrazo*." I didn't speak Spanish, but I figured it out—I had seen it all over Latin America. I gave him a big hug on both sides of his head. The next day, he said, "If you had not given me un abrazo, it would have meant that our relationship with Washington was estranged." Within the decade Nicaragua would be under siege and the United States' relationship with it would become very controversial, but, at the time, I was glad that some quick thinking and a timely hug prevented any diplomatic problems.

President Jimmy Carter caused the diplomatic problems in Nicaragua. When he defeated Gerald Ford in the presidential election, Carter immediately announced that the United States would not support any dictator, regardless of how much that leader loved the United States. Within months, the Shah of Iran was deposed by the Ayatollah, and a few months later the Sandinistas took over Nicaragua. After that, Somoza was assassinated in another country.

In my opinion, Carter's policy was wrong. I believe there are some countries that aren't ready for democracy. Prince Bandar of Saudi Arabia is a longtime friend of mine. He was the Saudi Ambassador to the United States and later the foreign minister to Saudi Arabia. He explained to me, "Welcome, most of my people are living in the eighth century. They're not ready for democracy. We are bringing them along as fast as we can."

Aside from that foray into international diplomacy, I honored my promise to Joanne, and focused my career on business. The people I had met in every level of the government continued to be a part of my life, and my interest in politics never waned. John Connally would have a long-term impact on my political life. I was always a staunch Democrat, but my political involvement would eventually be much more focused on the Republican side. When Connally was serving as Secretary of the Treasury in 1973, he talked me into becoming a Republican. He was in Houston on business when he said to me, "Welcome, we're not leaving the Democratic Party. The Democratic Party has left us."

After Hurricane Audrey hit Louisiana in 1957, I held a hearing in Lake Charles to dispute the U.S. Weather Bureau's reporting.

It was true. The Democratic Party had become more and more liberal and was dominated by union bosses and various special interests. Texas and the South had gradually shifted from the Democratic Party to the Republican Party, principally because of the civil rights movement of the 1960s. When we passed the Civil Rights Act of 1964, LBJ said to me, "Welcome, the Democratic Party has lost the South for at least a generation." That was three generations ago, and they have still lost the South.

But in 1961, both Texas and I were enthusiastic Democrats, and I was ready to come home to Houston and put all my experience and connections to work, this time for my family. Joanne and I had a vision of what success would look like, and I could practically taste it. But life still had a few important lessons to teach me. My wife had proven to me that she knew when to be patient and when to push, and her willingness to be patient as I ventured full-time into business was about to be put to the test.

5

Our First Development
Jamaica Beach, Galveston

Jack and I had long talked with our friends from our University days about partnering in the real estate business, but we knew nothing about how to get there. And we all had jobs: Johnny Goyen was executive director of the UH Alumni Association, Jack Valenti had an advertising agency named Weekly & Valenti, and Bill Sherrill was working for Roy Hofheinz, who was now the former mayor of Houston. Jack and I were busy with our jobs in the Dallas/Fort Worth area.

Below is the cover of the first annual report of the company that developed Jamaica Beach in Galveston. It was published in the 1960s when I was CEO.

In 1957, a 300-acre tract of land became available for sale on Galveston Island about halfway between the city of Galveston and the end of the island. The price was $500 per acre, and cash was required. Galvestonians did not believe in selling real estate on time.

When the 300 acres became available, I flew back to Houston and met with Bob Smith. After I had been his executive assistant, he had become a mentor, not only to me, but to our group. I proposed that he buy the 300 acres for cash, keep fifteen acres on the beach, and sell us 285 acres for a dollar down with no payments until we sold something.

It was definitely a Wilson deal, with a pitch worthy of my father, but I didn't realize until later how much that deal was tilted in our favor. Bob wanted to know where we were going to get the money to put in the streets and utilities. I told him that my plan was to go to a bank and pledge the 285 acres, on which we owed him the total cost, and borrow the money.

"Welcome," he said, "I don't know of a bank in the world that would do that." He suggested that we go to the bank and sign an unsecured note. "I'll guarantee it," he added. I went to Pete Rehrauer, the number-two man at the National Bank of Commerce, Jesse Jones's bank, who was known as the dean of Texas banking. Pete sat behind a big roll-top desk on the second floor of the Gulf Building. He quickly told me that he would fund any loan that Bob Smith guaranteed and would not even require that we furnish personal financial statements.

The five of us—Valenti, Goyen, Sherrill, Jack, and I—signed a simple, small, printed note; Bob Smith signed the back of it, and the bank provided $250,000 for improvements. And just like that, we were all in business together.

The partners had agreed to name the project Holiday Beach. Johnny Goyen was put on the payroll for $800 per month to run the project. He resigned from the alumni association and was replaced by my brother Jack. When I flew in for the grand opening, I was startled to discover that all of the brochures read Jamaica Beach instead of Holiday Beach. Jack Valenti, whose advertising agency created the brochure, decided that the name Holiday Beach was too wimpy. I raised no objection.

After the opening, the project immediately sold all of the best lots on the Gulf of Mexico beach, but then sales stagnated. After about a year, Johnny Goyen came to the partners and said that the dry land lots on the bay side of the island were too expensive, $1,250 each, and that we should cut the lots in half so we could sell them for $625. We re-platted, put in additional streets, and began to sell some lots.

About that time, Johnny ran for Houston City Councilman At-Large and was elected. Bill Sherrill then became the full-time executive to run Jamaica Beach. We decided we needed to dig canals and have canal lots, too, as developers were doing in Florida.

In the late 1950s, no one thought they needed a second home. It was a totally new concept. Mortgage companies would not make a loan on a second home, and insurance companies would not insure them. It was a miracle that we sold any lots at all. We sold lots for ten percent down with payments over ten years at six and a half percent interest. Needless to say, at half or full-size, selling the lots was difficult.

When Joanne and I made the decision that I would leave federal service to return to the business world, Jamaica Beach was the logical place for me to start. Even though I had been out of Houston for many years, I had remained the leader of our group. When I told the others my plan, they were enthusiastic about my return. My natural Wilson sales abilities, honed at *The Daily Cougar*, were about to be unleashed on Galveston's second-home market. I was to report for duty at the Jamaica Beach Corporation on September 9, 1961.

But nature had other plans. On September 7, Hurricane Carla entered the Gulf of Mexico and was soon upgraded to a Category 5 storm. By the time it made landfall in Port O'Connor on September 11, the devastation wreaked on Galveston was so extensive that people were not permitted to go to the west end of the island for three days. During that three-day period, the five Jamaica Beach boys met one night at Jack Valenti's bachelor pad at the Chateau Dijon Apartments off of Richmond Avenue. We took a poll on what percentage of houses would remain at Jamaica Beach when we finally got down to see the damage. Valenti and Goyen thought that none would remain. Jack and Bill said a quarter. I won the poll by guessing that half of the houses would still be standing. In fact, only one out of seventy-three houses were destroyed by the hurricane at Jamaica Beach. I ran an ad in the *Houston Chronicle* that said, "Hurricane Carla—1, Jamaica Beach—72. "Sales went from poor to zero. Even though the development had fared okay, the hurricane scared people away. I spent the next few months on repairs and building a new pavilion on the beach, where the first one had been totally destroyed.

TRYING TO STAY AFLOAT

When my family had first returned to Houston, I had gone to Meyerland State Bank and borrowed $3,000. I traded a home builder in the Meyerland subdivision three lots at Jamaica Beach as a down payment on a $35,000 house on the corner of Cheena and Balmforth.

Since the company had no money, I had to fend for myself. There was no money coming in from lot sales. Johnny Goyen proposed that I raise money for his reelection campaign and be paid a twenty percent commission. I jumped at the idea and quickly earned $10,000 for myself.

Then, in addition to Jamaica Beach, I started working on other big real estate development deals. For example, I was floating the idea of a high-rise apartment project in what is now called Midtown. I worked for months hawking that deal. The truth was that I knew nothing about developing Jamaica Beach, and my success was hampered by the fact that I still thought I was a big shot. While working for the federal government, I held the civilian rank equivalent to a three-star general. When I would fly to New Orleans to make a speech, my picture would be on the front page of the *Times-Picayune* newspaper. It took me a while to realize that in business, nobody cared who you used to be.

Jack and I getting ready for the 100-mile Houston Salt Grass Trail Ride in 1969.

Finally, in the late spring of 1962, nine months after I arrived during Hurricane Carla, I sat down and had a talk with myself. I said, "Self, you are no longer a big shot. You are a lot salesman. You are not a major developer, you are a salesman of lots at Jamaica Beach. It's time you got off your high horse and became a lot salesman, because that's what you are."

I had a button made up for my lapel that said, "I sell lots at Jamaica Beach." I wore it every day. I asked every single person I met for the next few months to buy a lot at Jamaica Beach. It worked. I began to sell lots. I went to Houston Bank and Trust and made a deal that they would lend me seventy percent of the face value of a contract for deed on the lot. That way cash could be generated from the sale at ten per- cent down, which otherwise would not even pay the sales commission.

Although I spent my weekends at Jamaica Beach selling lots, my main office was in Houston. I subleased a single office in the Bank of the Southwest building on the fifth floor, next to the Coronado Club, from Frank Sharp, a major real-estate developer, and began to add additional sales people. I ran ads in the newspaper. I talked Southwestern Savings and Loan Association into making loans on beach houses. FEMA, which had been formed out of my former role in the Executive Office of the President, had started issuing insurance policies against hurricanes. People gradually decided that a second home was not a waste of money.

And most importantly, I began to learn from my mistakes. I stopped being an ex-big shot, and I became a real real-estate developer.

BUILDING JAMAICA CORPORATION

When I became president of Jamaica Beach, I did not know what a deed of trust was. I thought Dun & Bradstreet was an intersection in New York. I had so much to learn.

Around 1963, I was sitting in the sales office at Jamaica Beach on a Saturday when the world's skinniest man walked up the front walkway. He introduced himself as Charlie Wilson. He had been hired by Temple Lumber Company in Diboll, Texas, to start a second-home division, build the second homes, and sell them. He came to see me because, by that time, Jamaica Beach was a thriving second-home subdivision.

Charlie and I joined forces and built spec houses at Jamaica Beach. I would put in the lot, Temple Lumber Company would build the house, I would sell the house, and we would split the profit. It was a bonanza for me, because I had learned that every time a house was built, we could sell five lots to the friends of the house owners. That started a long relationship with Charlie Wilson, who would later become a congress- man and, ultimately the subject of a best-selling 2003 book called *Charlie Wilson's War*. Charlie and I remained good friends through all his wild adventures, and he came to my office just six months before he died to inscribe a copy of his book to me.

As Jamaica Beach succeeded, my partners began to come on board as full-time employees. Bill Sherrill, who had returned to city hall after his initial stint as an executive at Jamaica Beach, returned and brought with him Eugene Mayer, the director of public works, and Ellis Allen, the tax assessor-collector for the City of Houston.

I persuaded my brother Jack to join us as head of advertising and pro- motion. Jack Valenti remained in Washington DC, and Johnny Goyen was working as city-councilman-at-large. To get office space, I made a deal with Lloyd Bentsen, then the President of Lincoln Liberty Life Insurance Company and later a US senator, to trade Jamaica Beach lots for the first year's rent in his new office building, the Sheraton Lincoln Center. It was a great location, because the first ten floors of the building were a Sheraton hotel with a private club on the second floor. We had swanky offices on two floors and a circular metal stairway in between. We could not afford the payroll, but I thought if we had good people we could make it work. I would make many mistakes in business by jumping in and believing that I could figure out the details of making it work later, but this time, the gamble paid off.

Texas banking laws had recently changed, and our group had invest- ed in a bank. I was chairman of the board and Bill was president. We also had a savings and a loan, an apartment project called Kingsbrook on the Katy freeway, and a retail center on Homestead Road. We changed the name of the company from Jamaica Beach, Inc. to Jamaica Corporation. Jamaica Beach, Inc. became a subsidiary that owned our projects in Galveston.

Our First Development

After Jamaica Beach's success, others thought that they would develop similar subdivisions. They thought it was easy money, and they were wrong. Terramar Beach opened, and, after the ten principals bought

Joanne and I on the way to attend a reception for the dedication of the Tiki Island Marina owned by partner, Bill Sherrill.

lots, they had great difficulty selling lots to others. We bought them out for cash because of our ability to finance contracts and deeds and lots. We bought Treasure Island in Brazoria County on the west side of the San Luis Bridge for the same reason. Then we bought Bermuda Beach and even Sea Isle, which had been the only subdivision on the island when we started Jamaica Beach.

My brother Jack came up with the idea of investment sales. Someone would buy a lot on a pre-development basis in a new section of one of our subdivisions before we even broke ground digging the canal. The idea was that after construction was finished, their lot would be worth more in value, and they could sell it at a profit. The program was initially successful, but after the investors were unable to sell the lots quickly because our sales people could not resell them, the program began to bog down. We were innovating as the world was rapidly changing around us. We were trying new deal structures and expanding our vision for the Jamaica Corporation as new opportunities rapidly came our way. If one program didn't work, we quickly came up with another one that would.

TIKI ISLAND

Bill Sherrill, one of the smartest people I know, noticed when he was driving back and forth to Jamaica Beach that there was a large tract of semi-submerged land on the mainland side just before you entered the Galveston Causeway. It was about 400 acres in size, and it was called Wilson's Pointe after a colonel in the Confederate Army.

Bill checked into it and saw that it was privately owned, with four different owners in Galveston. He conceived the idea of a canal community that would be forty-five minutes from Houston, instead of an hour and twenty-five minutes, like Jamaica Beach. He came to me with the plan, and I quickly subscribed to it. He went to work quietly buying up the four tracts of land at Wilson's Pointe.

In those days it was easy to get a permit from the US Corps of Engineers to dig canals. Today, because of environmental laws, it is almost impossible, particularly in marshland like Wilson's Pointe, where the land was only about six inches out of the water. Bill was successful in buying up all of the tracts, and he also bought the connection to the Gulf Freeway called Virginia Pointe, which is about ten acres with frontage on the Gulf Freeway, West Galveston Bay, and Jones Bay. Bill had a bridge designed to take traffic from Virginia Pointe to Wilson's Pointe.

He called the project Tiki Island. I was CEO of our company, and my brother Jack and I didn't think that the Tiki reference related to Galveston at all. We went to a naming expert, and he came up with the name Buccaneer Bay, which I thought was more appropriate to the island's history—rich with stories of Jean Lafitte and other pirates. Bill was adamant, however, and since it was his project, I concurred in naming it Tiki Island. Despite the name, it was an immediate success, because, thanks to the short period of time it took to drive to Houston, we could sell second homes as well as primary homes.

Today, there are several three-million-dollar homes on Tiki Island. A few years ago, I was sitting at the bar at Berryhill Tamales when a friend came in and said, "Welcome, weren't you the developer of Tiki Island?" When I said that I was, he asked, "What was the price you sold those two lots on the tip end for?" I told him that I remembered those

I am standing before the original fence put up at Jamaica Beach in the 1950s to stop automobile traffic on the beach. The State sued and won; the fence was breached.

two lots well, because they were the most expensive lots on the island, and I thought I sold them for $18,000 each. He said, "I just bought one of them for $500,000 cash."

I have to thank Bill Sherrill for his great vision to create something of extreme value out of marshland. We may not have been able to tie the name to the pirates' buried gold, but the Tiki gods were definitely smiling on that project!

After about six months in Washington, Jack Valenti called me and asked if I would buy him out of Jamaica Beach, our apartment projects, and our banks. I was happy to do so. Several years later Lew Wasserman, who was CEO of Universal Studios, went to LBJ and said that he want- ed to hire Valenti as president of the Motion Picture Association of America. He wanted LBJ's blessing first.

At first LBJ said "no way," and then, a few months later, spoke to Valenti about it. Valenti thought that it was a real opportunity for him, and asked LBJ's blessing for him to accept the job. LBJ reluctantly gave in, and Valenti became president of the Motion Picture Association of America for almost forty years. When LBJ appointed Bill Sherrill, who had been president of our bank, to the FDIC, Bill and I traded some assets around. He withdrew from the partnership when he went to Washington. Our group remained in close contact, even when across the country from one another.

OTHER PROJECTS

The Jamaica Corporation quickly began investing in a variety of interests, and that diversity continued as the members moved and changed. As my ability to finance deals increased, I saw opportunity everywhere. Very close to the city limits of Galveston was the Wayman Ranch, a 1,000-acre tract of land I had long aspired to own. Ultimately, I bought two tracts of land and got an option to purchase the rest over time. We started developing a project called Spanish Grant, which I thought was a great name for a Galveston subdivision.

Each project had an appeal to a different group, not because the properties were that different, but because people wanted to be where their friends were. We had a secret sauce in that we knew how to finance the lots when nobody else did, and we had also learned how to sell them. We would sell the lots on a contract for deed; the customers paid ten percent down and started paying monthly payments. After the first monthly payment, we could take that contract to the bank and borrow seventy percent of the sale.

Our investments were not limited to Galveston. In Houston, we worked on a deal that included a Marriott hotel project near the Astrodome, which was completed in 1965. The development of the Astrodome was a fascinating deal on many levels, and I'll go into it in detail later. For purposes of understanding the Marriott deal, what's important is that Bob Smith owned the land on which the Astrodome was built, and he still owned several hundred acres of land surrounding the stadium. Eugene Mayer, who worked for Jamaica Corporation, had the idea to build a major development on about 100 acres of Bob's land. The land stretched west from Fannin, past Greenbriar Street, and almost reached Main Street. There was a million square feet of land that fronted on Main Street that we decided to buy. It belonged to Claud Hamill. After a lot of negotiation, we finally signed the contract to buy it for three dollars per square foot. I financed the purchase with a loan from American General Life Insurance Company. Gus Wortham, chairman of American General, was personally involved in the loan.

We planned a hotel for the major tract and approached the Marriott hotel headquarters in Washington DC. Today there are over 5,500 Marriott hotels in the world, but at that time there were only four, plus one under construction in Chicago at O'Hare Airport. I made the deal, we dealt directly with J. W. Marriott and his son Bill Marriott, who was in his twenties. We were planning on building the hotel at the corner of Main Street and Braeswood Boulevard, but the architects who worked for Marriott chose another site, also owned by Bob Smith, just north of the tract that we had under lease. It was ten and a half acres on an island between the streets and the bayou. I went back to Mr. Wortham and got the hotel financed because Bob Smith had subordinated his land to the mortgage. I particularly remember the groundbreaking for the Marriott. There had been a lot of rain so we scheduled it at a private club on the top of an office building that overlooked the site. Welcome Jr., who was about fourteen at the time, rode in a chauffeur-driven limousine to the hotel's future location, shoveled some dirt into a box, and brought it to the club at the Fannin Bank building where the reception was being held. Bob Smith was in the middle with a shovel, and Bill Marriott and I got shovels out and posed around the dirt on both sides of him for the photographers. We had our groundbreaking, but with the added benefit of air conditioning and cocktails.

PREPARING TO GO PUBLIC

In the late 1960s the Jamaica Corporation had expanded from a single development to a multi-faceted company. We were urged to have a public stock issue. We were growing fast. So fast, in fact, that we didn't have time to raise all the money we needed or keep extensive records. Going public was the next step, because then we could acquire property by issuing stock instead of cash. The value would be there for the investors, but our cash flow would allow us to take advantage of the opportunities that were coming our way. We would also be able to borrow on our stock. Before we could do it, though, we had to go through an auditing process, which was complicated because of our seat-of-the-pants record keeping.

The underwriter for the public stock offering was to be Dominick and Dominick, D&D, from Wall Street. They were a small but prestigious Wall Street firm, and we expected great success. At their urging, we went out and bought large parcels of raw land. They said that we had to own plenty of land, otherwise investors wouldn't believe that we could keep doing what we were doing. I bought 6,000 acres in Freestone County, 3,000 acres in Bastrop County on the Colorado River, and an extra 3,000 acres in Galveston County.

But the timing was not right, and, from the years of experience I have now, I don't believe D&D knew what they were talking about. Owning raw land is a huge burden, because it has no income but demands a great deal of cash for debt service. You can always buy land when you have a use for it and can put it immediately to work. But, at the time, their suggestion was right down my alley because I loved to buy stuff.

The original partners of Jamaica Beach at the Democratic Convention in 1964. Me, my brother Jack, Jack Valenti, Johnny Goyen, and Bill Sherrill.

After a great deal of waiting, the audit was finally completed in early 1969, and the economy was booming. Richard Nixon had been elected president of the United States in November of 1968. When he took office in January, he announced some sweeping changes in the federal government. Then, in March of 1696, the Dow Jones Industrial Average dropped forty percent in five weeks. Our stock offering was due to go public on July 1, 1969. Instead, it was canceled.

My friend George Mitchell had also scheduled a public stock issue on his oil business. He had been expanding by using debt. His was scheduled for March 1, 1969, and it went off without a hitch. George was able to take his company public, and he became a billionaire. Caught by the stock market drop, the Jamaica Corporation had a disaster on our hands.

Owning all of that land, with no income and a big debt load, combined with all of the money I had spent in anticipation of going public, forced me to liquidate the company. It was a powerful lesson. You can't control the economy. Being long on raw land is a position that I never wanted to find myself in again.

It was a hard time, to say the least. Bob Smith, who had been such a great supporter, had had a stroke and was no longer in communication with us. With no capital, I had to find a new way of making deals. Remembering the lessons, I had learned from my family during the Depression, I knew that I could leverage my ability to see potential and sell it to people in a way that benefited us both. I knew I had a knack for real estate development, so, instead of hanging up my hat, I began going into real estate businesses that didn't require capital up front, like the brokerage business, and I began doing joint ventures with other partners. The Jamaica Corporation had given me a great deal of experience. Now it was time for me to use the tools I had to continue creating the life that I wanted for my growing family.

THE JAMAICA CORPORATION'S LASTING LEGACY

I'm very proud of most of my developments. Jamaica Beach and Tiki Island are each separate cities in Galveston County. They are both thriving. The 300-unit Foxhall Apartments on Katy Freeway, one of the first

In the 1970s Jack Valenti visited Houston and came by my office. Pictured are brother Jack Wilson, Valenti, and Johnny Goyen.

Our First Development

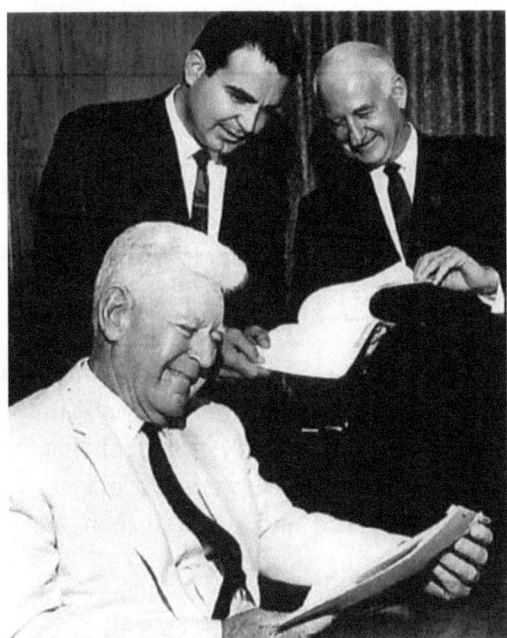

R. E. "Bob" Smith, my mentor and best friend, examines the sale documents for the sale of the Jamaica Beach Marina in 1969.

non-resort projects the Jamaica Corporation did when Johnny Goyen insisted we go into the apartment business, are still there, fully occupied, over fifty years later.

In the Jamaica Beach days I made every mistake known to man. In addition to experience and contacts, I also took the wisdom gained from my mistakes with me. I was down, but I never had the temperament to con- sider that I was out. It was time to roll up my sleeves and start over. From my perspective now, here's what I learned from those exciting times:

> 1. In the early days I thought I was smart enough and swift enough to handle anything. "I'll think of something" was my mantra. I came to realize that there are certain things over which we have absolutely no control; principally, the economy. If people aren't buying something, there is nothing you can do about it. So I

learned to know exactly what I was going to do before I jumped in. Today, we take very few risks of any kind.

2. You have to be willing to make a pitch that is highly favorable to you. You have to be willing to put yourself on the line to make the pitch. It was true when my father first told it to me, and it is still true. Few people are willing to go all-out with their pitch.

3. Never burn a bridge. Along the way, I have had people get mad at me, insult me, and call me names. I learned to just say, "I'm sorry you feel that way." Five years later, those same people are some of my best friends. If I had countered and insulted them, they wouldn't have ended up being supporters.

4. If you don't have the money, use partners. There are plenty of people who have money who are looking for deals that will make them money. Instead of trying to borrow 100% like I used to, now we just bring in partners. Owning a smaller percentage is better than having all that debt.

5. Never personally guarantee a note. I haven't guaranteed a note in forty-seven years. Structure the deal so that you don't have to. Make sure the partners have enough equity so you can get whatever loan you need without a personal guarantee.

See the second annex of this book for more of "Welcome's Rules of Order."

If I learned a little bit from each of my mistakes, today I must be the smartest real estate developer in town because I have made so many mistakes. Now I'm in business with my two sons, and we stick to one field. We develop industrial facilities, such as manufacturing plants and big laboratories. Some of the projects we own are half-million square feet. We own about four million square feet—ninety percent of which is located in metropolitan Houston. In over sixty years of developing real estate, I have learned the hard way how to be smart about it. But still, when I am asked what my favorite project has been, without hesitation I say, "Jamaica Beach."

6

How To Own A Bank For $600 Cash
Houston

William Shakespeare famously wrote, "Neither a borrower nor a lender be." I have been both. I became a banker almost by accident. After I resigned from my position in the Eisenhower Administration and moved back to Houston, I sub-leased an office downtown from Frank Sharp, a prominent real estate sub-divider who was the founder of Sharpstown—one of the area's first master-planned communities. The office was especially attractive to me because it was inside the new Bank of the Southwest building and next to the prestigious Coronado Club. The exclusive club, which had opened just five years earlier in 1957, was quickly becoming the place to be for Houston's business elite. I gladly placed myself nearby.

Frank came in one day and said that he had a commercial reserve in a subdivision on Houston's north side. If I bought it, he felt sure that I could get a bank charter. Banking in Texas boomed after the war, and Houston especially enjoyed the positive effects. I jumped at the idea, even though I had no financing, banking experience, or any of the other items needed for success. I thought the prestige of owning a bank would help Jamaica Beach

The year was 1962. I was thirty-four years old. I called the Jamaica Beach Boys together, and, as usual, the five of us were absolutely confident we could pull it off. I was to be chairman of the board, Sherrill was to be president, and the others would be board members. The commercial tract was on the corner of Homestead and Parker Road in northeast Houston. We decided on the name Homestead State Bank and immediately filed an application for a bank charter.

The Banking Commission in those days was comprised of the state banking commissioner, J. M. Falkner; the state attorney general, Will

I was Chairman of the Board of the Homestead Bank for which the Jamaica boys got a Charter in 1964. The name changed to North Side State Bank.

Wilson; and the state treasurer, Jesse James. The attorney general and I were acquaintances, and he quickly pledged his support to our application. The banking commissioner opposed the application on the basis that we did not have the experience or financial backing to make the bank a success. Although he was right, we continued our quest.

The determining vote turned out to be the state treasurer, Jesse James. The state treasurer was, at the time, an elected position, since abolished. We were unaware of it then, but it turned out that Frank Sharp, who was going to sell me the land for our bank, was a major contributor to Jesse James's political campaign. Frank called Jesse, and unlike Will Wilson, Jesse said "I've got to hear more about it before I decide." At the hearing where the vote was to be taken, I stood up and made my presentation. Since I couldn't talk about my banking experience or financial capacity, I instead spoke about Dwight Eisenhower, John F. Kennedy, and LBJ. As I spoke, I saw Commissioner Falkner lean over again and again to whisper into Jesse James's ear, assumedly trying to get him to vote no.

After the hearing was over, the attorney general and the banking commissioner cast their votes for and against, and then turned to Jesse. There was a long pause before Jesse said, "I think Welcome and these other young fellows can make a success of it. I vote yes."

GETTING STARTED

We had the charter but still no money for capital. We celebrated anyway. The next day, after seeing my picture in the newspaper in a story about the bank charter, a stranger called me to ask me to explain what a bank debit was. He had read in the financial pages that "debits" were up in Texas banks and wanted to learn more. I had never heard of a debit except in accounting class, but I confidently explained that it meant the number of checks clearing the banks were up in numbers. The next day I asked someone, and it turned out that I gave the right answer; a miracle.

Now that we had the charter, our next steps were to raise the money to capitalize the bank and apply to the FDIC for its approval to insure the deposits. For capital, we went to Judge Jim Elkins, the chairman of the board of the First City National Bank. We asked for a 100% loan against our stock ownership. My financial statement showed that I had a whopping $600 in the bank.

I knew Judge Elkins a little from my days as an assistant to Mayor Roy Hofheinz, but Johnny Goyen and Jack Valenti knew him well. When the three of us went to see him, I made the pitch. Judge Elkins asked me at the end of my pitch who was going to head this operation. I told him we would hire a professional to be the executive, but I would be the CEO and chairman of the Board of Directors. Then he asked me about my banking experience.

"None, except as a borrower," I responded.

The judge shook his head in amazement. "You're the man we need," he joked. He called in his vice president for banking relationships, Bill Keitt, and told him to look into our request. About a week later Keitt called to say that the bank would make a 100% loan to finance the bank stock if we brought in Walter Mischer, Sr., as the controlling partner over the bank.

Walter Mischer, Sr. was one of the most respected real estate developers and bankers of the time. Because he had been a big supporter of Mayor Cutrer, we knew him well. Mischer was a country guy with an accent so thick that was sometimes hard to understand him. But he was a brilliant businessman who had started off as a bulldozer operator and ended up with a big construction company. He eventually controlled an eleven billion-dollar bank. We liked and respected Mischer, but we had come this far without giving up control and intended to keep it that way. I told Keitt that I appreciated what his bank was willing to do, but we would seek financing elsewhere.

The next day Mischer called me and said that he was embarrassed by what the bank had said, and he wanted me to know that it was not his idea. He said "Welcome, why don't you come down and get with Gerald Smith and me, and let's see if Continental Bank can make this loan instead."

The next day Continental Bank agreed to make a 100% loan to finance our bank stock, guaranteed only by the thin credit of the five of us. Luck and connections triumphed over talent. The $600 my financial statement showed in the bank was probably an exaggeration.

Again, we celebrated. We thought that we had it made until a week later when the FDIC called to say that they were unwilling to provide deposit insurance for the bank. Well, I knew that under then Texas laws, federal insurance was not required; several very old banks in Texas did not have FDIC insurance. I called the regional director of the FDIC in Dallas and told him that the denial was not a problem. We planned to open and then re-apply in six months. When he saw what a great job we were doing with the bank, I told him, I was sure that he would grant us the insurance at that time. My confidence left him speechless.

We issued a news release announcing the new bank and held a groundbreaking ceremony for the building. Construction began as we busily sold small amounts of shares to friends, families, and people in the neighborhood.

A couple of months later, during the construction of the bank building, the regional director of the FDIC from Dallas telephoned me. He was very polite. He said, "Mr. Wilson, the chairman of the FDIC in Washington wondered if it would be possible for you to come to Washington to discuss opening your bank without deposit insurance."

"Of course," I answered and told him that I would bring a couple of directors.

The next week Bill Sherill, Jack Valenti, and I flew to Washington. The son of the FDIC's chairman had been Valenti's roommate at Harvard when Valenti got his MBA. I felt like a casual and friendly visit with the chairman would help us convince him that we knew what we were doing, and he would reconsider the denial of deposit insurance for the bank.

When we arrived at the FDIC office, the receptionist said that the chairman would greet us in the boardroom. She ushered us into a room the size of a tennis court with a huge board table. We were kept waiting for a while, and after fifteen minutes others began to arrive and take seats near, but not at, the board table. Soon there were almost twenty people seated next the table. A handful of others arrived and sat at the table. The chairman then walked in and after normal greetings suggested that we sit at the board table across from him. By this time, my anxiety was running high. It was apparent that the board of directors of the FDIC expected us to make a formal presentation. Even if I had known what I was doing and was an expert in the banking business, I would have been scared silly. As it was, I was petrified.

We sat down across from the chairman, and he leaned back in his chair and said "Well, Mr. Wilson, having made a failure in the real estate business with Jamaica Beach, I see you are now going to try your luck in the banking business."

The minute he threw out this insult, my apprehension and fear vanished. I leapt to my feet. Almost shouting, I said, "What do you mean, 'made a failure in the real estate business?' My real estate projects have been extremely successful and are successful today." I was mad. In rapid fire, I spent the next five minutes listing all of our successes and arguing that we were perfectly qualified to operate a bank. I then told them that the FDIC had made a grave error in declining our application for insurance. As I wound down, I noticed a wry smile on the chairman's face. There followed a forty-five-minute question-and-answer session, during which members of the board and its staff, acting like prosecutors, kept drilling down about my qualification and our operations. Sherrill and Valenti were speechless at the turn of events and my response to the chairman's opening question. After about ten minutes the shock wore off, and they both made great contributions to our case.

When the questions were over, the chairman thanked us for coming to Washington and walked out, followed by the others. We tried to assess what had happened but reached no conclusions about the success or failure of our presentation.

Ten days later I received a letter from the regional director stating that the FDIC had approved our insurance. It was only then that I finally pieced it all together. The staff of the FDIC had strongly opposed our application, but the chairman wanted to help us, perhaps because his son had been Valenti's roommate at Harvard. He threw out that initial insult in the hope that our responses would convince the staff that it should be approved. My impassioned reaction was just what he wanted. I learned that then that anger will reduce fear. I had been scared to death until he insulted me.

LEARNING FROM OUR MISTAKES

We celebrated the grand opening of the bank a few months later. I had just turned thirty-five years old. We all enjoyed being bankers for the first six months. Then we had our first bank examination by the Texas Banking Commission and the FDIC.

The state sent Ed Smith, later the chief lending officer at Allied Bancshares. After a few days of examination, Ed asked me to call a special meeting with the bank's Board of Directors. I asked him what this was all about, and he said that he would discuss it with the Board.

At the meeting, Ed announced that the bank was broke; unless we could put in another $250,000 of capital, the bank would be closed. The banking commissioner had predicted that we would have to learn from our mistakes, and our first mistake was hiring an operations officer instead of a loan officer as the top full-time executive at the bank. Our second mistake was who we hired to be our chief loan officer. After Ed Smith shocked me and the other directors with the news that the bank was broke, he went on to explain that our chief loan officer, a former car loan officer from the Bank of the Southwest, had made $250,000 worth of loans to anyone who came into the bank carrying a Bible. He had given a $25,000 loan to a bakery secured by pots and pans. When we organized the bank, we agreed that we would make no loans to our friends because we wanted the bank to be clean. Now we saw that many of our bank's loans weren't any good anyway.

I asked Ed to give us thirty days to solve the problem. He called the banking commission and reported back that they had agreed. That afternoon we reversed our previous policy and decided we were going to make loans only to our friends; people we knew could, and would, repay the loans.

Directors and Officers of Homestead Bank, posing with R.E. "Bob" Smith.

In those days, banks charged what was called add-on interest. For example, if you had a land loan for $100,000 that was a five-year loan at six percent interest, you would simply take the $100,000, add five years of interest at six percent, or $30,000, to the principal. The borrower would sign a note for $130,000 payable with no interest in monthly, quarterly, or annual payments for the term of the loan. This made the interest sound reasonable, although it was actually ten percent per annum. But the good part about it was that the banking authorities al- lowed you take the $30,000 in future interest and put it into immediate profit, which would add to the capital of the bank.

I rounded up about ten people that I knew could repay the loans and made them 100% loans to buy properties all over town. With the add- on interest I covered the shortfall in bank capital in less than thirty days. All of this was done with the full knowledge of the bank examiners and with their total approval. Bank accounting rules today do not permit such methods.

All of the loans were repaid, and I named Sherwood Crane, another University of Houston friend who was finance director of Jamaica Beach, as chairman of the executive committee of the bank. The bank prospered because we concentrated on consumer loans and high overdraft fees, which provided our biggest source of income. To my knowledge, we never made a bad loan again.

About six years later, I got into a severe financial bind and had to raise big money over a weekend. I called my friend Lamar Golden, from whom I had bought the Treasure Island Subdivision in Brazoria County, and suggested that he buy our controlling interest in the bank at three times book value. I told him that I thought I could get it financed by Bob Lanier, who owned five banks and seven savings and loan associations at the time. Lamar jumped at the chance, and I called Bob. I thought he would be willing to make the loan because he was a genius, and he would see a way to make it happen.

Before a bank will make a loan on controlling interest in another bank, the lending bank must understand the assets of the bank being purchased. In other words, are the notes in the bank's note cage worth what they say they are? Knowing that I had only the weekend to raise the money, Bob called the five presidents of the banks he owned and told them to meet him at my bank on Saturday morning. That weekend Bob and his five bank presidents went through every note we had. Late Sunday evening he called me and said they would make the loan. At ten o'clock Monday morning I went to Bob's biggest bank and picked up the proceeds from the sale. This transaction saved my financial neck. Bob would later become the mayor of Houston.

THE SHARPSTOWN SCANDAL

My foray into banking as an owner turned out to be a success. As a borrower, however, there wasn't always a happy ending. One of those times involved Frank Sharp, my landlord in the Bank of the Southwest building. Frank owned two small suburban banks: Sharpstown Bank and Oak Forest Bank. He also owned the town's most successful shopping center, Sharpstown Center, Houston's first fully air-conditioned mall. Somehow Frank convinced the Sharpstown Bank to issue new stock for his $10,000,000 equity in the shopping center. It was a complicated transaction that involved the principal of a Catholic school, Strake Jesuit.

My understanding is that it went something like this: Strake Jesuit invested ten million dollars in the bank, greatly increasing its loan limit. Moments later, Sharpstown Bank made an unsecured loan of the same amount to Strake Jesuit. Frank Sharp exchanged the bank stock now owned by Strake Jesuit for ownership of the Sharpstown Shopping Center. Strake Jesuit then settled its ten-million-dollar debt with the bank by conveying the shopping center to the bank, which was located on the same real estate. The regulators objected vigorously, but no laws or regulations in place at the time were violated, and the net result was that Frank Sharp now owned a bank with a very large capitalization and loan limit and still owned the shopping center through the bank.

The bank immediately began to make loans. Because it did not have excess cash for loans, the bank would require the borrower to purchase brokered deposits. If someone wanted to borrow a million dollars, the loan officer would furnish the customer with the name of a deposit broker who would agree to provide 100 certificates of deposit (CDs) for $10,000 each for six months in Sharpstown bank ($10,000 was the cur- rent limit of insurance by the FDIC). I myself soon owed them about three million dollars under such arrangements.

But banking operations and regulations were loose, and the bank officers were sloppy when it came to keeping track of who was renewing their CDs. Although all of my brokered CDs were in the proper number and current, other borrowers were not so diligent. Around Christmas of 1970, many CDs began to be withdrawn, and Sharpstown Bank developed a liquidity problem. In January the bank examiners came in and shut down the bank.

The FDIC found in the bank's records many loans from Sharpstown Bank to Texas state officials such as Waggoner Carr, who was then the Attorney General of Texas. Frank would make loans to elected officials so they could buy stock in his insurance company, National Bankers Life Insurance, based in Dallas. Then after a while the official would say he wanted to sell his stock, and Frank would arrange for a sale at a profit. Suddenly, the Sharpstown scandal was in full bloom. Later during the Watergate hearings, we would learn that the White House had directed federal agencies based in Texas—such as the Dallas Office of the Securities and Exchange Commission, the FBI, IRS, and others—to dig around to see what they could find on elected officials in Texas.

Frank Sharp wanted influence with elected officials to support a bill in the Texas State Legislature eliminating the need for a bank to have insurance from the FDIC by authorizing private insurance companies to ensure deposits. His plan was to have the National Bankers Life Insurance Company in Dallas, which he controlled, offer private deposit insurance to banks after the legislation was passed. Thanks to Frank's generous stock deals with the elected officials, his private FDIC insurance passed both the House and Senate in Texas. However, when the bill reached the desk of Governor Preston Smith, he vetoed it.

All of these various activities culminated in January of 1971 when the bank was shut down by the examiners and the SEC seized Sharp's insurance company. Indictments of Sharp and others soon followed, pushed forward by a federal grand jury in Houston. It was not good news later when I got a call from my lawyer saying that I had been subpoenaed to testify before the Houston criminal federal grand jury.

It was not a pleasant experience. First of all, I could not take my lawyer with me. Also, the three federal prosecutors, as well as any of the eighteen members of the grand jury, could ask any question they liked, whether germane or not. Although I had the constitutional right to re- main silent, I wasn't about to invoke that privilege. Pleading the Fifth would make me look suspicious, and besides, I had committed no crime.

I had been a witness in numerous civil cases before, and I had learned to give complete answers, even though they might be fuzzy. In other words, I tried not to give the other side the opportunity to ask me to go check my records and come back to testify again.

The lead prosecutor was an able lawyer named Ted Pinson. Although I had never met him before at the time, later we became good friends. I had been called for the simple reason that I was a big borrower at the bank. They gave me every opportunity to report my knowledge of any criminal activity. There were three FBI agents sitting at the back of the room, and during my testimony the prosecutor would occasionally tell one of them to check up on something I said. Like I said, it was not   a pleasant experience. So I answered questions about various elected officials, my borrowing, and used a lot of "gee whiz," "gosh," and "gee," and was finally released subject to recall. A week later they called me back, by which time I felt like I was on my game, and I got through the second interview with less pain.

But an amazing thing happened that year. Because of the Sharpstown bank scandal, nearly every statewide elected official was thrown out of office, including Governor Preston Smith, who had vetoed the Sharpstown Bill, and Ben Barnes, the former Texas Speaker of the House and then lieutenant governor, who had absolutely nothing to do with Frank Sharp or his bill. Dolph Briscoe, a rancher from Uvalde, was elected Governor of Texas.

I spent the next couple of years dealing with the receiver for the Sharpstown Bank because of my big loans. Interestingly, after the receiver finished his work of selling notes at a discount, liquidating assets, and selling the Sharpstown Center, the FDIC was repaid in full and the residual assets were handed back to Frank, with a value of about $6,000,000. In other words, the bank wasn't broke; it was just illiquid. Frank had a deal to testify against the elected officials and received probation. He made a lot of great deals during his business career, but his deal with the prosecutors may have been his best.

Most of the elected officials and insurance company officers made a plea deal with the prosecutors, with some serving short prison sentences and others paying a fine. But not Waggoner Carr. Waggoner absolutely refused to accept any plea deal, because he didn't feel that he was guilty. It was three years later when Waggoner finally went to trial and the jury proclaimed him innocent. In the meantime, he had lost his position as attorney general of Texas and most of his money. I have always admired Waggoner's decision to do the right thing and refuse to plead guilty.

A PROMINENT HOUSTONIAN

I also ventured into the savings and loan business for a time. Some years before, when I was developing Jamaica Beach, Sherwood Crane purposed to put together a group to organize a savings and loan association. My friend Lewis Cutrer was mayor of Houston and at my behest had appointed Sherwood as the director of civil service, a city department head. Bill Sherrill was serving as the mayor's chief of staff, and other close friends of Bill's and mine were scattered around as other department heads.

Sherwood's idea was that we would get a charter for a savings and loan, finance it by getting as many as 100 investors, and hire a well-known Houston appraiser to run it. None of us had much money, but I invested $1,200. Sherwood got the charter. We opened Colonial Savings Association, and it seemed to be doing fine, although I had little or no connection with it.

About a year later I got a call from Bill Sherrill who said that Colonial Savings was in a major public scandal. It was on all of the front pages of the three Houston newspapers. I sent down to the hotel in the building where my office was and had someone buy a Houston Chronicle. There was a huge headline on the front page that said, "Prominent Houstonians Involved in City Financial Scandal."

I laid the paper down, closed my eyes, and said to myself, "If I'm not listed in the paper it means that I am not a prominent citizen, but if I am listed that's even worse." I picked the paper back up.

Reading on, the story explained that it had been discovered that 100% of the cash in the City of Houston municipal employees' pension fund, firemen's pension fund, and police pension fund had been deposited in the Colonial Savings Association where Sherwood Crane, the director of civil service and a member of each of the three pension boards, served as part-time president.

I was listed among the "prominent Houstonians," but at least my name was not on the front page; it was on the jump page. I called Sherwood and he carefully explained that he had abstained from the vote to deposit the money in Colonial Savings. Somehow, he thought that would absolve him of any criticism.

Sherwood was one of the ablest business people I knew, then and later, and had tremendous capacity for handling problems. Later, as chairman of the executive committee at our bank, he did a wonderful job keeping the bank on the straight and narrow. But in this situation, I felt his judgment was flawed.

The mayor immediately fired Sherwood. The pension funds with- drew all of the money from Colonial, but it was done on an orderly basis so that we had time to replace it. I hired Sherwood full-time as CFO of Jamaica Corporation.

Sherwood continued to serve as president of Colonial Savings Association, and a few months later the Colonial board of directors voted in a split vote to remove him as president, along with several directors who were Sherwood's men. Since he was part of my group, I felt like Sherwood being ousted by the Colonial board would reflect adversely on me as well as on Sherwood. The head of the opposition was a prominent lawyer, who had convinced a majority of the Board of Directors that he should be president and take over control of the association. I met with him and proposed a truce. Since I only owned about $1,200 worth of stock, I can't say that my position was very strong. He declined.

I developed a plan; if I could get four of the directors to change their minds and vote with us, we could stay in control and throw them out. The odds were not good because the four directors were adamant. I went to see each of them and talked at length about Colonial and their aspirations for it. I designed a plan for each director. For one, I promised to greatly increase the amount of appraisal work that he would be hired to do for Colonial. To another, who was a lawyer, I promised all of the legal work for processing loans. I don't remember what promises I made to the other two, but at the end of the day all had given me their secret pledge.

I went to my friend Walter Mischer looking for the $600,000, big money at the time, that it would take to buy out the opposition so we could have peace going forward. I also needed to increase my personal ownership to become the largest shareholder. Because the bank examiners had begun to crack down on financing financial institutions, he said that he could only lend me $500,000, leaving me $100,000 short.

I talked to various other banks and got a similar answer. Mike Halbouty, a very prominent geologist and oil man and a friend of mine, owned North Side State Bank. The president was a legendary banker named Willie Wells; his son Mike Wells was later chairman of the Houston Livestock Show and Rodeo. I went to see Willie and told him that Colonial Savings Association would deposit $100,000 in his bank if he would also make a $100,000 unsecured loan on a note signed by six of us. The six were my Jamaica Beach group: Jack Valenti, my brother Jack Wilson, Johnny Goyen, Bill Sherrill, and me, along with

Sherwood Crane. The loan could not be secured by the cash, but I promised to leave it there as long as the loan was outstanding. Although our credit didn't justify the unsecured loan, Willie agreed.

At the next meeting of the board of Colonial Savings Association, the board voted out the opposition and elected me chairman. Later that day I offered again to buy out all of the dissenters, and they accept- ed. The financing was already arranged. Colonial Savings continued to prosper, and later I stepped down as chairman of the board and turned it back over to Sherwood, although I continued as the largest shareholder. Some years later Sherwood bought me out.

OTHER FINANCIAL FORAYS

The housing boom of the sixties caused most savings and loans to prosper, and my partner Bill Sherrill saw an opportunity for a federal savings bank charter. A federal savings bank does not have stock; it is actually owned 100% by its depositors. However, the group that controls the association is eligible for fees, management contracts, and the like, and that makes it very profitable.

There was one big federal savings bank in Houston named Houston First Federal; they had recently converted to a state charter so that the control group could actually own the association. Therefore, there was no big federal savings bank in Houston. Bill got busy and organized a group that included the six of us along with a prominent lawyer named J. Searcy Bracewell, Jr., a former state senator. Also, in our group was Stanford Alexander, the young chief executive officer of Weingarten Realty, for whom the real estate center at University of Houston was named in 2013.

We filed our application, and the Houston First Federal Savings group filed a bitter opposition to it. We had the Federal hearing, and no decision was made. At the end of the day we talked ourselves out of it because it was becoming increasingly more difficult to make any serious money with a federal savings bank. As usual, I was to be chairman, but Bill Sherrill was to be the principal executive, and he decided it wasn't worth the trouble.

Around 1970 my financial-institution enterprises were all doing well, and one of my bankers called me and said that the fourth largest bank in Dallas was for sale, and he believed I ought to buy it. He said he would finance my purchase. It was Exchange Bank and Trust located on Harry Hines Boulevard in the north part of Dallas. Armed with a commitment for a 100% ten-million-dollar loan, I flew to Dallas and started negotiating with the owner of the bank, a former attorney general of Texas named Gerald Mann. The bank owned their fifteen-story building and seemed to be prospering. We quickly reached an agreement, signed a contract, and I sent in a squad of auditors to check the books of the bank.

I've made some stupid decisions in my time, and my decision to make a public announcement regarding our contract to buy the bank ranks at the top. Self-aggrandizement got in the way of good judgment; I wanted the world to know that I was buying the fourth largest bank in Dallas. I thought bankers loved other bankers, and I was anxious for the world to know about it as soon as possible.

The reaction in Dallas was explosive. "Who is this Houston promoter coming to Dallas to buy an important bank?" At the time all Houston banks were owned by Houstonians, all Dallas banks were owned by Dallasites, and no out-of-state bank owned any banking institution in Texas. After my public announcement, Gerald Mann called me up.

"Welcome, you've made a big mistake," he said. The three big banks in Dallas were First National, Republic National, and Mercantile Bank. Their CEOs were among the most influential men in the state of Texas. Each called the banking commissioner, who called the bank that was going to finance my stock and threatened to close his bank if he made the loan. So, began a sixty-day period, during which I flew from Houston to Dallas to Austin to Houston to Dallas twenty times.

After my bank financing got shot down, I went to my lead real-estate bank, the Houston Bank & Trust, where my friend Charles Bybee was chairman of the board and CEO. Bybee agreed to make the loan in the form of six loans of $1,700,000 to each of the six of us, each loan secured by one-sixth of the bank stock. The next day the chairman of the board of Mercantile Bank in Dallas called Bybee and threatened to call his loans at Mercantile if Bybee made the loan. Bybee withdrew. Mann was still trying to save his deal, although he probably thought he was dealing with an idiot. He told me that he had an out-of-state banker who would finance my purchase if I could include at least one prominent Dallasites in my group.

I called John Murchison, whom I knew slightly. He was the son of the well-known oil man Clint Murchison. I met with John, and he seemed interested. He sent a team of auditors over to examine the bank. About a week later, he called me in to say that he was unwilling to do the deal because he thought that I was paying too much. I called on various other Dallasites and realized that the Dallas business community had closed ranks. They were dedicated to the proposition that I was not going to succeed in buying a Dallas bank.

Gerald Mann suggested I call on a certain up-and-coming businessman who had something to do with the computer business. Computers were brand new at the time, and few people even understood what they did.

"I've never heard of him," I said.

"Well," said Mann, "His company occupies the entire high-rise building next door."

"Do you mean Ed's?" I asked. There was a big sign on the building that said E. D. S.

"E. D. S.," he said. "It stands for Electronic Data Systems."

Jack Valenti was the MC when Homestead Bank opened. I am behind and at my right is Bill Sherrill, who was president of the Bank.

"I have nothing in common with a computer guy," I said, adding "and I don't want to get involved with one."

The computer guy at whom I turned up my nose was Ross Perot, who would later become a billionaire. Ross would have made the perfect partner, because he didn't give a hoot what anybody else in Dallas thought. He always fought the status quo and the establishment. After sixty days of attempting to buy Exchange Bank and Trust, I concluded that I would not be welcome in Dallas, even if I succeeded, and called the deal off. I was happy to get out of Dallas with my skin.

Six months later, John Murchison bought the bank. For the same price. Ross and I later became friends, and his son Ross Perot, Jr. and I were inducted in the same class of the Texas Business Hall of Fame in 2011. Although I certainly didn't get inducted because of the way I handled the Exchange Bank deal, the whole affair was an important learning experience.

LOOKING BACK

I have not owned a financial institution in over forty years. About six months before he died, Walter Mischer visited me in my office. At that point, Walter and I had been friends for fifty years and frequently partners. Walter had taken a small bank named Continental Bank in Houston and built it into a statewide multi-bank holding company called Allied Bancshares, now Wells Fargo Bank. I had developed 8,000 subdivision lots; Walter had developed 150,000. Walter had financed my first apartment project. He had financed my bank and my savings and loan. We had made a big success in the home-building company Dover Homes. Welcome Jr. and I brought money from England to match with Walter's in forming a home-building company that was a major success.

Sitting in my office that day, Walter and I both in our eighties, he and I agreed that we knew too much about what could go wrong in business for either of us to ever bring ourselves to make a loan. We concluded that if we owned banks today, we probably wouldn't make a loan to anybody.

The Astrodome
Houston

The Astrodome, famously nicknamed the "Eighth Wonder of the World" and home for some time to the NFL's Houston Oilers and MLB's Houston Astros, opened on April 9, 1965, just over half a century ago. Vacant since 2008, for the last decade its fate has been a hot topic of discussion in Houston, and only recently has it been granted landmark status by the Texas Historical Commission. Both sports teams have moved on—the Astros to a newer stadium in downtown and the Oilers to a different state. Proposed ideas for the empty stadium have ranged from a hotel and waterpark to an indoor parking lot, but no one can agree.

The Astrodome started with a man named George Kirksey, who had an advertising agency in Houston. George was a baseball fan and had campaigned for years to get Major League Baseball (MLB) to Houston. Houston had a farm league team under the St. Louis Cardinals named the Houston Buffalos, commonly called the Buffs. They played in a small stadium at what is now Cullen Boulevard and the Gulf Freeway.

George Kirksey rounded up Craig Cullinan and eight other Houston business people to join the endeavor. Craig was the grandson of Joe Cullinan, the founder of Texaco who was early to the Spindletop oil field in Beaumont, Texas, and helped birthed the modern oil industry. Kirksey and Craig Cullinan called on multiple civic leaders to try to develop support for the concept of an MLB team. In order to add excitement, they also proposed that it play ball under a domed stadium, which at the time few people thought was feasible.

Judge Roy Hofheinz had been defeated in the Mayor's race in 1955 after three years in office. As executive director of the United Citizens Association, the organization that was going to get him re-elected along with a slate of eight City Council candidates, I had gone down in defeat with him. In early 1956, George Kirksey approached Bob Smith and asked him to get involved in the fight for an MLB team for Houston. Bob told him to go see Hofheinz.

Kirksey was excited by Bob Smith's response to his proposal. After his defeat in the mayoral race, Judge Hofheinz was looking for an enterprise in which he could engage with Bob, his best friend and close ally. When Kirksey and Cullinan walked into Hofheinz's office, history was changed.

As a former Harris County Judge, Hofheinz proposed that Harris County sell bonds to build the stadium. It was estimated to cost about thirty-five million dollars. They formed a company named Houston Sports Association that would obtain an MLB franchise and sign a for- ty-year lease on the domed stadium. The annual lease payments would equal the debt service on the bonds. Bob Smith and Hofheinz would put up all of the money to organize the team, but they gave Kirksey, Cullinan, and the eight other promoters a ten percent carried interest, one percent each.

I had experienced Judge Hofheinz as a bold politician, but now I realized that he was also one of the most creative and effective business people I had ever run across. It took several years, but in the early 1960s a bond election was held and passed by the voters of Harris County. I believe the bond issue passed because of the great reputation of Bob Smith. In addition to his success in the oil patch and his philanthropy, he was a civic leader of the first order. Hofheinz's terrible defeat in the mayor's election of 1955 had cast him into semi-disgrace. Bob Smith furnished sixty-five percent of the cash for the enterprise, but he gave Hofheinz an option to buy up to a total of fifty percent of their joint stake in the Houston Sports Association, which owned the lease to the domed stadium and was soon to be granted an MLB franchise.

The investment group decided to name the new Houston baseball franchise the Colt .45s. Bob Smith and Hofheinz owned 200 acres near South Main at Braeswood, and they agreed to sell it to the county as a location for the stadium at their original cost-plus four percent interest.

After the voters approved the bond issue, a contract was immediately let by the county for the excavation for the stadium. It was Hofheinz's position that people would pay more for tickets if they walked in and walked down instead of up. In his experience, seats you walked down to access were more expensive. In order to have more of them, he had a deep hole dug so the entrance level would be about midway up the stadium. There were delays in the designs and delays in selling the bonds, so the big excavation was left dormant. Spring came, and it filled with water. The newspaper columnists called it Lake Elliott after Bill Elliott, the county judge who sponsored the bond issue. After some delay, the contract was let and construction began.

The Colt .45s started playing baseball in a temporary wooden stadium called Colt Stadium, built in what would become the parking lot of the domed stadium. The temporary stadium seated 33,000 people and was built for one season, although it remained in place, standing vacant until the 1970s and has since been dismounted and rebuilt in Mexico for a baseball team there.

Soon, the Colt's Manufacturing Company filed suit against the Houston Sports Association for trademark infringement for using the name Colt .45s. Remarkably, no one had talked to them about using the name. Hofheinz had thought that they would be pleased.

It was time to find a new name. Hofheinz wanted to name the team the Houston Stars because of NASA and the new focus on aeronautics in the city. Bob Smith was unalterably opposed. He thought the name was braggadocios. It was one of the few times when he put his foot down on a Hofheinz plan. After a couple of weeks, Hofheinz came up with the name Houston Astros, which Bob Smith approved. The name of the team gave the innovative new stadium the name Astrodome, and it was dubbed the "Eighth Wonder of the World."

In a survey taken by the Houston Post, fifty-three percent of the Houstonians polled were confident that the domed stadium was not going to work. They were sure that the roof would collapse as soon as the super-structure underneath was removed. I remember when the construction was almost finished, and it came time to remove the super-structure from the dome. As they began to bring down the super-structure the roof came with it…one foot, two feet, three feet, five feet. We were all sweating. The super-structure was lowered eleven feet before the roof stopped coming down with it.

I am standing next to Johnny Goyen and Archie Bennett, Sr. at the opening of the Astrodome. President Lyndon Johnson, Ladybird, and Hofheinz are on the first row.

The Astrodome opened in April of 1965. The Astros played and beat the New York Yankees' all-star team, including Mickey Mantle and Roger Maris. I always suspected that they threw the game. We were not in the American League like they were, and it didn't matter a lot to them: They were the New York Yankees. Lyndon B. Johnson was president and happened to be in Texas at the LBJ Ranch at the time. He and his wife Lady Bird attended the game. I was in the owner's box as a guest of Bob Smith and Hofheinz. The Houston Post ran a picture on the front page the next day of LBJ, Lady Bird, Hofheinz, and me watching the game. Also, in the photograph were Johnny Goyen—my longtime partner—and Archie Bennett, Jr., who was married to my sister.

INNOVATION AND INGENUITY

An unexpected dilemma occurred after the Astrodome opened. The windows in the roof let in so much sun during an afternoon game that the outfielders could not see fly balls because of the glare. Fly balls were dropping everywhere. It wasn't long until Hofheinz decided to paint over the plastic windows on the southwest side of the dome. That solved the outfielders' problem, but very soon thereafter the grass on the field, which had been thriving with the sunlight, began to die.

Hofheinz, being the creative genius that he was, called Monsanto Chemical Company and asked them to do research on an artificial grass that could replace the real grass growing in the Astrodome. A few months later they came back with a solution, which they tested at Colt Stadium next door. Hofheinz said he would give them an order to make the product to install on the entire floor of the Astrodome, but he want- ed the Houston Sports Association to get a royalty off of the sale of the product to third parties in the future. After much wrangling, Monsanto said that they were unwilling to give a royalty, because they had paid for the research; however, they would name the product AstroTurf. Today, artificial turf is popular in many professional sports stadiums and even in some people's backyards.

Along with AstroTurf, Hofheinz's involvement in the stadium resulted in another wildly popular invention—the stadium suite. In the 1960s this was an unheard-of concept. Today no stadium could survive without them. After the Astrodome was constructed, there had been an area on the seventh level above the crow's nest seats that went unused. Hofheinz decided to construct what he called Sky Boxes. Each one had twenty-four or thirty stadium seats over the field and a small room behind the seats with lounge chairs, sofas, a bar, a table, and a butler in a tuxedo. Whoever bought a Sky Box had the privilege of paying for thirty tickets per game for eighty-one games each year, plus the cost of food and drinks.

Being the easiest mullet in the room, I was the first person to buy a Sky Box from Hofheinz and Smith. It was box number one, right behind home plate but high in the sky. Hofheinz had managed to turn the worst seats in the house into the most expensive, and people were clamoring to buy them.

ROY HOFHEINZ AND BOB SMITH

The deal for the Dome had been set up so that Hofheinz had the option to buy part of Bob Smith's stock share. When he exercised the option, he would own forty-five percent instead of twenty-five percent. The option was to expire six months after the Astrodome opened. Six months came and went, and Hofheinz didn't even mention it. The ownership remained with the Kirksey group owning ten percent, Hofheinz about twenty-five percent and Bob Smith sixty-five percent. Twenty months went by, until one day at a Board of Directors meeting, Hofheinz said "Bob, by the way, I'm going to be exercising my option on the stock, and I'll be sending the papers over in a week."

Bob, caught by surprise, didn't say anything.

The next week, the transfer documents arrived, along with a cashier's check for the cash needed to pay Bob back at cost plus four percent interest. The option had expired twenty months earlier. Bob's lawyer and other advisors were outraged. When the option had been granted to Hofheinz, there was no assurance that either the Astrodome or the Astros would be a success. But long after the option had expired and the stock had proven to be a great investment, Hofheinz wanted to buy the stock.

At that time, Bob Smith and I went every day at one o'clock to the President's Health Club downtown to work out. Bob believed that working out was an important way to stay fit and relieve stress, and he made a big impression on my own exercise habits. Sitting in the snack bar afterward, we'd order a Vita-C Cool health drink, and Bob would pull the cashier's check out of his wallet. We would both look at it and try to decide what to do.

From my position on the edge, I noticed the tension that had been growing over these many months. Since the Astrodome opened, Hofheinz had been hailed far and wide for the success of the enterprise. His picture was on the cover of Time Magazine. He was a national darling, and sportswriters from coast to coast were interested in talking to him. And all this time Bob Smith's name was seldom mentioned. Having known Bob for so long, I knew that if Hofheinz would simply give Bob some recognition and thanks, he would be glad to reinstate the defaulted option. But that didn't seem likely to happen; Hofheinz had also developed a habit of being critical of Bob at Board meetings, treating him as though he was old and out of touch.

Three weeks later, after the next Board meeting of the Houston Sports Association, Hofheinz walked over to Bob and said "Bob, you never did sign those papers and send them back."

Bob said "Well, Judge Suhr, my lawyer, doesn't think I should accept it, since the option expired twenty months ago."

Hofheinz blurted, "Bob, are you gonna welch on this deal?"

Well, that did it. Bob said something to the effect of "You buy me out, or I'll buy you out" and stormed off. Bob Smith's word was his single most valuable possession, and to be called a welcher was the greatest insult anybody could hurl at him.

Bob Smith's favorite quotation was from the poem "The Cremation of Sam McGee" by Robert Service. It is "A promise made is a debt unpaid." (By the way, that's my favorite quote as well.)
I tried to get Hofheinz on the telephone to tell him that a simple apology was all that would be required to put the incident to rest and solve the problem, but I didn't hear back from him. I was not surprised. It was always difficult to get him on the phone.

A few days later Hofheinz's lawyer called Bob and said that Hofheinz would have a proposal for him in a few days. A week later a contract arrived that said that Hofheinz would buy Bob out by paying him his exact cost for his sixty-five percent of the stock, without interest, but would give him a ten percent carried interest in the Houston Sports Association. In other words, Hofheinz would give

Smith back the money he had invested in his portion of the team but leave him with ten percent ownership.

The kicker, however, was that Hofheinz wanted six months to be able to do it. Bob was certain Hofheinz would not be able to do it, so he immediately agreed to the plan. Without paying a nickel, Hofheinz now had another six months option to own eighty percent of the Houston Sports Association, while George Kirksey and friends and Bob Smith would own ten percent each. It was a tense six month, and Hofheinz never gave any indication whether or not he would be able to pull it off. Ultimately Hofheinz went to Houston Bank and Trust and borrowed the money to purchase Bob's stock. On the last day of the six month period, Hofheinz showed up with the cash. Bob was very disappointed, but he fulfilled his part of the deal.

I later asked Bob Smith who he planned to have run the Astrodome and the Houston Astros if Hofheinz had failed to raise the money to buy the controlling interest. He said, "Welcome, you, of course." I was stunned. I knew more about atomic fission than I did about running a baseball team. If I had known that during the six-month period when we were waiting for Hofheinz, I would have been sweating bullets.

MOVING FORWARD

Six months later I bought Bob's ten percent of the Astros because his wife Vivian wanted absolutely no connection with Hofheinz after what had transpired. Bob's health was also failing. I became a director of the Houston Sports Association. Hofheinz and I had remained friends, and I had no desire to tell him how to run the ball club. From the first board meeting I started working on getting Hofheinz to reconcile with Bob. Simultaneously I was talking to Bob about how regretful Hofheinz was, how he overreached, and how Hofheinz missed him. Although I hadn't exactly heard that from Hofheinz, I thought it was true.

To Hofheinz, I would say things like Bob Smith was terribly hurt and disappointed, and in my view all it would take was an outreach on Hofheinz's part to get the two back together. Within four months I had made substantial progress and felt like I was only a couple of months away from a total reconciliation. At the time I was also running seven subdivisions, a bank, a savings and loan association, six apartments

Here, I am standing with Senate Majority Leader Lyndon B. Johnson at a political rally in 1960 in Houston. (LBJ was running for President)

projects, and an American stock exchange company, so I only had limited time to worry about Smith and Hofheinz.

Then Hofheinz had a stroke that affected him dramatically, and Bob's health deteriorated more as he lost his ability to speak. I had to abandon my reconciliation plans because Mrs. Smith was doing all the speaking for Bob, and she was very protective of her husband.

In the meantime, the country went into a recession in 1969, and the Dow Jones Industrial Average fell forty percent. My business suffered, as did the Astros. Hofheinz began to have difficulty making the payments on his debt at Houston Bank and Trust, which by that time had been bought by Joe Allbritton, merged with Citizen's State Bank, and renamed Houston Citizen's Bank & Trust. Hofheinz had built the Astroworld amusement complex adjacent to the Astrodome and other projects, which were also a drain on him financially. He was in a wheelchair and quite incapacitated. The federal bank examiners had classified his loan at Houston Citizen's Bank, and if they wrote it off, it would close the bank.

At that point Ben McGuire, a famous Houston mortgage man, approached me and said that he was interested in buying my ten percent of the Houston Astros. I desperately needed the money, but I suspected that McGuire was acting for Hofheinz. I thought I had better talk to Bob Smith's people. I met with Billy Finnegan, Bob's number one man, and told him of the offer to buy the stock. I asked if Mrs. Smith would object if I sold it, or would she want to buy it back herself. Bob himself no longer made these decisions. Bill Finnegan told me he said sell it. Mrs. Smith still wanted no part of Hofheinz or the Astrodome stock.

Deep down, I still felt like Hofheinz was the real buyer, so I called Helen Johnson, another lawyer in Bob Smith's office. She said, "Welcome, sell the stock. Mrs. Smith would have absolutely no interest in anything connecting with Hofheinz."

I asked Helen if I should talk to Mrs. Smith about it, and she said no. I wish now I had ignored this advice, but I didn't.

About that time, Ben McGuire confessed that Hofheinz was the real buyer, and I started negotiating with the president of the Houston Sports Association. I still owed about a million dollars on the stock to the same bank, the Houston Citizen's Bank and Trust. Joe Allbritton, the chairman of the board and principal shareholder, called me and urged me to sell the stock because Hofheinz was unable to pay his note, or refinance his Houston Sports Association stock, unless he controlled

100% of the stock or had an agreement from every shareholder giving up their rights to vote. The new lender, Ford Motor Credit Company, would not make the loan to pay off the bank on Hofheinz stock unless I sold or gave up my voting rights.

Joe Allbritton was my principal banker and Hofheinz's as well. My financial strain increased, so I decided to sell. The sale occurred in October of 1971. Hofheinz's empire was saved by a fifteen percent interest per annum note.

A few years later, during some recession I'm sure, he defaulted on the note, and the Houston Sports Association was taken over by Ford Motor Credit Company. A year later they sold to marine industrialist John McMullen and a group of others from Houston.

Had I held onto my ten-percent share of the stock, today it would be worth more than two hundred million dollars. But that's not the part that bothers me when I think about the Astrodome. Neither of Bob's lawyers mentioned to Mrs. Smith that I had called for advice before selling the stock. Later, in a book written about Hofheinz, Mrs. Smith was quoted saying she didn't feel the same about me after I sold the stock. That, and the fact that Bob never got the credit he deserved for his role in developing the Astrodome, are my two real regrets about the whole deal.

Many years later, Bud Adam's, who owned the Houston Oilers proposed that the county spend about one hundred million dollars to upgrade the Astrodome. The county declined and Bud moved the team to Tennessee and they are now the Tennessee Titan. Also, many years later the Astro's base- ball team was moved to Minute Maid Park in Downtown, Houston. The Astrodome was closed.

After sitting vacant for many years, amid cries to tear down the Astrodome, Harris County Judge Ed Emmett got behind a plan to convert the under- ground part of the Astrodome into a parking garage and sell $100 million dollars' worth of revenue bonds to pay for it. The Astrodome was saved. I now serve on the Board of Directors of the Astrodome Conservancy, which is developing a plan to use the surface in the Astrodome above the parking garage.

8

It's Right To Support Civil Rights
Houston

Houston in the early 1960s operated much like the rest of the South under the Jim Crow laws that had been put in place after the Civil War. At City Hall and places like Foley Brothers department store, there were two water fountains side by side—one marked "white" and one marked "colored." It was the same with the restrooms; in public places, there were separate restrooms for blacks. A private business, however, was not required to provide a separate restroom, so in most places of business, such as restaurants and services stations, blacks were not permitted to use the facilities.

If a black person were traveling, even to downtown, he or she would have to plan ahead and know where to find a bathroom when need- ed. There were separate schools, separate colleges, and separate universities. The University of Houston had no black students, no black athletes. They attended the Texas State College for Negroes, renamed Texas Southern University in 1951. No one used the words "blacks" or "African Americans"; in formal society and polite circles people said "negroes," and many whites used a variety of much harsher names.

While there were black-owned businesses in Houston, the job opportunities for blacks in the white world were limited to being maids, janitors, laborers, and infrequently a truck driver. In stores that whites patronized, there were no black clerks; at white banks, no black tellers; and in white offices, no black secretaries. Like the large majority of the white population, I didn't worry about the segregation, because I was not really affected by it. I didn't necessarily think it was right, but I considered it someone else's problem.

In the 1950s when Judge Roy Hofheinz was mayor of Houston, he would frequently send me to make speeches when he was invited but could not attend. Many times, they were at African American churches or gatherings. I would always include some remarks about the Hofheinz

Administration recognizing the "plight of the negroes" and explain that we were working for more justice. In effect I would say, "Hang in there; things will get better."

In the early 1960s, I was chairman of the board of a bank and a savings and loan association. The bank was located in northeast Houston, which had a substantial black population. Many of them were moving into decent $10,000 houses for the first time. It was unprecedented to hire African American bank tellers at a white bank, but I decided to do it. I could hire college graduates who were good looking, well dressed, highly intelligent, and eager for a job—excellent employees. The problem black college graduates had in those days was a lack of professional jobs available to them. Mine was also the first white bank to have a black member of the Board of Directors. His name was Mack Hannah, Jr., and among his many accomplishments, he had founded the first black-owned savings and loan, Standard Savings & Loan. I was not trying to help the civil rights movement; I was just trying to help my bank. I saw an opportunity, and I went after it.

Throughout the South there was substantial race-related violence. The police unleashed dogs on peaceful demonstrators. All over the South integration was causing major problems. Lunch counter sit ins took place across the South, a visible yet peaceful action by African Americans demanding equal service.

Going back to the early days of Jesse Jones, Houston's leaders have al- ways addressed problems head on. One of the famous occasions was when Jesse Jones called seven bank presidents into his office on the top floor of the Gulf building, the headquarters for the National Bank of Commerce, which he owned, and proposed that the seven banks come to the aid of an eighth bank in Houston which was failing because of the Great Depression. It took several hours, but at the end of the meeting everyone agreed and the bank was saved. Houston has always had that spirit.

So, during Mayor Cutrer's administration, when some well-dressed college students from the Texas State College for Negroes, now Texas Southern University, arrived at the Foley's lunch counter and sat down to order lunch, the mayor called me, his go-to guy, to help sort things out.

Over the next week, Monday through Friday, the students would catch the bus downtown and go to Foley's lunch counter, the Walgreen's lunch counter, and similar places, and sit on the stools waiting to give their order. No one would take their order, since it was against the rules, and probably against the law. The students would sit there politely for two to three hours with photographers from the newspapers hovering around them, along with television news cameras.

We knew we had an explosive situation on our hands, and we did not want the negative publicity that accompanied such occasions in other Southern cities like Birmingham, Atlanta, New Orleans and Little Rock. We called a meeting of all of those businesses that had lunch counters downtown. We also included members of the Restaurant Association and other civic leaders. At the meeting a man named Bob Dundas, at the time vice president for advertising at Foley Brothers, made the pitch that if all of the lunch counters downtown desegregated at the same moment, we could probably avoid fireworks. Speed was the strategy, and for the plan to work, we had to have the cooperation of the news media.

It took two hours of discussion to persuade those at the meeting that this plan made sense. We had all spent a lifetime operating under the old set of rules. I called the editors of the three daily newspapers: the Chronicle, the Post and George Carmack's Houston Press, and others called the radio and TV station news departments.

I don't know what the response was from TV and radio, but the three newspaper editors I contacted agreed to report the situation, but to downplay it. There would be no banner headlines about desegregating the lunch counters in Houston.

On August 25, 1960, at noon, the students, who by this time had been brought into the plan, arrived at about five or six different lunch counters in downtown Houston and were served lunch at these all-white establishments for the first time in history.

THE CIVIL RIGHTS ACT

In the spring of 1963, Jack Valenti called me and said that Vice President Johnson was going to be in Houston, and he wanted me and "the guys" to come by Valenti's house on Sunday to visit. "The guys" were my brother, Jack, our Jamaica Beach partners, and Archie Bennett, who had just married my baby sister, Beverly.

After Valenti had handled the advertising in Texas for the successful 1960 Kennedy-Johnson campaign, he and LBJ's former assistant Mary Margaret, who he had married after the election, had moved to a house on San Felipe near Kirby Drive in River Oaks. At this point, we had all been involved with LBJ for about fifteen years, since he was first elected to the US Senate from Texas in 1948.

It was a Sunday afternoon, and Joanne and I drove over to Valenti's house. We were the last to arrive, and everyone was drinking wine except LBJ. He was sitting next to the fireplace in the living room in an overstuffed chair. He was drinking decaf coffee—one cup after another. I grabbed a glass of wine, walked over, and sat down in the chair next to him.

Trying to think of something of significance to talk about, I asked him what his prediction was about the Kennedy civil rights bill in Congress. JFK had introduced the civil rights bill, but it seemed to be going nowhere. In those days, Congress was 100% controlled by congressmen and senators from the South, including Texas. Civil rights was not a popular subject in the South, and Kennedy's civil rights bill was dead on arrival.

After I asked LBJ to comment on the legislation, he was quiet for a moment. I could tell he was trying to decide whether I was important enough to deserve a full answer.

I must have passed the test, because he turned to me and said, "Welcome, let me tell you a story. When we were campaigning, the vice president's campaign entourage was traveling through New Mexico in 1960. Welcome, you know how New Mexico is; you travel for two hours seeing nothing but cactus and then you come up on a service station in the bend of a road. You stop at the station, go to the bathroom, fill up with gas, and have a Coke. We saw such a station, and that's what we did."

He continued, "After about fifteen minutes, we got ready to leave and one of the girls on the staff was missing. She worked in the Majority Leader's office in DC. We looked everywhere in the service station but could not find her." Then he said, "Welcome, it turned out she was a

It's Right To Support Civil Rights

In the 1960s, a group of black TSU students sat down at the Foley's store's counter and asked to be served. (Houston Chronicle files).

half block behind the building, squatting down behind a bush to go to the bathroom, because she was black. They would not let her use the ladies room at the service station."

LBJ grabbed my knee with his left hand and he pointed his right fin- ger in my face and said, "Welcome, that is wrong. That is wrong." I will never forget his next words. He said, "And when I am in a position to do something about it, I am going to."

In November of 1963, just six months after our conversation, Kennedy was assassinated, and LBJ became President of the United States. Seven months after that, in the late spring of 1964, against all odds, he passed the Civil Rights Act of 1964. The following year he passed the Voting Rights Act of 1965. Later, he passed the Fair Housing Act of 1968.Beginning with the 50th anniversary of the 1964 Act, some national leaders have given credit to JFK and Martin Luther King, Jr. for getting the civil rights bill passed, but the credit goes to LBJ.

HOUSTON'S EQUAL RIGHTS ORDINANCE AND LGBT RIGHTS

LBJ's clarity on the importance of civil rights, my recognition in business that race did not define a person's ability to succeed, and the experiences I had with Houston's peaceful desegregation all helped me realize how important it is for communities to overcome prejudices and work together for the common good. After the 1960s, my understanding on this topic continued to evolve as my businesses became more successful and I became more involved civically.

While my experiences with people of other races allowed me to drop many of my prejudices, there were still areas where I did not have enough experience to understand that there was still a need to open my mind further. One area where experience has provided me with more understanding is the LGBT community.

For about the first fifty or sixty years of my life, I was convinced that the gay lifestyle was a voluntary activity. In the small towns where I grew up, most of us thought that gay activity was extremely uncommon. The truth is, of course, that gays and lesbians have always been part of the population, but they were in the closet. In Brownsville, I knew of only one gay man. The common wisdom of my teenage friends was that if a gay man tried to pick you up in a bar, you were supposed to hit him.

So, in the 1980s when a long-time, loyal, able employee, who was about thirty years old, came in one day and said he was coming out of the closet, I was not prepared to handle the conversation properly. He said he was gay and that he wanted me to hear about it from him and not through a third party. He was divorced and had two kids. I made it clear that under the circumstances, I had no choice but to fire him.

I was the only employer he had ever had. He was hard working and able. He was very conservative in his dress and manners. I was able to get a friend of mine who was more enlightened than I to hire him. Today when I think about it, I recognize how unjust that was, and I'm ashamed of myself. With the understanding and experience I had at the time, however, I thought it was the right response.

My education was to continue. In the spring of 2014, I was a member of the Greater Houston Partnership (GHP) when Houston mayor Annise Parker proposed a civil rights ordinance. Her rationale was that Houston was the only major city in America that did not have one. Many business people took serious objection, on the basis that Houston didn't have a civil rights problem. Why search for a solution for a problem that doesn't exist? I was asked by the leaders at the GHP to be part of a small policy group to figure out what to do in the situation. When we first met, I was not surprised that over half of those present raised serious objections to the new ordinance. However, in typical Houston fashion, after an hour of discussion it was determined that we would be better off to work together with those on the other side than to have a confrontation.

Initially, there were about two-dozen items in the draft ordinance that we found unacceptable. We voted to work to correct those items so we could support the ordinance. Our biggest issue was the call for a "civil rights commission." We saw this as a continual opportunity for activist-generated publicity without a proper procedure for confidentiality, time for response, or other procedures that would keep the situation from being misinterpreted.

Although the ordinance covered a broad range of groups, including blacks, Hispanics, and American Indians, the mayor's main objective was to expand civil rights to include protection against discrimination of gays, lesbians, bisexuals, and transgender people. These groups were not then protected by federal law, and our wonderful mayor, who is a lesbian, was anxious to fill this void.

The GHP chairman was Paul Hobby, and our president was Bob Harvey. Bob Borchoff, owner of the Adobe Restaurants and a major leader at the GHP, initiated the discussion with the mayor and her city attorney. Immediate progress was made because the mayor was realistic enough to understand that if she could get the business community's support, passage of the ordinance would easily follow.

After several weeks of discussion, the mayor came and met with our group at GHP along with her city attorney. She both outlined her plan and thanked us for working with her. At the end of the day, an ordinance was produced that we could support. And we did.

In May 2014 the ordinance came before the City Council and was adopted twelve to six. In the process of pulling together the business community, Bob Harvey of the GHP reached out to eight major business organizations, including the Houston Apartment

Association, the Houston Restaurant Association, the Houston Hotel Association, the Houston Association of Realtors, and other similar organizations. Initially, all had grave misgivings about the ordinance. But, as had happened before, after discussing it for an hour or so and considering the alternatives, all agreed to move forward to fix the ordinance instead of fighting over it.

Unfortunately, however, when the ordinance went to a public vote in November 2015, it failed sixty-one percent to thirty-nine percent. One of the hot-point issues in the civil rights ordinance was the use by transgender people of the bathroom for the sex with which they identify. To many, this meant men could use the women's restroom. More than any other provision, this was the flash point that caused many religious groups, especially African American religious groups, to passionately oppose the ordinance. When we discussed this issue, it was stated that if someone looks like a woman, dresses like a woman, and acts like a woman, they should be using the ladies' restroom. During the negotiations for the civil rights ordinance, one of our negotiators explained that a transgender person with whom he had been discussing the ordinance told him that there are twenty-three shades of gender assignment. I have no reason to question that.

So, we at the GHP added a good-faith provision to the ordinance that simply said if a restaurant, in good faith, believed a male was entering the ladies' restroom dishonestly, they could stop him without repercussions. For example, if someone was dressed as a woman but had a beard, he could be stopped from entering the ladies' restroom.

In finally reaching the decision to support and improve the ordinance, we at the GHP were comforted by the fact that in other cities across America, where similar laws had been enacted, there were seldom any complaints filed. The opposition, however, focused solely on the bath- room portion of the ordinance, calling it the "Sexual Predator Protection Act" and promoting the tagline "No Men in Women's Bathrooms."

The fight will continue. Under the Houston City Charter, only 17,000 signatures have to be obtained in order for a city-wide election to be held on any subject. The advocates for this ordinance could easily pull together 17,000 signatures.

Like America, Houston has come a long way on the matter of civil rights, and we still have more work to do. Change will come one heart at a time, and civic leaders can make it happen faster by engaging the business community. It is possible for people to change their opinions, when they are given opportunities to work together to better their communities. I began life with all the prejudices of the small world I lived in, and as I gained experience, I dropped those beliefs.

When I judge people today, it is not because of their race or sexual orientation. After all my experience, the only real prejudice I believe I still hold is that when I first meet someone and he or she uses poor diction and grammar, I think less of that person. And I am certainly prejudiced against those who use profanity. Anyone can choose to learn how to communicate clearly and respectfully.

9

Thirty Years On River Oaks Boulevard
Houston

Wherever we lived, adventure seemed to follow us, and our kids kept us on our toes. When Welcome Jr. was about five years old in 1956, we were living in Bellaire, TX on Braeburn St. I was in Brazoria County at Bob Smith's hunting lodge, the Mad Island Slew. We were there duck hunting with Bob and Mayor Roy Hofheinz. It was then that I was running the Civil Defense Department for the city of Houston and Harris County, and I also had the title of assistant to the mayor so I could go speak for him when he was unavailable. I remember the trip well because sitting in the duck blind with Mayor Hofheinz as ducks would approach, he would say "Don't shoot, don't shoot, don't shoot...wait until they're right on top of us. Don't shoot until I tell you to."

I was crouched down watching the ducks and suddenly I would hear *bang bang*. That was Hofheinz shooting. Then he would say "shoot," by which time the ducks had passed over us.

After the morning shoot, we went back to the headquarters building, and I got a telephone call from Joanne. She was at the hospital, and apparently Cindi was having her stomach pumped out because she had swallowed ant poison by mistake. My wife wanted me to get back to Houston.

The mayor's chauffer was a police officer named Lt. Sam Clauder. He was a cousin of my uncle, Otto Clauder, who married my mother's sister, Alberta. The mayor told me to take Sam and get back to Houston. With the sirens in the mayor's limousine blaring, we went back to Houston at eighty miles an hour, and I was dropped off at the hospital. At the hospital, there were news reporters from the Chronicle and the Post, who were reporting on the incident because I was public figure.

I am standing in front of our home at 1808 River Oaks Blvd. where we lived for thirty years. Welcome Jr., Cindi, Pam, Craig and Joanne were raised here.

It turned out that Welcome Jr. was having a tea party in the garage with his two sisters, Cindi and Pam, and, unbeknownst to him, was serving them ant poison which he had found in the garage. The total amount that Cindi had taken was minor. So, although her stomach had to be pumped out, there was no lasting effect. The next day, a photograph of Welcome Jr. and Cindi was on the front page of the Houston Chronicle.

Later, in Denton, TX, Welcome Jr., Cindi, and Pam, were still the only kids we had. They spent most of their time playing barefooted in the neighborhood. On two separate occasions, I had to remove a nail that had gone in the bottom of Welcome Jr.'s foot and was sticking out the top. And nails weren't the only things the kids had to maneuver.

In the back of our house in Denton was a vacant lot that belonged to my friend George Deutsch. With his permission, I built a stage about four feet off the ground. It was about twelve feet square. My kids and my brother Jack's kids, Charlene and Kathy, would organize shows where the neighborhood kids would sing and dance and put on shows, just like we had done when we were kids. One day, Cindi came running into the house saying that a rattlesnake had been seen near the stage. I went to the garage and got a hoe and went back to the group of kid performers. As they carefully watched, I cut the snake into four or five pieces. They were startled to see that after I had cut off the snake's head, the rattler was still rattling at the other end of the snake.

In the mid-1960s, we were living in Meyerland, a subdivision of Houston. One day that year, I kissed Joanne goodbye and left for work. She had beautiful shoulder-length dark hair. When I returned after work, I found a short-haired blonde in her place. No preparation. No conversation about it. There it was. Her hair was close-cropped and barely covered her ears. In high school, I had broken up with my first girlfriend after two years because she cut her hair.

At the time of the hair-color change, the Houston Chronicle did a feature article about her, and she appeared in a full-page photograph on the front page of the home section in a picture taken at our canal home at Jamaica Beach. She looked wonderful, and the house did, too. I realized that Joanne had always had an eye for what looked good, whether it was her hair, her clothes, her art, or her homes.

From the early days of our marriage, when we lived in our first little apartment, Joanne has used this ability to make our space an inviting home. From apartment to apartment, and house to house, as our for- tunes rose and our furnishings became finer, that warm quality of home has always been present in our lives, thanks to her vision and her willingness to act on it.

In 1965, we began thinking it was time to move out of Meyerland. It took me nearly an hour to drive to work every day.

Freeways were still a thing of the future, and traffic was slow. We had been blessed with the arrival of two more children, Craig and Joanne, and the seven of us needed a bigger house. Our daughter Cindi was using the dining room as a bedroom, and Welcome Jr. slept in the garage, which had been remodeled into a private bedroom and bath.

When we began the quest for a new home, I told Joanne that I would never again live more than ten minutes from my office. Because my office was downtown, that presented a limited area in which we could live. It would have to be the Houston Heights or River Oaks. In those days, River Oaks was not nearly as expensive as it later became. Small houses were for sale in the neighborhood at remarkably low prices, around $30,000 to $40,000. We found a real-estate agent who was a private independent broker. He was very good, primarily because he and Joanne communicated well. In those days there would never be more than half a dozen houses larger than 6,000 square feet on the market in River Oaks. Today there are many more houses on the market in any price category in the neighborhood, in any price category.

We looked at a number of different houses, but nothing seemed to fit our family. We saw one house that looked big from the outside but was actually small. It was only one room deep with small rooms, which Joanne did not like. As with many of the houses in those days, it had low ceilings, or at least ceilings that felt like they were too low for us.

Then we received a call saying that Candace Mossler was going to put her house up for sale, and we could go look at it if we wanted. Candace Mossler was the widow of Jacques Mossler, who had been a major investor in Houston. He had become wealthy and lived on a five-and-a-half-acre tract on Willowick in River Oaks in a house that was more than 9,800 square feet.

Mrs. Mossler had just been acquitted of murdering her husband. She was tried with her nephew and presumed lover, a man named Mel Powers, in Florida where the murder had occurred. The prosecution alleged that she had sent Mel Powers to Florida to murder her husband and then fly back. She hired the prominent Houston defense lawyer Percy Foreman, who won acquittal for both Mossler and Powers.

Back in Houston after the trial, she offered her house for sale. It was a grand house on a big piece of land, and the restrictions in River Oaks provided that you could sub-divide a piece of land that you owned if it was not less than one acre. Being a sub-divider, I figured I could sell three of the acres for other home sites and end up with a very low-cost basis in the house. I was very interested.

The house was quite nice, although it needed a great deal of work, as did many houses in River Oaks at the time. It had a very spacious yard, swimming pool, and all the things you would expect from an expensive house. The price as I recall was $250,000, a great deal of money in 1965. When I walked through the dining room, however, I saw a mammoth portrait of Jacques Mossler ominously looking down from the high-ceilinged room. I knew he had been murdered, so I felt very uneasy. As we walked into the library, to get my mind off the eerie painting, I turned to the real estate broker and asked, "Who built this house originally?"

"Oh, that's very interesting," he said. "It was built by the president of Hughes Tool, the famous early Houston industrial company." I felt better that the head of such a well-known company had lived in the house before all the drama. The broker then went on to say, "As a matter of fact, he committed suicide in the very room we are standing in."

That did it for me. There was the murdered Jacques Mossler staring down from the dining room and a suicide in the library. This was too much for me. I felt it was an unlucky house. But the problem was, I had made a hand-shake deal to buy the house.

My problem was solved when my lawyer called me a couple days later and said that Mrs. Mossler had informed him that the deal was off if I did not close the next day. I replied that I probably could meet her de- mand, but I was not going to be forced into doing so. The deal was off.

I was so glad not to have to choose between my word and living in a haunted house that I didn't think much about why she cancelled the deal. When I later learned more about the situation, I decided that what had happened was that she had learned that no one wanted her as a neighbor. It turned out that she had signed a contract to buy a condominium in a high rise; but, after the other residents objected, the owner canceled the deal. Then she had gone to a subdivision and contracted to buy a big house there. The property owners' association had a town meeting and threatened the developer if he sold to her.

Seeing that she was going to be unable to buy another house, she elected to stay where she was and cancel my contract.

Also unbeknownst to me at the time, one of the River Oaks neighbors who wanted her out had a hand in helping me secure financing. After we struck our hand-shake deal to buy the house, the lawyers got on the phone and decided that, since we were all honorable people, no signed contract would be necessary. We would go directly to closing.

I received a call from the chairman of the board of the MD Anderson Foundation. I had met him before, but we weren't more than acquaintances. His name was John Freeman, and he was a named partner in Fulbright, Crooker, Freeman, and Bates (and later Jaworski). He told me that the MD Anderson Foundation was interested in making a loan to me on the house. I thought that was somewhat interesting, since their foundation had hundreds of millions of dollars and I had never thought of them being in the mortgage business. He said the foundation was anxious to make loans to qualified buyers on good properties, and he invited me to come down to the law firm and meet with the other members of the Board. I met with all of them. They didn't bother to run a credit report on me; they just approved the loan on the spot.

It turned out that a partner at Fulbright Crooker was Candace Mossler's next-door neighbor. He was so anxious for her to move out of the neighborhood that he had arranged for the foundation to make me the loan so that we could have a quick closing. While I appreciate all the faith that the neighbors had in me, I have always been grateful that that deal didn't work out. If it had, not only would I have avoided the library, but we would have also missed out on living in the house of our dreams.

THE HOUSE OF OUR DREAMS

After the failed attempt to buy the Mossler house, we went to see a house owned by Judge John Arthur Platt, a business associate of wealthy oil and lumber baron J. M. West. West was a wealthy oilman who built a ranch south of town in what would become the Clear Lake area. Years after West's death, Humble Oil acquired the mansion and much of the ranch land. The land ultimately became Clear Lake and

NASA's manned spacecraft center. The mansion served for many years as the Lunar and Planetary Institute. Four of the first ten homes built in River Oaks back in the twenties were built by his family.

West's main home was on River Oaks Boulevard at Del Monte, across the street from his sister. She had married Judge Platt who built the house that we were looking to buy. West's son "Silver Dollar Jim West" lived two blocks south, on the corner of River Oaks Boulevard and San Felipe, and his brother Wesley lived around the corner on Chevy Chase.

Joanne liked the Platt house immediately, because it had a huge living room, a grand dining room, and all of the bedrooms were large. Famed Houston architect Joseph Finger designed the French Renaissance-style home around the same time that he designed Houston's city hall. The house had not been remodeled since it was built in 1937, but it had tremendous potential. It was not listed for sale, but the owners were planning to ask $200,000 for it. I offered them $180,000, and they accepted. We signed the contract on the house around the first of April in 1966.

After we closed, I took the entire family to see the house. I'll never forget that visit. All the Platts' furniture had been removed from the house, and on the walls, you could see where pictures had formerly hung. As we walked up the stairs, our three-year-old son Craig said, "I can't live here; I can't live here! Too many ghosts." We would all, including Craig, come to love the house as much as Joanne did.

The house was large, but not large enough in Joanne's mind for a family of seven. She began the process of remodeling and enlarging it; $650,000 later in expansion and remodeling costs, we moved in, with the house still incomplete. She added an additional 1,200 square feet as a master bedroom wing on the first floor. She also installed a mammoth swimming pool, enlarged the kitchen, and converted the porte-cochere into a lovely morning room and family dining room. The larger formal dining room was next to the living room. She also remodeled the servants' quarters in the garage. She hired a renowned Houston decorator, Herbert Wells, and spent almost a year buying furniture for the now 9,000-square-foot house.

I had recently made a good profit on two transactions, one in Spring Branch and the other near the brand new intercontinental airport. Those two deals generated about $700,000, which we used to expand the house and buy furniture.

During the first year in our new house, I was negotiating with John Mecum to take over his subdivision in Galveston County called Flamingo Isle. He invited the negotiations. He had owned about 7,000 acres for many years. Three or four years before, he had started building canals. It was located on the mainland very near the causeway to Galveston Island. Although some of his children had built houses there, he never actually offered the lots for sale to the public, even though seven million dollars had been spent.

Our negotiations stalled because his way of making a deal made no sense to me. One day he said, "I heard you bought a new house on River Oaks Boulevard. Tell your wife that if we make this deal, I'll give her enough French antique paneling to panel the entire house, upstairs and down." John and his wife had been to France and bought the antique paneling out of an old castle for his wife's antique business. In spite of the pressure from my wife to make a deal, we did not. The paneling slated for our house ended up on Montrose Boulevard in the ballroom of the boutique hotel La Colombe d'Or. Even without the paneling, Joanne made our home lovely.

**I am standing in front of our house on River Oaks Boulevard in the 1970s.
I decided the grey beard made me look old, so I shaved it off soon afterward.**

FAMILY LIFE

From the first days we began discussing marriage, Joanne was clear about how she wanted to raise our family. When she saw that her parents were spoiling Welcome Jr. as a baby, she had put a halt to it by packing him up and moving to Japan. She knew instinctively what was best for our son, and she augmented her natural good sense with book after book of respected experts' opinions. I have always trusted her knowledge on what would be best for the kids.

It has often been said that my wife raised our five kids as five only children. My parents had always lived in a three-bedroom house; my brother and I lived in the second bedroom, and the third bedroom was reserved for guests. But Joanne, who had grown up as an only child, felt strongly that each child should have a private bedroom. In Meyerland, after Craig and Joanne were born, we first converted the dining room into a bedroom, and then we built a suite in the garage with a bath. One of the things that Joanne liked best about the new house in River Oaks was that each of the kids could have a bedroom.

The kids' bedrooms were on the second floor and included the previous master bedroom, which my wife and I did not use because of our new bedroom suite on the first floor. As the oldest girl, Cindi was the first occupant of the old master suite. As each older girl moved out, the next oldest took over the suite. Initially, our youngest daughter, Joanne, had a bedroom directly above our downstairs bedroom suite, which was connected by circular stairs which we installed so she could come down every night and get in bed with us, as all preschoolers do.

As we always had at our previous homes, we had fire drills. Knowing that speed was essential to surviving a house fire, I would make the kids exit the house quickly for the fire drill, typically to the front yard. This was very important no matter the size of our houses, but in a three-story house like the River Oaks Boulevard one, it was even more crucial, because a fire in the stairway could have caused one of the kids to hesitate and die. We were very lucky that we never had to put our drills to the test.

Welcome Jr. was fifteen years old when we bought the house in River Oaks; little Joanne was eighteen months. Over the next thirty years, we raised all five kids there. Living on the Boulevard put us at the center of a wonderful neighborhood, introduced us to many dear friends, and provided us with more memories than I can begin to describe.

Joanne lived the longest in the house on the Boulevard. She remembers using the cushions from the sofas on the third floor to slide down the stairway. Because the cushions had plastic covers, they made a good sled. She also remembers lying on the top of the stairway at night and listening to receptions and parties that we had while she was supposed to be asleep. We frequently gave receptions for visiting celebrities, and others, for charity events.

We converted the former ballroom on the third floor into a recreation room for the kids where they played ping-pong and other games. During my hard-financial times in the 1970s, the playroom came in handy. I moved my office from downtown to the third floor of our home. There were about five people, including me. Six months later the River Oaks Property Owners Association telephoned me about the situation. I told them that to call it an office was an "exaggeration," but I moved the office out.

Many of our wonderful memories of the house were made in the backyard. After we put the pool in, Joanne designed a beautiful

My wife Joanne was quite a gourmet cook when we lived on River Oaks Boulevard.

wrought-iron fence to go around it so that our small children would not fall in and possibly drown. When the pool was finished and we had our first swimming party, Craig, four at the time, easily slipped between the bars of the fence. His sister Joanne was only two and a half. So at great expense we paid to have an additional bar welded between each fence picket to make the gap small enough to keep our smaller kids safe.

We installed a trampoline in the backyard, and our kids would spend hours on it with their friends from the neighborhood. We also had a small foot-cranked merry-go-round for the smaller kids, which remind- ed me of the merry-go-round that my father had built for us as kids on the beach in Corpus Christi. As my younger kids got older, they would go faster and faster. We had a jungle gym set that the kids could climb on, and we turned the servants' quarters over the garage into male and female dressing rooms for the pool. Our backyard became a paradise for kids from preschoolers to teenagers.

The biggest outdoor area at our house was the side yard. It was roughly 100 feet wide and 180 feet deep. It is most remembered for the many, many touch football games that we organized for family and friends. I was always the quarterback on one team, and Welcome Jr. was always the quarterback on the other team. Welcome's team usually won.

In the corner I built a fort where Craig and Joanne and their younger friends spent hours playing cowboys and Indians. As a child, Joanne's favorite game was hide-and-go-seek. To this day she remembers the best places to hide in the house and not be found. The best was upstairs in the linen closet on the second floor. Another one was underneath the round living room table, which had a tablecloth that reached the floor. And yet another was behind the suits in my dressing room.

Joanne also loved playing in the butler's pantry with her mother's collection of tiny demitasse cups and silver spoons. She played store by putting price tags on clothing in the third-floor storage closets. The big house provided great fun for a little girl, but it could also be scary. She was afraid of pictures of old dead people. Pictures of my wife's grand- parents scared her. Whenever she entered the room on the second floor where my wife kept her office in later years, little

Joanne would run through the room and run down the circular stairs to get away from the photographs.

Various family members, have worked out at the Houstonian Club for many, many years. Joanne is pictured on the right.

HOLIDAYS AND SPECIAL EVENTS ON THE BOULEVARD

When we first moved in, one downside to River Oaks was that the majority of the residents were older; very few young families lived there. At Christmas time the five kids and I took pride in putting up the outdoor decorations. At first, we were one of only four families in River Oaks to put out Christmas decorations. Our decorations went along River Oaks Boulevard as well as our Del Monte Drive frontage. We had lights in the trees, lights in the bushes, lights over the doorway, and lights on the roof, which was accessed by a small porthole on the third floor. My daughter Joanne recalls sitting on my legs when she was eight as I thrust my body out the small window to hang lights outside the house. Had she stood up, I would have fallen forty feet.

Despite the neighbors' lack of enthusiasm for lights, we decorated every year for the next thirty years. Now, as the neighborhood has

TOP: Joanne and I visited the French Quarters in New Orleans in the 1970.

BOTTOM: Jack Valenti, President of Motion Picture Association, asked me to escort movie-star Gina Lolabrigida to a Paramount Pictures banquet in New York.

turned over and new families have moved in, the area is filled with so many beautiful displays that people come from all over at Christmas to drive down the twinkling streets.

Other holidays brought other traditions. I had a famous Frankenstein mask that I wore every Halloween. It was a plastic mask that fit over my entire head and looked remarkably like Boris Karloff in the movie. I would put a black coat on backwards and black pants. Each Halloween I would make a Frankenstein-like stagger down the sidewalk, making noises. The kids were petrified of me. To this day, Welcome's girls, Christina and Courtney, shudder when talking about me as Frankenstein. Later, I lost the mask, so my great-grandchildren have not had to suffer through Frankenstein.

And the fun wasn't just in our house. We discovered that there was a great deal going on in the neighborhood. One big annual event was the tennis tournament. Since before World War II, River Oaks Country Club at the north end of the Boulevard has hosted a professional tennis tournament in the spring. During the seventies, my kids had many exciting times during the tournament. Trolleys carrying spectators to their cars ran up and down the street, and it seemed like everyone we knew was in the neighborhood. It was a very friendly atmosphere. In those days, the second-tier players were housed in people's homes in the neighborhood. Tennis was not a high-dollar sport, and only the major stars like Björn Borg could afford to rent a hotel room. One year, two Australians playing in the tournament stayed at our house. The kids were thrilled, especially my three girls. Later Craig was a ball boy at the tournaments.

With my political interests, Joanne's philanthropic work, and all the family events, we had more parties than I could count at the house on River Oaks Boulevard. One particularly meaningful celebration was our daughter Joanne's wedding in May of 1994. Joanne married Howard Castleberry at St. John's Church, and the reception was held in our backyard. It was a beautiful occasion, and the weather was great.

SCHOOL DAYS

In addition to wanting a wonderful home for our family, Joanne also insisted that our kids should go to private school. In 1963 when Welcome Jr. was about twelve, Joanne enrolled him at The Kinkaid School in Houston. The following year Cindi and Pam joined him there. When Craig and Joanne each reached age three we enrolled them in Kinkaid preschool. Our family had a long run at Kinkaid. The year Joanne graduated, after fifteen years at Kinkaid, Welcome Jr.'s oldest daughter, Christina, enrolled in pre-school. All of Welcome's children were "lifers" there, and in 2016 we completed fifty-three consecutive years of having students at Kinkaid School without ever missing a single semester.

We enjoyed having our kids' Kinkaid friends over to the house. At some point during the early years there, someone came up with the idea of the Indian Guides. The concept was that instead of turning your sub-teenage kids over to a Scout Master, each father would accompany his boy to meetings so that it could be a bonding experience. My son Craig and I were deeply involved in Indian Guides. We would frequently have meetings of our troop at our house on the third floor in the playroom. I thought it was as wonderful program and of great value to the fathers and the sons.

With Wilson kids in five grades, our house was always busy. There was always something going on and sometimes the fun came with complications, which might have seemed like problems at the time, but are now some of our favorite stories.

When Craig was in high school, he had a party. He thought it would be a grand idea to turn the heat up in the pool to make the whole pool a Jacuzzi. It worked. The temperature was about 100 degrees. The electric bill that month was outrageous.

Other parties were not so expensive. For instance, when Cindi was in high school, we had the Baccalaureate service part of the graduation at our house. It was a Sunday afternoon with tables in the side yard decorated from magnolias blossoms from our own magnolia trees. I can still see Welcome Jr. high in the magnolia tree clipping flowers for the tables and dropping them to his brother and sisters below.

In 1968 we hosted the Kinkaid/St. John's football game after-party. The game, an annual rivalry, was held at St. John's that year, which is just down at the southern end of River Oaks Boulevard. Kinkaid had won, so everyone was in a great mood and ready to party. Because it was November and cold, the party was held indoors. It had been raining, and the band and guests tracked mud in from the outside. As more people arrived, more mud was tracked in the house. It was a great time, but I had to refinish all of the floors after the party was over. Many, many teenagers dancing the night away with muddy shoes was more than our floors could handle.

Later, college friends would come to the house. My son Craig held fraternity parties at the house when he was a student at the University of Texas. They were usually fundraisers, so parents were invited. The fraternity boys, who had little taste, would buy cheap wine, which they would auction to the parents. These parties raised a lot of money, but purchasers like me did not get much of a bargain. Craig was president of the fraternity while he was at UT, and the parties were well attended. Jim Baker, who would become a notable Secretary of State among other achievements, was a member of Craig's fraternity in college and came to our event one year with his son. And to this day, I will have major executives mention coming to my house as UT students.

THE NEXT GENERATION OF ENTERTAINERS

When we moved into the house we had planned to put the piano on the third floor, which was to serve as a recreation room for the kids. But the day we moved in, the movers could not get the piano up the narrow stairway to the top floor, so I told them to put it temporarily on the second floor landing, and we would figure out how to get it to the third floor later. It was there for thirty years. On Sunday mornings I would go to the landing on the second floor and wake the kids up by playing the piano. Frequently I would sing as well. Cindi particularly remembers the song "Moonriver," which was featured in the movie *Breakfast at Tiffany's*.

Although I could only play a half a dozen song on the piano, I could cord any song. My father had taught me to play by ear in Corpus Christi when the family got a baby grand piano. My brother became an accomplished pianist, again, by ear, but I always struggled. So, I adopted the plan of chording on the piano and singing.

The piano was a big part of our lives. We made each of our kids take piano lessons, starting at age six or seven. When we lived in Meyerland, at 6 a.m., Welcome Jr. would spend thirty minutes practicing on the piano, followed by Cindi at 6:30 and Pam at 7:00. Because they all took

Joanne and I with our five kids in the living room; (Welcome Wilson, Jr., Joanne Castleberry, Craig Wilson, Cindi Proler Ray, Pam Wilson).

piano from the same teacher, the songs that Welcome practiced one year, Cindi would play the next. Trying to sleep with the piano playing was a problem!

I wanted the kids to continue the Wilson family tradition of being entertainers, so I made every child pick a popular song to play on the piano or sing. Joanne picked "Blue Eyes Crying in the Rain" by Willie Nelson. Each Christmas Day in River Oaks we would have a reception for 100 people or so, and one of the highlights was singing Christmas carols together. We even had a Wilson Family songbook. I remember that Ben Love, a prominent banker, would come and sing at great length...only sometimes on key! I still play the piano infrequently either at home or at the ranch, but regrettably, I'm the only family member who still does.

FAMILY FITNESS

Another feature of the annual party was the athletic contest. All who wanted to participate, mainly young people, would compete in about ten exercises, such as push-ups, deep knee bends, and more. I always won the push-up contest. For the one-armed push-ups and the one-legged deep knee bends, I did not even have an opponent in the contest.

I have remained interested in fitness since Bob Smith and I began going to the President's Health Club downtown in the early sixties. Bob had been a boxer, and he insisted we all join the health club. I was the only one of our group who went regularly. Bob would call me every day at one and say, "Mr. Welcome, it's time to go." I would meet him, and we would work out. He was about seventy-five and I was about thirty-five, but he was fit. His example got me into the routine.

When he had a stroke and stopped going, I went through a short period when I wasn't working out. Then one evening, I was talking to my friend Jimmy Lyon. He said, "Rod Peddie and I run a mile every morning at the Lamar High School track. Why don't you join us?"

I said, "I'd like to do that."

"Fine," he said. "Tomorrow morning, 6 a.m."

When I called him the next morning and woke him up, he barely remembered why I was calling. We met at the track and I started running, but I could only go about a quarter of a mile. As I got back into shape, I could eventually do a twelve-minute mile, but it was exhausting. I mentioned my running habit to my lawyer one day, and he said, "It would be easier if you ran it in eight minutes. It's the length of time that's wearing you out." This was great advice. Soon Lyon and I were running three miles six days a week, and we kept that habit until he died twenty-three years later. Welcome Jr has been my workout partner since James died.

Lyon also had a full gym in the basement of his house, so we would work out as well. I knew how important it was to stay in shape, and I wasn't going to let myself slip again. But it was Joanne's influence that really kept me on track.

Around 1975, my wife announced that she wanted to be a runner, too. I was startled, because she had never been athletic. She would show up in the morning to run with Lyon and me. At first she could run only a block and a half before needing to walk for a while.

I had a "pat her on the head" attitude about it, but pretty soon she was running the entire three miles with us. Then she began to run longer. I tried to keep up, but when she reached four miles I stopped running with her. She continued and ended up running six miles, six days a week, which she continued for thirty five years.

In the 1980s, she signed up for the Houston Marathon, a 26.2-mile race. After American Frank Shorter won the marathon at the 1972 Olympics, more cities began hosting their own races. Houston's first marathon was held in December 1972, with only one female, a fourteen-year-old girl, participating. Running wasn't yet a popular sport, and most people believed it was crazy for anyone to run that far. I agreed, and thought Joanne wanting to run a marathon was a ridiculous goal.

Undeterred, Joanne went out unannounced two weeks before the marathon and ran twenty miles. She wanted to be sure she wouldn't be embarrassed at the race. A week before the marathon, she ran twenty-six miles. Fewer than 1,000 people ran that year. Today around 13,000 runners participate in the marathon in Houston, plus another 13,000 that run the half marathon. In her first marathon, Joanne won the race for her age group. But, because she had lied about her age, she

I ran three miles at Memorial Park six days a week for thirty years (Joanne ran six for thirty-five years). Below I am shown finishing a 10k race (6.2 miles) in Houston.

did not get the trophy. That was fine with her, because the last thing she wanted to hear was someone announcing, "In the fifty-five-year-old category, Joanne Wilson is the winner." She later ran another marathon and several half marathons.

Because of her marathon activity, Kenneth Schnitzer, the developer of the Greenway Plaza office building complex in Houston, made Joanne a member of the board of governors for the Houston City Club, which he had founded. She served for about ten years.

Fitness had become a core value for our family. On a family trip about ten years ago we were in a sailboat off of the coast of Costa Rica, and I decided to have a push-up contest for members of the family. My wife won in the girls' category with forty-one push-ups. It looked like she could've gone on forever. After forty-one, she looked up and said, "Is that enough?"

I was required to give up running in the year 2000 when I had a hip replacement, but Joanne continued to run. She still jogs three miles at Memorial Park, four days a week. The other two days she lifts weights with a trainer at the Houstonian Club. When George H. W. Bush was President of the United States, she used to run with him at Memorial Park.

When Joanne joined the Board of the Houston City Club, I started to work out there, too, doing aerobics and getting groups together to exercise. Michelle McCarrel was my first aerobics instructor. Wherever I am, it is my nature to gather groups together. Whether it was business deals, family parties, or just working out in the gym, ever since Dean Nelson pointed out my leadership abilities, I have always been an organizer. But once Joanne started running, she soon surpassed me as the fitness leader in our family. I am so proud of her accomplishments as an athlete and a leader, and I know that our entire family has benefited from her determination that we stay healthy and fit.

Along with fitness and running, another activity we enjoyed as a family was waterskiing. At our beach home in Jamaica Beach, it was very popular. I would take the neighborhood kids and go to West Bay, or the Intracoastal Waterway and water ski. It was a great physical experience for the kids, and when we went, I would ski with Welcome

Jr. running the boat. Living near the coast and having a home there had many benefits, but, as I had experienced many times, it also made us vulnerable to storms.

HURRICANE ALICIA

When you spend thirty years in a home on the Texas Gulf Coast, the odds are that you will face several major storms. Hurricane Carla had impacted my business career when we first moved back to Houston, but the storm that was most memorable to us as a family was Hurricane Alicia in 1983. As the storm raged during the night, one by one each of our five kids came downstairs and got in bed with us. We ended up with seven people in our bed, even the teenagers.

Hurricane Alicia had a major impact on our home as well. Our one- acre lot had approximately fifty major trees. We lost a dozen of them during Hurricane Alicia. The morning after the hurricane, went to the side yard to check things out and found a seventy-five-foot-tall pine tree with a two-and-a-half-foot trunk leaning at about a fifty degree angle toward the house. We had already seen major trees fall over the day after the hurricane because of the wet soil and broken roots, and this pine looked like it was ready to go at any moment.

I jumped in my car and rode through River Oaks looking for a tree company. I located Roy Rivers Tree Service, a company which had done work from time to time at the house. I quickly made a deal with Roy to come over and cut down the tree from the top before it fell over on the house.

Thirty minutes later he had not shown up, so I got in the car and went back. Roy told me he couldn't do it because others had offered him more money to go to their houses first. I didn't tell him what I thought of that, but I offered him $500 to stop what he was doing right then and come over and spend thirty minutes solving my problem. He accepted and came over with two men.

Incredibly, one man wearing spikes on the sides of his boots scram- bled to the top of the tree carrying a rope and a chainsaw. He cut off the top ten feet and lowered it down by rope to the ground. Then he came down the tree a little and cut off the next six feet and did the same until he was down to a stump, which was only about ten feet high. The tree-men knew that the slight weight of a human being was nothing compared to the weight of the tree and his climbing would have little to do with whether or not the tree would tip over. Personally, I thought it was an unparalleled act of bravery.

We lost live oaks in the front yard that were forty feet high and huge. But even after all the fallen trees had been removed, the lot still looked wooded. We had kept the large pine from crushing our house and our yard, despite the loss of trees, was still beautiful. Others were not so lucky, and the storm caused one tragedy that I have never been able to forget. A tree in the back corner of our lot had been blown down, and it stretched across the southbound lane on River Oaks Boulevard. Sometime in the middle of the night a teenager came speeding along the Boulevard, crashed into the tree, and died. To this day I still won- der what I might have done in the middle of the night that could have prevented his unfortunate death.

MANAGING THE HOUSE

A large house with seven people living in it requires help to keep it running smoothly and looking its best. When we first moved in, we had four servants—three maids and a gardener. My wife complained that she had no privacy because all of the maids liked to talk to her. After about five years, she determined that it would be more efficient to hire a lawn service and just one maid for the house. We got along fine.

For a short while during the 1970s, I served as the lawn service. I was carrying fifty million dollars of debt, and I was having trouble making payments, so I started mowing the lawn myself. I figured that bankers who lived in modest homes might resent someone who lived on River Oaks Boulevard who could not make his payments promptly. I decided that if they saw me mowing my own lawn, they might be more sympathetic.

Although we had staff working at the house, Joanne always did all of the cooking. At breakfast the seven of us would sit down at a big round table in the morning room to eat. We would all eat dinner together as well. On Sundays we would usually have an elaborate Sunday dinner in the formal dining room.

Joanne had no experience in the kitchen when we married, but in her typical way, she determined to learn. She ventured further into the kitchen when we were stationed in Japan, and, upon our return to Houston,

The cover of a brochure when the River Oaks Boulevard house was put up for sale in 1996.

she got recipes from a friend, Mary Beech, who was married to the mayor's executive assistant, Gould Beech. Joanne loved Julia Child. She watched her show and had all of her cookbooks. She developed a love for cooking, and from that modest beginning, she went on to learn how to prepare some of the finest French food in Houston. Joanne's talents in the kitchen and the many hours she has spent preparing wonderful meals have contributed immeasurably to the family's happiness, and mine personally. Joanne's talents and hard work created the home of our dreams on River Oaks Boulevard. The environment, the food, the hospitality: she made everything top notch. During these years, she also made second homes for us in Galveston and at our ranch. Wherever we live together, it feels like home because of her efforts. I will always be thankful that she put her foot down and told me that I needed to leave Federal service and go back into business. If I hadn't listened to her, our family would have led a very different life.

FRIENDS AND NEIGHBORS

Not only was our home important to us, but our neighbors were wonderful, too. I fondly remember so many of them, and they each had stories that could fill volumes. To give you a feel for the neighborhood, here are some of my favorite memories of the friends and neighbors we had in River Oaks. Many were prominent Houstonians, while others were nationally known. I did some deals with a few, and some were dear friends. River Oaks Boulevard has always been full of characters, and I am happy to have been one of them.

Ben Woodson: After we lived on the Boulevard for a year or so, Ben Woodson, the legendary chairman of American General Insurance Company, bought the house next door and tore it down. Ben, whose nickname was Woody, and I got off to a rocky start when he cut down the trees in his yard that shaded my yard from the west sun. He promised to plant more trees that would substitute. Although it took about twenty years, the trees he planted did the job.

Bud Adams: The owner of the Houston Oilers-turned- Tennessee Titans, Bud lived down the street on Del Monte until his death in 2013. He lived a few doors down from my friend Dr. Denton Cooley, the famous heart surgeon.

John Moran: The founder of Hycel, a pharmaceutical company, John lived across the Boulevard and was a great friend. One of the memorable occasions in my life was when John invited five guys including me on a one-week trip on his yacht in the Caribbean Sea. We had a great time.

Jimmy Lyon: My best friend and neighbor James E. Lyon joined us on that trip. Lyon lived at the corner of River Oaks Boulevard and San Felipe just one block from my house. Lyon and I were inseparable for twenty-three years until he died of pancreatic cancer in 1993. Sometime during our friendship, he and I decided that we were going to learn tennis. We both played but poorly. Lyon was extremely self-conscious, so he was un- willing to practice if anybody else was watching. Accordingly, we would sneak over to River Oaks Country Club and play tennis in the dark on the clay courts. After six or seven months we gave it up but continued jogging six days a week.

Bob Lanier: Bob, who was mayor of Houston in the 1990s, bought a house built by "Silver Dollar" Jim West, that many considered a masterpiece of architecture. He tore the house down and built a big colonial house across the Boulevard from Lyon.

Oscar and Lynn Wyatt: The Wyatts bought the Cullen mansion on the west side of the Boulevard next to the River Oaks Country Club. For the thirty years we lived near one another on the Boulevard, Lynn and I were always planning, but never pulled off, a major Halloween party, complete with coffins and more.

Harry Holmes: Harry was both one of the richest men I knew and one of the tightest. As a Houston city councilman, he bought four acres next to the River Oaks Country Club from Hugh Roy Cullen, who owned the big house across the street. Harry's father was Cullen's drilling contractor. At the time I was an assistant to the mayor of Houston, Judge Roy Hofheinz. Harry Holmes was a political opponent of Hofheinz, so when a reporter discovered that city crews were out installing the curb- cut on River Oaks Boulevard for Harry Holmes' house, we all got in the mayor's limousine and drove out there to make the most of the publicity about the event. Harry explained that he was using the city crew only to be sure it was done right, and he planned to reimburse the city.

Harry built what I considered a nice home on the Boulevard. I later discovered to my shock that the structure he built was not a house but the garage apartment. Then he built a huge colonial mansion that is now occupied by his wonderful son Ned. In spite of his frugality, Harry was extremely generous. When I ran out of cash while remolding my house, I went to Harry and he lent me $50,000 to finish the work.

Years later when my company faced a major financial crisis, I happened to bump into Harry on Travis Street in downtown Houston. I told Harry that I needed help. He said, "Come into my office." We then walked into the lobby of the National Bank of Commerce and stood at one of the tall tables where bank customers filled out deposit slips. I explained to Harry that I had until four o'clock to raise $100,000. I told him that I had some miscellaneous collateral, none of which would be available in time for my deadline. Harry didn't say much but then reached in his pocket and pulled out a very small checkbook that said Mr. & Mrs. Harry Holmes on the checks. He wrote me a check for $100,000, which saved my neck. A few days later I gave Harry a second lien on a few things and signed a promissory note for the money. What a great neighbor he was to me.

Carolyn and Harold Farb: Carolyn and Harold bought the J. M. West home from my friend Frank Briscoe, a former district attorney of Harris County. Frank had bought the house from legendary oil man J. Collier Hurley, who spent his father's fortune over many years and ended up in bankruptcy. Afterward, Collier proposed to have a public auction of his furniture in his yard on River Oaks Boulevard. The River Oaks Property Owners came unglued. He called me and asked if I, as his neighbor, objected to his attempt to salvage something out of going broke. I told him I had no objection. Armed with that, he made a deal with the Property Owners Association to limit the auction to one day. It was a big success.

Years later, Carolyn and Harold Farb moved in and lived there for a number of years. After their divorce, Carolyn, who was and still is a major social force in Houston, remained there for a while.

Frank Sharp: Frank lived on River Oaks Boulevard toward Westheimer.

John Connally: After he left the governor's office of Texas, John lived on the south end of the Boulevard while he was managing partner of the Vinson & Elkins law firm.

Claude Hamill: Claude lived on a huge tract of land on the Boulevard. I bought a piece of land from him on South Main, but when Prudential Insurance Company, with whom I had arranged the financing, pulled out at the last minute, he refused to give me a short extension on the earnest money contract, stating that he would rather take my $250,000 earnest money and sell the land again. I scrambled around and went to see Gus Wortham, chairman and CEO of American General Insurance Company. Gus was financing my hotel, and after several days of putting me through rigorous grilling by himself, his partner Mr. Barrow, and the wonderful J. W. Link, his other partner, Gus made the loan in time for me to close on the property.

Merlyn Christie: A partner in the oil company of Christie, Mitchell & Mitchell, Merlyn lived on River Oaks Boulevard at San Felipe across from James Lyon. I liked Merlyn a lot, not only because he was so friendly, but also because I considered him an immaculately dressed businessman. The other two members of the firm were Johnny Mitchell, one of the most interesting and flamboyant of all people in Houston, along with the legendary George Mitchell, who not only created the Woodlands community but also adapted hydraulic fracturing to the production of national gas and oil from shale formations.

General Maurice Hirsch: My next-door neighbor on the Boulevard was General Maurice Hirsch. General Hirsch headed a major law firm in Houston and was one of the most respected leaders in the community. Maurice was forty-five years older than I. Maurice was president of the Houston Symphony for many years and held many other major leadership positions in Houston over time.

What I remember about Maurice most was his ability to stand up and make an extemporaneous ten-minute pitch about anything, even into his nineties. I vowed at the time that when I was ninety I would be able to do the same. So far so good.

10

I Owe Everything To Having Good Partners
Houston and Beyond

Thanks to my father's intuition, my brother Jack and I moved to Houston in 1946. Dad's confidence in the city and his belief that it one day would become the business capital of the world has proven accurate. My father expected that for us to succeed here, we would need self-reliance, guts, and determination. I would add to that formula that for business success in Houston, you also need able partners. I have had many.

In the 1920s, during Houston's early boom led by Jesse Jones, Houston welcomed newcomers in business. It remains that way today. In my experience, if you go to Dallas and succeed, you are resented. If you come to Houston and succeed, you are applauded. When I came to Houston there were 600,000 people in the metropolitan area. Today there are six and a half million people here, most of whom have come because of the opportunities the city presents.

I've had many partners over the last seventy years, and I certainly owe a great deal to them for whatever business success I have had, as well as much of my personal happiness. In the beginning of my career, two men who were more than partners were there for me. Now, my two grown sons are also far more than partners to me. Having people whom I could trust by my side made both the hard times and the good times better.

Far more than a partner, my brother Jack was by my side first and longest. At the time of his death in 2003, our offices were next to each other, and we had many projects in the works. For over seventy-five years, we did everything together. There were only two short times when we were apart: during World War II when he served in the Army Air Corps and then five years later when I was in the Navy during the

Korean War. Except for those brief episodes, we spent our lives together.

In college, Jack was my partner in Wilson, Goyen & Wilson, the advertising agency that received commissions for selling ads in The Daily Cougar. Jack was my partner in Jamaica Beach, Tiki Island, Bermuda Beach, Sea Isle, Terramar Beach, Spanish Grant, Treasure Island, Kingsbook Apartments, Fox Hall Apartments, Villa Marina Apartments, Halifax Corporation, Homestead Bank, Colonial Savings Association, Aberdeen Petroleum Corporation, Indian Bayou, and Summerfield Estates.

Being Jack's younger brother had a lifelong impact on me. He is probably the reason I am so aggressive. When I was about four years old, Jack learned that he could convince me to do and say things that he was too shy to do or say, even if it was just approaching a stranger and asking a dumb question.

As time went on, I began to get credit for having nerve and being assertive. I liked that, so I continued. Today my specialty is telling people things they don't want to hear. This includes pitching a deal that is heavily in my favor. Jack had a great influence on my life.

The other man who had a great impact on me from my early days was R. E. "Bob" Smith. Many people thought that Bob was my partner, but that never was the case. Bob helped me 100 times, but it was always by providing me with money when I needed it. To start Jamaica Beach, Bob lent me and my partners the money to buy the 300-acre tract on Galveston beach for cash, and then we signed a note for 100 percent. Then when we sold a piece of property, I would pay him part of it on the note. His only benefit was that he kept fifteen acres out of 300, so that if it turned out to be a success, which it was, maybe the fifteen acres would go up in value. He co-signed my note at the bank numerous times. Bob was a true friend, and I will always remain grateful for his belief in me and his generosity.

JOHNNY GOYEN, JACK VALENTI, AND BILL SHERRILL

The first group I think of when I look back on my partners is my friends from the University of Houston. I developed strong ties with Johnny Goyen, the president of the student body; Jack Valenti, a former president of the student body; and Bill Sherrill, the president of the freshman, sophomore, and junior classes at UH.

The four of us and my brother Jack became known as the Jamaica Beach Boys, and we developed Jamaica Beach, bought banks, started savings and loan associations, built apartment projects, and pursued a variety of other opportunities. Each of these men had so much talent, as evidenced by their ongoing success—Sherrill as a member of the Federal Reserve Board in Washington DC, Jack Valenti as an assistant to the president of the United States and then forty-year president of the Motion Picture Association of America, and Johnny Goyen as may or protem of Houston for twenty-two years. We spent wonderful and exciting years together.

WALTER MISCHER

A later partner whom I greatly admired was Walter Mischer. There was not a bad bone in Walter's body, and he was an inspiration when it came to leadership and real estate development. One of the most admirable things about Walter was his desire to leave some room in a deal for the buyer to also make a profit. He had no interest in squeezing the last dollar out of every deal.

The Jamaica Beach Boys and I went to Walter to finance several projects, including an apartment project called Kingsbrook Apartments on I-10 at Chimney Rock. This project was one of my big learning experiences. Walter said that he would do the construction loan, but then it turned out we didn't have enough equity. In fact, we had no equity, to be honest. So, Walter said that he knew a doctor who wanted to invest in something with a group of other doctors. He asked me to talk with them. Dr. Tom Anderson became our partner with the equity, and then his bank furnished the loan.

The bank president said, "I'll tell you what. If you use Bedford Construction Co. then we won't even require you to have a bond. We have that much confidence in Bedford, and that will save you about $30,000." So, we hired Bedford. Halfway through the construction, they went broke. Every Friday I was out at the construction site writing checks to pay the subcontractors; it was a disaster.

It later turned out that president was taking kickbacks from Bedford. He went to jail.

We had some cost overruns because of that, but we got the job finished, and I learned a lot about partnerships. There were eight partners in the project, including me. We each had a twelve-and-a-half-percent ownership. The partners included a mortgage broker, an operator, and a good promoter, plus the five Jamaica Beach Boys. My idea was that everybody would do an equal share, and we'd have a very successful project. This was my first apartment project, and the minute the project got into trouble, nobody would do anything except the Jamaica Beach Boys.

As head of the group, though, you can't abandon the thing. That is when I learned about structuring partnership. If a partner only owns twelve and a half percent, they don't have enough riding on it to roll up their sleeves, write the checks, and do what needs to be done. So, I bought out all the partners except Valenti, Goyen, my brother Jack, and Sherrill. We went on to build 1,000 apartment units over time. Mischer was very helpful.

Another great quality Mischer had was that he always took a big-picture approach to business. Jimmy Lyon owned a piece of land on Buffalo Bayou at Chimney Rock. He put the land up for sale as a high-rise location. Sure enough, somebody from Yugoslavia, who came to Houston to become a real-estate developer, signed the contract to buy the land for a high rise. Tanglewood, a nearby subdivision, was upset at the idea of a high rise right in the middle of their beautiful neighborhood. Of course, they had no control over it because it was unrestricted land. Joe Jamail, the prominent plaintiff's lawyer, was the principal spokesman for Tanglewood residents. A major controversy arose.

We went down to City Hall and before the City Council; Jimmy Lyon and I made speeches. I was supporting Lyon because he was my friend, but I kept saying to myself, I wish we weren't here. We appeared before the City Council knowing they did not have the power to tell Lyon what to do or what not to do. After our speeches we walked to the elevator lobby on the second floor of City Hall. Lyon and Joe Jamail had words, and things got very contentious.

After Johnny Goyen died, the remaining Jamaica Beach partners gathered to dedicate an office in the UH Alumni Association named after Johnny, a founder of UHAA.

Lyon decided that we needed to call all the developers in Houston together so they could stand up for what we believed to be right. The meeting took place in the boardroom of the River Oaks Bank and Trust. Probably forty major developers attended. Lyon made his pitch, after which someone got up and said, "We are going to commit suicide if we do this! We should dodge this bullet, otherwise we'll bring zoning to Houston as sure as the world." Everybody else got up and said the same thing. We had expected everyone to get behind us at the meeting. That didn't work out very well.

Afterward, Walter Mischer called me and said, "Welcome, we have got to stop this. Why don't you and I buy the land?" I told Walter that I didn't have much cash. He said he would put in ninety percent of the money. I agreed and went to Lyon and talked him into selling it to us at the same price he had been promised from the high-rise developer.

We were going to develop it as low rise, two-story townhouses. We plotted it in tiny twenty-five-foot lots. Then before we actually bought the land, we told the neighbors there would be twenty-five lots. If they found buyers for ten of the lots for cash, we promised that we would

ALWAYS WELCOME

TOP LEFT: At my brother Jack's beach house in Galveston. Circa 1975

TOP RIGHT: In pajamas in Denton, TX. Circa 1959

RIGHT: Exercising at the Houston City Club. Circa 1980

BOTTOM: With my nephew Dennis Frost in a staged bank hold up to promote the Saltgrass Trail Ride. Circa 1979

I Owe Everything To Having Good Partners

TOP LEFT: Receiving awards for my appointment by President Eisenhower to a federal post. Sherwood Crane and Bill Sherrill were partners.

TOP RIGHT: Brother Jack and I perform in the house of Houston Mayor, Roy Hofheinz. Circa 1954

LEFT: Joanne and I in the first year of marriage at the home of her parents on Branard Street in Houston. Circa 1950

TOP LEFT: Brother Jack, me and partner Johnny Goyen at the movie premiere in Houston of "Big Hand for the Little Lady." Circa 1966

TOP RIGHT: Joanne and I on the back porch of the Triple W Ranch in Waller, TX. Circa 2010

ALWAYS WELCOME

TOP LEFT: Posing with Dudley the burro at the Triple W Ranch. Circa 2012

BELOW: Joanne and I in my favorite sport shirt. Circa 1980

BOTTOM LEFT: Brother Jack and I preforming in the Cavalier Theater for UH Frontier Fiesta, 1947.

Finishing a 10-kilometer race. Notice the cigar in my hand. Circa 1975

I Owe Everything To Having Good Partners

TOP LEFT: With my sister, Beverly Smith, my mother, Irene Wilson, and my brother, Jack, at my sixtieth birthday party in 1988.

TOP RIGHT: Joanne and I attending a reception in Denton, TX. at the country club. Circa 1960

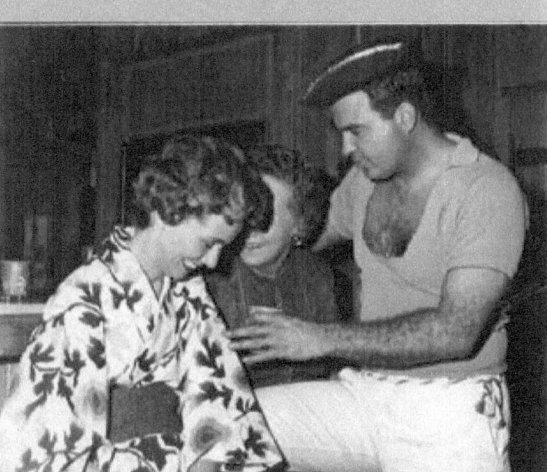

MIDDLE LEFT: With brother, Jack in Corpus Christi. TX. Jack is seated. Circa 1934

MIDDLE RIGHT: With my assistant at a company costume party. Circa 1969

RIGHT: The official observer group of the Hydrogen Bomb test at Bikini Atoll in the Pacific. I am second from the left on the front row, 1956.

ALWAYS WELCOME

Here is am with what was left of my beard. I had to darken the moustache. Circa 1985

TOP LEFT: I was given a pair of chaps by the UH Board of Regents at a black-tie affair when I stepped down as Chairman. Circa 2011

RIGHT: On the Saltgrass Trail Ride, Circa 1965

ABOVE: Joanne and I at our sixtieth wedding anniversary at the River Oaks Country Club in Houston, Texas. 2009

BOTTOM LEFT: Partner Johnny Goyen, Joanne and I at a reception in Galveston, TX. Circa 1965

BOTTOM RIGHT: In my office in downtown Houston. Circa 1965

I Owe Everything To Having Good Partners

: The Wilson boys, Jack and I, pulled a sled on the beach in Brownsville, TX. to attract girls in Junior College. Circa 1945

TOP LEFT: In the Board of Regents Regalia for UH graduation. Circa 2010

TOP MIDDLE: Meeting Jackie Kennedy in Houston, the night before the assassination. Circa 1963

TOP RIGHT: Joanne and I at home on our sixtieth wedding anniversary. Our daughter Pam took this picture in 2009.

RIGHT: Jack, an unidentified friend, and our cousin Lester Ralph in a sleazy bar in Tampico, Mexico. Notice I am wearing a tie. Circa 1948

TOP: Jack Wilson, cousin Billy Ray Armstrong, and me, in Brownsville, TX. before a Willis automobile. (later Jeep) Circa 1940

BOTTOM LEFT: Me, my sister, Beverly Smith, mother Irene Wilson, and brother, Jack Wilson, at Jack's beach house in Galveston, TX. Circa 1985

BOTTOM RIGHT: On the Saltgrass Trail Ride. Circa 1975

In the side yard of the house on River Oaks Boulevard in Houston. I grew the beard for the Saltgrass Trail Ride.

I posed in front of our house on River Oaks Boulevard for the Bicentennial of the United States in 1976.

I Owe Everything To Having Good Partners

TOP LEFT: My mother and father at the rodeo in Houston. Circa 1962

TOP RIGHT: Joanne and I. Circa 1995

LEFT: Joanne and I in Aspen, CO. Circa 2001

BOTTOM: In 2017 Warren Buffet was inducted into the Texas Business Hall of Fame. I attended and Warren is passing along a fake secret.

buy the land, put in a subdivision, and solve the problem. Our plan worked. Even Jamail bought two lots. Everybody came together. That is the way we do things in Houston.

That was in 1982, however, and a year later, oil plummeted to ten dollars a barrel. Houston business hit the skids. We were stuck having sold only ten lots. I finally sold the subdivision to another friend named Walter Scarborough, who built it out and made a big success of it. By that time the crisis in the economy was over.

Mischer was always the guy seeking a compromise solution. He had some of the world's greatest phrases. He used to say, "Look, this deal has been in trouble for years. All I am trying to do is to get back to shore." Or he would say things such as, "I don't want any more cheese, I just want out of the trap." The one I like, and still use when I get a new opportunity to do something different after a deal flops, is "You get another kiss at the pig." Welcome Jr. and I still say that today.

JIMMY LYON

Jimmy Lyon was my one of my best friends for twenty-three years. We met in the early 1960s when I had some business propositions for him. Lyon came to my office with a colleague, and I made my pitch to him. I don't remember what my deal was, but I remember being very impressed with James Lyon because of his ability to articulate. As always, he did most of the talking. There was one phrase that he used several times that caught my attention. It was "being in the catbird seat," which meant being the person who held control. He was a very important figure in my life from 1970 to 1993 when he died.

Lyon, as opposed to Walter Mischer, felt like if he didn't get the last dollar out of every deal it was somehow a failure. Lyon was one of the kindest men I've ever known, but he felt that business was a game and the winner should take all. He always adopted an impossible position when negotiating anything. In his later years he would call me into deals that I had nothing to do with only because I was the one person alive who could talk him into making a deal. Many times, when a deal was proposed, whoever was on the other side would say, "Welcome, I'll do this deal with Jimmy as long as all of my dealings are with you so that Jimmy and I can remain friends."

Lyon was one of the great business characters of Houston. He made most of his money as a real-estate developer. He built the Flagship Hotel in Galveston as well as many, many Houston apartment projects and subdivisions. We developed a downtown office building together, 801 Travis. Although he ran his bank, River Oaks Bank & Trust (ROBT), very conservatively, there was nothing conservative about him in his real-estate developments. He had the most imaginative business mind I have ever seen. All of our partnerships were based on a handshake, never a written agreement.

Typically, our partnerships would go like this: after he made the first two million dollars on a deal, I would make the third million dollars. After that we would split fifty-fifty. Neither one of us had to put up any cash because of his wealthy reputation, plus the fact that he was the owner of ROBT. My role was to oversee our financial requirements and make the deal work, either by using other people's money or by selling the deal simultaneously with our purchase. We did very well with that formula for twenty-three years.

Our last large deal after he developed pancreatic cancer was in 1990 in the middle of the real-estate crash that started in the 1980s. Most banks in Texas had gone bust. ROBT was one of the few healthy banks in the state, because Lyon never lent out more than thirty-eight per- cent of the bank's cash in loans. The rest of the cash was always in government bonds. Lyon had pledged his bank stock to the Bank of the Southwest and borrowed seven million dollars, which he used to support his lavish lifestyle.

When the Bank of the Southwest went broke in the 1980s, the Federal Deposit Insurance Corporation (FDIC) took it over. They called in Lyon's note secured by his bank stock. Lyon owned about sixty percent of the bank, his former wife Ann owned twenty percent, and the public owned twenty percent.

After a couple of years of trying to collect the overdue loan from Lyon, the FDIC gave notice in 1990 that they were going to sell his stock at public auction in thirty days. Lyon called on me to drop every- thing, find a buyer for the bank, and close the sale by August 30, 1990 (30 days away). It was about the fifth largest bank in Houston at the time. We met to develop a strategy. We settled on Compass Bank as the best prospect to buy it. This Birmingham, Alabama-based bank had big plans for Texas. They had purchased one small bank in Dayton, Texas, and hired Charles McMahon as the chairman and CEO for its Texas operation. Charles had already been talking to Lyon about buying ROBT.

I called Charles and said we were ready to deal. A whirlwind of negotiations, certifications, and loan division followed, but on the thirtieth day, we closed the multi-million-dollar deal and paid off the FDIC. Our deal was for cash, because Lyon didn't trust other people's bank stock. I spent the next three years selling the residual assets from the bank, along with most of Lyon's personal investments. Compass Bank's stock is now worth several times the cash he got. However, the sale made him more liquid than at any time of his life.

We were together a couple of hours every day, often running or exercising. I still miss Lyon and our regular runs. In 1990 Lyon was diagnosed with pancreatic cancer, and the doctors gave him six months to live. They suggested that he not be treated because the treatment was very painful, and it wouldn't save his life. When they gave him the death sentence, he was overextended everywhere. His many real estate projects were all in trouble because of the severe recession in Houston in the 1980s.

We also had a dozen other loose ends to tie up, including the sale of a subdivision north of town called Lakewood Forest. The problem was that Lyon had many very large debts outside of the debt on the bank stock. Two and a half years after he developed the cancer, long outliving the six months the doctors had predicted, we had liquidated all but some condos in Colorado and a high-tech instrument company he purchased from some friends. He bought the company by paying some cash and giving a big promissory note, secured by stock. As time began to run out and Lyon became less and less able to function, I would sit with him for several hours each day as he lay in bed.

The day before he died I was sitting there next to his bed, and he motioned for me to lean over. He was so weak that he could neither sit up nor speak except in a hoarse whisper. I leaned over and he said, "We owe a promissory note to the people we bought Ruska Instruments from."

I said, "Yes, it's several million dollars."

"They know nothing about the financial condition of my estate," he said. "Why don't you call and ask if they would take a twenty percent discount if we paid it off this afternoon."

I thought for a minute and said, "Lyon, that is a great idea."

He leaned up and said in a loud whisper, "Do I have to think of everything?"

From his deathbed, on the day before he died, Lyon made a half million dollars.

JACK TROTTER

Jack Trotter was my partner in various enterprises, and in the earlier years I had no idea how much he really knew about business. I remember asking Walter Mischer one time who he thought was the wisest businessman in town. Without hesitation he said, "No doubt, Jack Trotter." He added that whenever he had a business problem that was unsolvable he would go see Trotter, and Trotter would furnish a solution in about ten minutes. In 2007, I was talking to John Duncan of Houston, whose companies had owned Paramount Pictures and other major enterprises. Duncan said, "I owe everything I have to Jack Trotter." A strong endorsement.

It was Trotter's idea that we should take the Jamaica Corporation public in the late 1960s. And it was a good idea. Not only would we be rich, but also the financial strain on the company would be over. It took almost three years' work to prepare for the stock offering. When Nixon's actions plunged the stock market down, and our public stock issue was cancelled, the company never recovered, and two years later we liquidated it. I learned the hard way that you can't control the economy.

My other involvements with Trotter were more successful, however, and the last enterprise I did with him had a particularly happy ending. It involved Jack Valenti.

Valenti had been Trotter's very close friend and of course was my partner and friend as well. Valenti was also close to Welcome Jr., and my son Craig was his godson. When Valenti died in 2007, Craig, Welcome, and I got with Trotter to figure out what we should do to honor him. We quickly focused on the School of Communication at the University of Houston.

Valenti's job as president of the Motion Pictures Association of America was all about communications: lobbying, promotion, and public relations for the movie industry. Previously, as an assistant to President Johnson, Valenti's role was to communicate with the rest of the federal government. He was the author of five books and was the greatest public speaker I have ever met in my life. In his early career, Valenti had been a columnist for the Houston Post, was the head of one of the largest advertising agencies in Houston, and was an adjunct professor of advertising at the University of Houston. Eastern Europeans watched American movies because Jack Valenti negotiated and lobbied the permit for them. That introduction changed the way Eastern Europeans thought about America and helped end the Cold War. He had spent his entire life in communications. So, Trotter and the Wilson boys decided that changing the name of the UH School of Communications to the Jack Valenti School of Communications was a fitting tribute.

I was chairman of the Board of Regents at the time, and I talked this over with the president of the University of Houston, Renu Khator. I learned that there are three criteria for awarding such an honor, and at least one had to be met. First, the honoree has to have made a major leadership contribution to the University of Houston over many years. Second, he or she could be a UH alumnus who has attained national or international stature as a result of outside achievements. Or third, the honoree had to be someone who has provided a major capital contribution to the school.

In Valenti's case, the first two categories were covered. He had made great contributions to UH as president of the student body, an early president of the Alumni Association, a columnist for the Daily Cougar, and an adjunct professor. Additionally, he served on the university's first Board of Regents after it became a state institution, having been appointed by Texas Governor John Connally. Valenti had also received an honorary doctorate degree from the University of Houston. In the second category, his outside achievements on the national and international level were legendary.

We felt that we should raise at least three million dollars so that all three criteria were covered, not just two. With Trotter's help we convinced the grandson of Lew Wasserman, who had been president of

Universal Studios, to give us $300,000. We also raised $300,000 from the Hearst Foundation. Then Lance Funston came forward and offered to give one and a half million dollars. Valenti was Funston's friend and mentor and had helped him get into the Harvard Business School and become an official with the FDIC. Trotter and the rest of us raised a total of three and a half million dollars. The Jack J. Valenti School of Communications was officially announced on April 25, 2008.

SHERWOOD CRANE

I met Sherwood Crane around 1947 when he was active in the UH Alumni Association (UHAA). I was serving on the association's Board of Directors when Sherwood became chairman. I'll never forget one board meeting when another director who had spent his entire University of Houston career speaking out against the "clique" was especially abrasive about Sherwood and his leadership of the association. Since my friends and I were always in the clique, we had never gotten along well with this fellow. A few minutes later, Sherwood announced that there would be a short break and we would reconvene in ten minutes. Sherwood picked up his chair and started walking toward this man with the purpose of beating him over the head with it. We all jumped in and restrained him. Sherwood did not tolerate personal attacks.

Sherwood was one of the most effective leaders that I had ever known. When our bank got into financial troubles, I assigned Sherwood to straighten it out. He did. Sherwood never made a bad loan. He became chairman of the Executive Committee of the bank.

Sherwood served the Jamaica Corporation as chief financial officer. His responsibilities had nothing to do with accounting but solely focused on arranging loans. He and his able assistant Nancy were a very effective team. When Sherwood left the company around 1970, he and another vice president started building resort subdivisions in Arkansas. They were very successful.

RALPH FITE

In the late 1990s, I developed a relationship with Ralph Fite, who had been with Wells Fargo Bank as an energy lender. His grandfather was one of the founders of Houston's Second National Bank, which later became the Bank of the Southwest. I was immediately impressed with Ralph's knowledge of the banking industry and his focus on getting a deal done. We organized a semi-partnership in a spin-off called River Oaks Financial Services Inc. (ROFS), which specialized in financing single-tenant industrial buildings for our company and third parties. It has been a profitable relationship. Ralph also now serves as the director of finance, a department head, at our company Welcome Group, LLC. I admire Ralph for his strong political views. He was an early member of the Tea Party and is a strong advocate for small government and limited government regulations. He is a Republican Party precinct chair- man on the west side of Houston.

DAVID THOMAS

One of the smartest partners I have had was David Thomas. We met when he dated a family friend, Kristi Hoss. David talked Welcome Jr. and me into moving into the top floor of a Galleria-area Houston office building that he had just bought with his Dallas partner, we are still there. Welcome, David, and I made the perfect trio. David and his partner, Robert Neely, had just raised a fund to invest in real estate. My brother Jack would identify office buildings to purchase, and then David, Welcome, and I would negotiate the contract to purchase. Ralph and I would provide the debt financing to make the purchase, and Welcome would lease up the building. Robert Neely's job was to provide the cash equity. He was good at it. We had a great run for about five years, and then the FDIC ran out of buildings to sell, and we all went on to other things. Although our business relationship is limited these days, David still offices with us and remains a very close friend.

JASON AND RYAN WASAFF

Jason Wasaff, my brother Jack's grandson, partnered with my son Welcome and me in Wilson Wasaff Group, LLC. This company does tenant representation, principally in office leasing. Jason attended the Marine Military Academy in Harlingen, Texas, on a football scholarship. The marine academy transformed Jason. He lost thirty pounds and developed the greatest zeal for life that I had ever seen in a man. Jason let no obstacle stand in his way. Although kind and generous, Jason rolled over all opposition to success. Jason died unexpectedly in 2016 at the age of forty-four.

Ryan Wasaff, Jason's brother, is our semi-partner in another company, Welcome Realty Advisors, LLC. Ryan has what I call the "touch." The "touch" is that rare ability to make a deal. Ryan is an artist in his handling of the other side's negotiating principal. Ryan had zero experience in real estate when he joined us twenty-one years ago. He quickly learned about the construction business and how to get customers. Over time, Ryan has negotiated more than 200 deals for our company. I will say it again. Ryan has the "touch."

JOHN DUGGAN AND CHARLES CHURCH

In the early 1990s, Walter Mischer saw Houston coming out of a long recession, and he decided it was time to go into the house-building business since all the previously existing ones had gone broke. He asked if I thought John Duggan, Welcome Jr.'s partner in London, would put up five million dollars to start the company. Duggan was a successor to Charles Church, who had previously been a partner of ours. Welcome Jr. was very close to Duggan, who was about his age.

We brought Duggan to town, and Mischer outlined his plan. After Duggan put up the five million dollars, we all became partners in this enterprise, with Welcome and me on the Board of Directors. We named the company Dover Homes, and we grew it to the point where we were building about 650 houses a year before we sold it to KB Home, a national firm.

John Duggan was one of the most interesting partners I have ever had. He was born and raised in Ireland and moved to the London area as an adult. There he worked for the Charles Church Company, which built houses in London. I was always intrigued by the fact that the company ran two-column, six-inch ads on the front page of the London Times.

In 1981, the exchange rate between the British pound and the US dollar was very favorable to the pound. When Charles Church decided that he should come to America and make some investments, he select- ed Houston. In 1981 I received a voicemail from him from the Galleria Plaza Hotel, saying that he wanted to meet with us about investing. In

With my best friend of twenty-three years, Jimmy Lyon, next to a polar bear that he shot in Alaska. Jimmy died in 1993 of pancreatic cancer.

1981 there were many such messages from people who had no money but wanted to somehow become an investor.

I talked it over with Welcome Jr., and we decided that we would be willing to waste a breakfast on this guy. At the breakfast Church announced that he wanted to come to Houston and invest about ten million dollars in good property. That got our attention. He also suggested that Welcome and I become partners in his investments, which we did.

That was the beginning of a long and profitable relationship. Although I stepped out of the partnerships after the first two transactions, Welcome went on to become the full-time CEO of Church's American company. Two weeks after the first meeting with Church, John Duggan, his CEO in London, arrived to handle the details of the investments. Duggan made it clear to me that since he and Welcome Jr. were closer in age, he would prefer to have most of his dealings with Welcome Jr.

Over the next fifteen years, Welcome and I shot pheasant with Church and Duggan in England, Scotland, and Ireland on numerous occasions and had many very pleasant visits to their homes. Church was an aviation enthusiast and restored and collected more than a dozen World War II planes. He died flying a restored World War II Spitfire fighter plane. When Welcome became the president of his company in America, Charles's wife Susie picked out many priceless antiques for Welcome's office. Those antiques, including a 200-year-old partners' desk from the Bank of England and a 300-year-old secretary's desk, remain in our office today.

When Church was killed in the plane crash, Susie shut down the company, and John Duggan became the CEO of two large public property companies in London. After Welcome became the president of his new American operation, Welcome bought 25,000 acres near Phoenix, Arizona, to build a bedroom community. After seven years of assembly, design, and planning, and when the Arizona authorities had finally approved the permit for the master-planned community, Welcome sold the entire tract at a substantial profit to another developer. Duggan was great fun. He came to town about once every four months when the business was active and later would come about every two years. The last time he came in 2005, he announced that a growth had been found in his head that made him dizzy. After several operations over the next few years, his doctors announced that it was hopeless.

"I'll never forget when I came to Houston in 1981," Duggan said over the phone the last time I spoke with him. "Two large chaps came to the Westin Galleria Hotel and changed my life." Then he said, "I'm in desperate trouble. There is a new lump in my head above the right eye the size of a tennis ball, and I only have six or eight weeks to live. You and Welcome have been my great friends. I have been so lucky to have your friendships. Twenty-nine years is a long time.

Without you I would have never known Walter Mischer or Dover Homes." Duggan had not told anyone that he was dying and wanted to go quietly.

"There are some things in my will for the Wilsons," he continued. "You are blessed with a great family." He was leaving us 100,000 shares in a company on the Frankford Stock Exchange, worth about one euro per share.

He had also designated a monthly allowance to go to his children Chris, Lucy, and Alex, whom he hadn't told that he was dying. He told me that he was very touched when I mentioned his name at our sixtieth wedding anniversary party at River Oaks Country Club in 2009, and that all of our family members had given him such happiness.

He added, "The Pope will make me a Papal Knight in March if I am still alive. That will make me a Count in Italy." And then he said, "Senior, I respect you very much. Look after your family."

The next day John Duggan was dead. I think of his dying words frequently.

WELCOME WILSON JR. AND CRAIG WILSON

Today my two principal partners are my sons, Welcome Jr. and Craig. Welcome has been my partner for at least thirty years, and Craig for almost fifteen. Welcome Jr. is now the CEO of the company, and Craig is the COO. I am happy to say that we have never had a single disagreement. One of the reasons is that I never treat them like sons. I treat them like partners. They do the same with me. How lucky I am to spend hours each day with my two sons. We are all workaholics and happy as larks.

I owe a lot to all of my partners. I learned so much from each of them, and I couldn't have done it without them. Welcome, Craig and I have all benefited from the experience these men have shared with me through the years, and I think about them often. Like my neighbors on River Oaks Boulevard, they are a powerful and interesting collection of people, and I am richer in every way because they have been in my life.

11

Up To My Eyeballs In Politics For Seventy Years
Houston, Austin and Washington DC

Many times during the seventy years that I have been an adult, I've had people say to me, "I don't want to get mixed up in politics." Not only do I think that is totally wrong, but I even think it's stupid. Every citizen of America is obligated to be involved in politics by at least voting in every single election.

Politics is power. Politics is influence. I have profited greatly from my involvement in politics, and I am proud of it. I became interested in politics when I was in school, and my early interest has only gotten stronger throughout the years. For over sixty years, my role in politics has related to fundraising.

In 2007, when I was chairman of the Board of Regents of the University of Houston, I appointed myself chairman of the University of Houston Political Action Committee. Under Texas law, a state PAC is able to make contributions to elected officials and candidates for office. We support eighty-three elected officials in Texas, including the governor, lieutenant governor, attorney general, controller, many state senators, and even more state representatives.

When I got involved, the PAC had been around for about twenty-five years but typically was raising about $50,000 each election cycle. Shortly after I took over, I had a meeting with former Lieutenant Governor Ben Barnes and Ken Bailey in Ken's office downtown. Ken is a big plaintiff lawyer who was a UH quarterback years earlier. Ben Barnes made a speech to me. "Welcome," he said, "you ought to be raising $500,000 every biennium to make the UH PAC the largest and most powerful in the state of Texas." So, I took on the task of a 400% increase in the amount of money raised each biennium. We succeeded, and now almost five biennia later we are still raising $420,000 each time.

When President John Kennedy came to Houston to announce NASA, Mayor Lewis Cutrer put me in charge. I am on the left side with black hair.

We give significant money to the governor, lieutenant governor, attorney general, and state controller, but we also contribute to sixty members of the house and senate who are either members of the Houston delegation or key members of appropriations, higher education, and other important committees. It has made a difference in state government in Texas. When I began my activity, I used to get a warm handshake when I met important elected officials. Today I get a bear hug.

TOP: Joanne with Texas Governor Rick Perry and me at the Hotel Zaza in Houston, Texas.

BOTTOM: Joanne, President George W. Bush and me in Houston during George Bush's reelection campaign in 2004.

MY INVOLVEMENT IN THE PRESIDENTIAL CAMPAIGNS

As a young man, I had the great opportunity to serve in the administrations of Presidents Eisenhower, Kennedy, and Johnson, and those experiences gave me a clear indication of how important the Presidency is. I became very interested in supporting the candidates who I believed could make a difference.

When Richard Nixon was elected president in 1968, I was one of the major supporters for the Democrat nominee, Hubert Humphrey. In Texas I could not convince the oil people to vote for Humphrey because he had spoken out early on against the depletion allowance. Although Humphrey gave me every assurance that he would not tamper with the depletion allowance, the oil people of Texas went for Richard Nixon. Six months after Nixon was elected, the depletion allowance was eliminated, a major blow to the oil industry.

I was not involved in the Nixon White House, but I had many friends who were. Years later, when Richard Nixon was impeached, it was revealed that there was a conspiracy in the White House to defeat elected Democrats in Texas. Although I was not conscious of it at the time, after it was revealed, I thought back on the many occasions where I saw it actually happening.

About once every six months, a representative of the FBI or the SEC or the IRS would come to see me and say something to the effect of, "Welcome you're bound to know of some corruption going on in Texas. You are a major contributor, always in cash, and you're bound to know of some corruption."

I would always say something like, "Gee whiz, I don't know anything." In retrospect, it was obvious that the White House had an organized campaign using federal agencies to entrap elected officials in Texas.

After Nixon was thrown out of office, his vice president, Gerald Ford, was not elected president. Instead Jimmy Carter became the president of the United States. I thought Carter was one of the worst presidents we've ever had. Inflation became high, and the prime rate went to 21.5% per annum. Today the prime rate is 3.5%. The worst effect that Carter had was on international affairs. His first day in office, he announced that the United States would not support any dictator, regardless of how much that dictator might love the US. Within a month there was a revolution in Iran, and the Shah was thrown out of office. The radicals took over, and the situation remains a disaster to this day.

Somosa, the Dictator of Nicaragua, was thrown out by the Sandinistas. As the Republican Party began to rise in Texas, my best friend Jimmy Lyon became a superstar. Lyon was a Republican when there were less than a dozen in all of Texas. In a book written about the Ronald Reagan campaign of 1980, Lyon is given credit for saving the campaign by making a critical loan to Reagan for the campaign when Reagan began to slip. It's hard to imagine now, but Ronald Reagan was extremely controversial when he ran for president. He had been an actor in Hollywood and was not well respected.

When I decided to vote for Ronald Reagan, I had to decide that anybody as president was better than Jimmy Carter, because supporting Ronald Reagan was "out there." As it turned out, Ronald Reagan was one of the best and strongest presidents America has ever had. I give him total credit for ending the Cold War. Although it happened a year after he was out of office, it was his policies that broke the Soviet Union and reduced their support all over the world.

After Reagan's presidency, I supported George Herbert Walker Bush for president. George is one of the most decent human beings I have ever known. He and Barbara are still close friends, and we see them frequently. I was a big supporter of George W. Bush, too, although I was not directly involved in his campaigns.

In 2008, when I was determining where to place my support, my close friend Pat Oxford, managing partner of Bracewell & Giuliani, introduced me to Rudy Giuliani. Rudy had been the mayor of New York and transformed the city. No one obeyed the traffic laws in New York. People would stream across the intersection although the light was red, and taxicab drivers sped everywhere. On the subways in New York, you could not see out the windows because there was graffiti on every square inch of every window on every train. Within six months, the graffiti was removed from every window and stayed off. People began to respect red lights, and traffic began to move in Manhattan. In the end, Giuliani did not get the nomination, I supported John McCain in a tepid manner, and Barack Obama was elected president.

TOP: Texas General Land Office Commissioner George P. Bush with me in my office in 2016.

BOTTOM: Texas US Senator John Cornyn with me in Houston, 2013.

I am with Rudy Giuliani, the former Mayor of New York City, when he was a candidate for the presidential nomination of the Republic Party in 2000.

At the end of Obama's first term, Rick Perry, then governor of Texas, decided at the last minute to run for president. In August of 2012, he recruited Welcome Jr. and me to help him raise money. In six weeks, we and others raised eighteen million dollars for his presidential campaign. It was a phenomenal achievement. Because of painkillers taken after back surgery, the debates did not go well, and Rick dropped out of the race.

Prior to Rick's entry, Welcome and I had signed on to Mitt Romney's campaign. In January of 2012, we explained to Mitt that if Perry got into the race, we would be transferring to him. Mitt said he understood completely; it would not be a problem. Welcome and I went to Mitt's summer home in La Jolla, California, and spent the weekend with him and his lovely wife, Ann. We also were in Las Vegas for Mitt's formal announcement for the presidency. After Perry dropped out, we rejoined Mitt's campaign. It was ultimately unsuccessful, and Obama was reelected.

Texas Senator Ted Cruz visited in my office shortly after his election in 2012.

In 2015, Rick Perry, who had just left the governor's office, called Welcome and me and asked us to be on his national committee to run for president in 2016. I thought Rick had a great chance because he had been governor of a very successful state economically and he was a military veteran. And he was smart and good looking. As usual, my responsibility was principally fundraising, and in my judgment, I was only modestly successful. Because he was doing so poorly in the polls, with sixteen people running for president, Rick dropped out.

After Rick dropped out, Welcome and I were torn about whom to support. Welcome had been in school with Jeb Bush at Kinkaid, but Ted Cruz, the senator from Texas, had come to our office in December of 2014 for a couple of hours after he was elected Texas Senator. Then Heidi Cruz, Ted's wife, called me. She had been a friend for several years, and we both served on the board of directors of the Greater Houston Partnership. Heidi was head of Goldman Sachs for four states. She was smart. She was rich. She was powerful. And she was beautiful. I quickly signed on for Ted. Welcome Jr and I served on his national committee. My assignment was to raise money from previous Rick Perry supporters. It was reasonably easy to do because after the election was over, Ted Cruz was guaranteed to be either the president of the United States, the vice president of the United States, or the senator from Texas. I was startled by Ted's early progress. When I joined his campaign, he was in the single digits in the polls but quickly grew to the double digits.

I held a fundraiser for Ted in October of 2015 at a breakfast place on Washington Avenue in Houston. Heidi was there with the pollster who worked for the campaign. Heidi and the pollster explained to me that Ted would be leading the polls in Iowa by mid-December. I doubted their confidence. I was startled on the twelfth of December to see that Ted Cruz was leading the polls in Iowa, ahead of Donald Trump, Ben Carson, and six or eight others, who were in the single digits. He won, but came in second for the nominations. By May, Ted's numbers had dropped, and he officially left the race.

REPUBICAN DEBATE AT UH

Besides the impact that fundraising can have on a campaign, I've also been fascinated with the debates since Joanne and I watched the first one, between John F. Kennedy and Richard Nixon, on our television in 1960. The debates have been a major game-changer in American presidential elections.

In the first debate, Richard Nixon refused to use makeup. As a result, he had a five o'clock shadow and looked terrible. On the other hand, JFK was good looking, had a wonderful smile, and was a skilled debater. Nixon lost the debate and lost the race for president.

In the most recent election, the debates took another turn. They became personal and vicious. Donald Trump set the tone of the debates with his harsh criticism of his opponents, calling them names such as "Little Marco" and "Lying Ted." In spite of it, he won the election.

I had the opportunity to personally attend a presidential debate in late February of 2016 held at the University of Houston campus. Arrangements

Presidential Republican nominee Mitt Romney with Joanne and me in Houston in 2012.

had been made months before by NBC to have the debate at UH, but NBC angered Donald Trump and the Republican National Committee, and NBC's debate was canceled. CNN was selected to pick up the debate and announced they would still hold it in Houston, but the exact venue was up in the air. At the last minute, UH was selected again, and the de- bate was held in the Moores Opera Center.

I was lucky to get one of the twenty-five tickets that they gave to the University of Houston to cover the thirty members of the administration, the ten members of the Board of Regents, the ninety members of the faculty senate, the forty members of the student government, and the 42,000 students. My seat was in the balcony, and Moores Opera Center had never looked more beautiful. CNN put in indirect lighting so the walls were all lit. Moores was selected because of its beauty, although Cullen Hall had double the number of seats. I was fascinated by the Trump supporters in the audience. They would not only clap, but they would also jump up and scream. I felt like I was a part of history by attending the debate.

With President Donald Trump, in Houston when he was running for President in 2016.

In late June 2016, my friend Tony Buzbee held a fundraiser for Donald Trump. Welcome Jr. and I both attended and gave big money. I had my photograph taken with Donald, and although I knew his previous wife, Ivana, it was the first time I met him. He seemed very nice. Welcome Wilson III, currently a freshman at Southern Methodist University in Dallas, also attended and was in the photograph with me.

Politics is a part of who I am. I believe it is why I am well known. The relationships I have developed with politicians are what made big things happen for me. The governor of Texas appointed me to the UH Board of Regents. Eisenhower appointed me to oversee five states. LBJ appointed me a special ambassador. My relationship with JFK opened many doors for me. I have also known three other presidents personally. How did I meet Walter Mischer? Raising money for Lewis Cutrer.

How did I know Jesse Jones, Judge Elkins, and Gus Wortham? All through politics. If you are politically well-connected, it opens doors, and once those doors are open, opportunity awaits. You can keep the city going, you can build the Eighth Wonder of the World, you can create communities. Nothing is free. I learned that from my family during the Depression. You have to earn it. My connection with politics gave me the opportunities that I have received, and I have worked hard to turn them into something worthwhile for me, for my family, and for my community.

12

Leading The Cougars
University of Houston

I'm frequently quoted as saying the three passions in my life are my family, my country, and the University of Houston. Even today, I spend at least of a quarter of my time each day on University of Houston matters. My only official title now is chairman of the University of Houston Political Action Committee, but I am frequently involved when anything controversial comes along.

I served as chairman of the UH System Board of Regents from 2007 until 2010, but getting appointed didn't happen quickly. Fifty years ago, Preston Smith was governor of Texas. My friend Jimmy Greer had ap- plied to be a regent at the University of Houston to replace Jack Valenti when he left for Washington DC with LBJ. Johnny Goyen asked me to call the governor, whom I knew, to ask him to appoint Jimmy.

I called the governor during the day, and he called me back at home, around dinnertime. After I made my pitch about Jimmy, he paused and said, "Welcome, I was going to appoint you to the Board of Regents of the University of Houston. Tell me what you want me to do. I'll either appoint you or Mr. Greer."

I paused. Being on the UH Board of Regents, and then becoming chairman, had been my highest goal since 1947 when I first met Hugh Roy Cullen, who served as Board chairman in the 1940s. I had gone home that day and told my brother Jack that someday I would have that role. Jack was sitting at the table eating beans at the time, something we ate a lot of as students, and didn't even dignify my comment by looking up from the bowl.

I told the governor, "Appoint Jimmy this time, and appoint me next time." Preston Smith was not reelected, and there was no next time.

I am sitting outside Ezekiel Cullen's building at the University of Houston shortly after being elected chairman of the UH Board of Regents. Note the Cougar.

When Rick Perry became governor in the year 2000, I approached him at a fundraiser and asked to be appointed as a regent. It took me six years to convince him, and it involved a lot of begging. Lynden Rose, the governor's friend and a UH regent, played an important role. In August 2007, after I had served for a little over a year, the Board honored me by electing me chairman.

FIRE IN THE BELLY

I often say that my proudest moment as chairman was hiring Renu Khator as president and chancellor. She has been a game-changer for the University of Houston. At the first board meeting after I became chairman, we were tasked with the job of selecting a new president and chancellor. Our previous officeholder had been hired by his alma mater, Auburn University, as president and had resigned. I scheduled a meeting for the Board to discuss the candidates at a hotel downtown, in the hope that the press would not be present. It worked.

Welcome and I had been on a red-eye flight back from Los Angeles and arrived about 1 a.m. and checked into the same downtown hotel. We had been in LA raising $600,000 for the UH Jack Valenti School of Communications from the Hearst Foundation and the Lou Wasserman Foundation. I was somewhat groggy the next morning, but at the first break in the meeting I went to the corner of the room and did forty push-ups with my feet in a chair, and that made me more alert.

Leroy Hermes, my predecessor as chairman, served as chairman of the search committee, and they did an excellent job. The committee had brought forth three very qualified candidates to be president and chancellor. Based on their resumes, the board seemed to favor candidate number two, who had already been president of two universities of more than 30,000 students.

Renu Khator was the last candidate we interviewed. She was provost at the University of South Florida, where she had held every position in academia. She had been an assistant instructor, an instructor, an assistant professor, an associate professor, a professor, a department head, an associate dean, a dean, and spent three years as provost, the number two slot in university hierarchy.

All three candidates made impressive presentations, but when Renu Khator finished she turned to me and said, "And, Mr. Chairman, I have fire in the belly."

Well, that did it for me. Fire in the belly is exactly what we needed, and she certainly has it. After two hours of vigorous discussion, the board unanimously authorized me to negotiate a contract with Renu Khator. She was reasonable, and our long-distance negotiation took less than thirty minutes. She took office on January 15, 2008, and we've had a wonderful relationship ever since.

GETTING TO WORK

Soon after her arrival, I was asked to go before the faculty senate of the law school and outline my top three priorities as chairman. The chancellor accompanied me. I told the faculty senate, "My three priorities for the University of Houston are: Number one—Tier One Status for the University of Houston. Number two—Tier One Status for the University of Houston. Number three—Tier One Status." They laughed but got the message. I must admit now that I only had a foggy notion of what Tier One status meant. In those days, even the term couldn't be agreed on. Some called it "Top Tier Status," some called it "Flagship Status." But Dr. Khator knew exactly what it meant and exactly how to get there. Three years later, the Carnegie Foundation designated the University of Houston as Tier One.

When I became chairman, there was disharmony at the Board of Regents table. Three of the regents felt their voices were never heard. In the first few Board meetings, I let those three dissidents speak at great length. I allowed them each to talk as long as they wanted to talk. That convinced them that they were part of a team, and the disharmony on the Board disappeared.

I made a list of my immediate objectives. In my tenure as Chairman, we made great progress on some, modest progress on others, and no progress on a couple. Here they are:

Objective: Hire a World Class Chancellor/President. This was accomplished in the first ninety days.

After she had been at UH about eighteen months, I learned that Presidency of Purdue was available. I called the Chancellor and said "Wait right there, I'm coming right over." When I got there, she explained that she had been contacted by the search committee but declined to be interviewed.

A year later, I heard that the Presidency of the University of Florida was available. She has two daughters living in Florida and served for many years at the University of South Florida. I immediately called the chancellor. She said that the Chairman of the Regents at Florida had asked her to fly over to be interviewed, but she declined. She went on to say that he had flown to Houston with the outgoing President and they had just left her office that day, having failed to convince her to apply. Then she said something reassuring. She said "Mr. Chairman, where else would I have the opportunity that I have right here at UH to make a real difference. I'm not going anywhere. I'm going to stay right here and make this university the university it's destined to be." Since that conversation, I've been less uptight about her leaving.

Objective: Tier One Status for UH. This was my overriding objective, and UH joined with six other universities in Texas to push for legislation that would authorize a vote on a constitutional amendment to provide funds to create more Tier One universities in the state. When Bill Hobby was lieutenant governor of Texas, he had created a $500 million fund for higher education. The legislature was to add to that fund every two years, and when it reached two billion dollars, the income from the fund was to be distributed. Four legislative sessions later, not one dollar had been added.

I teamed up with the former Texas lieutenant governor, and we campaigned statewide to pass a constitutional amendment that would redirect the income from that fund to help the seven universities in Texas that were designated as emerging Tier One universities. It was the National Research University Fund (NRUF). Our campaign for the amendment was successful, and it passed by a large majority. I was the statewide treasurer of the campaign endeavor. The legislature created stiff criteria, and the chairman of the Senate Education Committee told me later that he thought it would be at least five years before any university was eligible to receive part of the funds. The University of Houston reached that goal in one year.

The criteria included were difficult but specific. In order for one of the seven universities to qualify for money, it had to meet five out of those seven criteria:

1. 200 PhD graduates every year
2. Research expenditures of $45 million or more a year for the previous two years

3. $400 million in endowments
4. High SAT scores for the freshman class
5. Active membership in the Association of Research Libraries or a Phi Beta Kappa chapter
6. A specific number of faculty who are members of national academies
7. Excellent graduate schools

In the following legislative session, the method of distribution of those funds was determined, and I was disappointed that much of the income was set aside for universities that would be entering in later years. I felt that any emerging university that was close needed all of the money possible in order to keep it moving. Although I did not prevail, it did increase funding to UH by about $12 million a year. A couple of years later, Texas Tech qualified. In 2015, three other universities in Texas reached the goal set out in the constitution amendment: University of Texas-Dallas, University of Texas-Arlington, and North Texas University.

Now that the Carnegie Foundation has designated the University of Houston as a Tier One University, the next rating agency is TARU, which stands for Top American Research Universities. Although we have not yet reached all of their standards, we are very close. For ex- ample, they require a 15% annual giving rate of all living alumni. The University of Houston currently has a 13.4% giving rate as of 2017.

I think we will be there soon.

Objective: Change the name of the School of Communication in the College of Liberal Arts and Social Sciences to the Jack J. Valenti School of Communication. To change the name of a school at UH, you have to meet only one of three criteria: the per- son must make a large contribution to the success of the University of Houston itself, the person must have made a major success in his own field unrelated to the University of Houston, or a large contribution has to be given to the university either by the person or in that person's name. Valenti met not one but two of the criteria.

Welcome, Craig, and I, with Ted Dinnerstein and Jack Trotter, were successful in our campaign to raise three and a half million dollars, so that not two but all three criteria could be met. We named the building in which the Valenti School is located The Lance Funston Communication Center, since Funston had so generously donated $1.5 million in honor of his mentor and friend. (Funston has since donated an additional $100,000.) My son, Craig, is deeply involved in advancing the school. Jack Valenti was his godfather.

Objective: Create a real estate program in the Bauer College of Business. More than any other city in America, Houston is a real estate town. I had long thought that the University of Houston ought to be an education leader in that field. I called a meeting at Gerald Hines' offices in the Galleria with a representative from each area of real estate: brokerage, apartments, retail, office buildings, development, leasing, finance, and others. At the meeting, Art Warga, dean of the UH College of Business, and I made a presentation to create an undergraduate real estate program in the college of business. The group was very enthusiastic, but by the end of the meeting they had convinced us that what was needed was a graduate rather than an undergraduate program.

They said that all of their top people had a bachelor's degree and needed the opportunity to get a master's degree in real estate. It was at that meeting that the graduate real estate program at the Bauer College of Business was born.

Because I had other fish to fry, we didn't make a lot of immediate progress toward this objective. Then one day I got a call from Joe Slovachek, a Houston lawyer and a UH graduate. Joe said plainly, "Are we going to get the real estate program going or what?" The next day I set up a meeting with Joe, the dean, and Dan Bellow, chairman of the Greater Houston Partnership. Soon, the program was under way.

John Walsh had been working as a consultant for the University of Houston. John had been president of the Friendswood Development Corporation, owned by Exxon Mobil. It was among the largest real estate development companies in the world. He had supervised a thousand apartment projects, thousands of retail centers, and many hotels and master-planned communities located all across America.

I went to John and proposed that he head up the graduate real estate program as the full time executive. John said that he would think about it. The next day he called me back and accepted the position but said that he would do it for three years only. But he would serve without pay.

John is one of the most effective human beings I have ever met. One day in my office, I asked him to what he attributed his effectiveness. He said to me, "Chairman, it's because I am nonthreatening."

I think he's right. He has a way of getting things out of people that they never planned to give. We immediately raised big money, thanks to John, and crafted a list of adjunct professors from the industry to create what we called a "practice-based" program. John was responsible for getting a large financial gift to create the UH Stanford Alexander Real Estate Center.

Objective: Change the name of the University of Houston-Downtown. When I first became a regent at University of Houston, I was approached by a nice lady at the Houstonian Club where I worked out every morning and was asked if I would participate in a survey she was conducting on higher education in Houston. I told her that I would be glad to participate and set a time for her to come by my office.

Her first question to me was "When you think of universities and colleges in Houston, who do you think of?" I quickly answered with UH, Rice, Texas Southern University, Houston Baptist University, and St. Thomas University. She asked me to think again to see if I had omitted any university. I kept racking my brain and said I could not think of any other four-year colleges in Houston.

She said, "What about the University of Houston-Downtown?" Of course! I had forgotten all about it. In 2006, The University of Houston- Downtown (UHD) was the second largest university in metropolitan Houston, with almost 14,000 students. It has a separate president from the University of Houston, separate deans, separate policies, and has been a successful university for over twenty years.

I decided right then and there that for University of Houston-Downtown to get the recognition that it deserved, it needed a new name. I talked to Max Castillo, who was president of UHD, and he agreed with me. I started quizzing my business associates about UHD and all wrongly thought it was simply another campus of the University of Houston. I met with the faculty there, and some were not enthusiastic about changing the name. Then I met with a group of students from UHD, and I was startled when one of the students said, "You mean we are not a branch of the University of Houston?" UHD is part of the larger University of Houston System, but it has no direct connection with the University of Houston itself.

In Regalia I spoke at the graduation at the UH Bauer College of Business in May 2009.

ALWAYS WELCOME

I was interviewed in the radio booth at half time at a UH Cougar out-of-town game while I was chairman of the Board of Regents.

Max Castillo ran a contest at UHD to pick a new name, and after much time it came forth with the name University of South Texas. I didn't like it. Not only did it conflict with the South Texas College of Law, also in downtown Houston, who were outraged at the thought of us using their name, but growing up in Brownsville, Texas, 400 miles south of Houston, I did not accept the idea that Houston was in South Texas.

The University of Houston Downtown is a wonderful institution. Most of their students work full time and take years to graduate. The first time I was invited to speak at a UHD graduation, I said to myself, "Minute Maid Stadium is too big for a graduation (35,000 seats). The crowd will look wimpy." When I got there, there were 25,000 people in the stands to support 1,200 graduates. Cousins, uncles, relatives from everywhere came to see their graduate get their degree. I would say that 90% of them were the first in their family to get a degree.

At a Board of Regents meeting, Renu Khator presented me with an eightieth birthday cake. In the background are regents Nelda Blair, Carol Ray, Lynden Rose and Dennis.

I'll never forget a graduation of UHD when a middle-aged woman came through the graduation line holding her diploma. She walked up to me and said, "Mr. Chairman, it took me seventeen years, BUT I GOT IT!"

The remaining project stalled, but I have not given up.

Objective: Revitalize Frontier Fiesta at UH. LeRoy Melcher, the founder of the UtoteM convenience store chain in Texas and a major contributor to UH (Melchor Building for the Bauer Business College and the Melchor Studio Building for Houston Public Media), was a longtime friend of mine. For many years, he would call me and say, "Welcome, we've got to bring back Frontier Fiesta." Around 2005, Frontier Fiesta came back with only modest support. When I was a student, sixty years before, Frontier Fiesta dominated the spring semester. Over 1,000 students were involved in everything from construction of saloons to singing and dancing. (No alcohol served.)

When Renu Khator became president of the University of Houston, she immediately became a superstar with the students. I'll never forget the first time I took her to Frontier Fiesta in the spring of 2008. After a reception in Frontier Fiesta city hall, we decided that we would take in a couple of the shows. We walked over to the first one and walked in the back, toward the front of the room. When the students saw her, the entire audience of 200 leapt to their feet and gave her a five-minute standing ovation. I knew then that we had made the right choice for president. Today Frontier Fiesta has regained much of the stature of the old years and is a major spring enterprise at UH.

In its heyday during the 1940s and 1950s, Frontier Fiesta was nation- ally renowned, featured on the cover of LIFE magazine as "the Greatest College Show on Earth" and attracted show biz luminaries the caliber of Humphrey Bogart.

Objective: Beef up the University of Houston Political Action Committee (UH PAC). The most important governmental body of UH to the Texas Government: The Legislature, the Governor, Lt. Governor, the Attorney General and the Controller. The UH PAC has been around for twenty years or more, and I had been a contributor for most of those years.

When I became a regent, Nelda Blair, a Regent and Mayor of The Woodlands, was chairman of the UH PAC. When I became chairman of the Regents, she asked to step down and be replaced by me as chair- man of the PAC. I accepted.

Early on as chairman, when I was invited by Ken Bailey to meet in his office with former Lt. Governor and Speaker of the Texas House, Ben Barnes, I had been challenged to raise $500,000, not $100,000. Bailey had told me that if I would raise at least $300,000, he would give another $100,000 for the current year, which I did, and he did.

For the first time, the UH PAC began to give serious money to candidates. We still give big contributions to the governor, lieutenant governor, and Speaker of the House, but more importantly we give serious money to state senators and representatives who are on key committees that affect UH.

Our goal the last four biennia have been to raise $420,000 for each. We have met that goal each time, but not without a great deal of hard work. One of my first moves after I became chairman of the Political Action Committee was to hire Andrew Biar and Strategic

Public Affairs. I felt like we needed professionals to both raise the money and keep from violating the Texas Ethics Commission's many rules. The UH influence in the legislature and among the top government offices has been increased tenfold. In 2017, Andrew resigned and has been replaced with Elizabeth Blackmore and Blakemore and Associates.

Objective: Enmesh UH in the Houston Business Community. This goal has been achieved. In 2008, I talked the Greater Houston Partnership into making Tier One Status at UH one of its three main priorities for three years in a row. Today the business community is deeply involved in all aspects of UH. President Khator created an energy advisory committee on which the CEOs of every major oil company in America sit.

Latha Ramchand, the present dean of the Bauer College of Business at UH, has also done a wonderful job in tying in the Houston Business Community to the college of business. In my early time as Chairman of the Regents, the Greater Houston Partnership made me chairman of the Higher Education Committee. I am now a Director Emeritus of the Greater Houston Partnership, and that organization continues to give UH solid support.

Objective: Obtain a Medical School for UH. Early on as chair- man I met with the president and chairman of Methodist Hospital, as well as the dean of the medical school at Cornell, Anthony Gatto. Dr. Gatto used to be my personal physician when he lived in Houston. Both Methodist and Cornell enthusiastically endorsed the idea of a medical school at the University of Houston. Methodist Hospital would furnish the residencies, and Cornell would furnish the faculties. Both made it clear, however, that all of the money would have to come from the University of Houston. The idea would be that in the first years, Cornell would issue the degree. After a couple years, the degree would be changed to a joint degree from Cornell and the University of

ALWAYS WELCOME

When stepping down as a Chairman of the Board of Regents, I was presented with a "Cougar Maximus duster" by the UH Frontiersmen organization.

Houston. After a number of years of success, the final objective would be to issue degrees from the University of Houston.

Because of their unwillingness to furnish any funds for this objective, however, the idea languished. In about 2014 the medical school idea was revitalized, and President Khator hired Stephen J. Spann as dean of the planned medical school. The problem of residency has been solved with a deal that was made with Hospital Corporation of America, a major private hospital chain in America, owning more than 230 hospitals and surgery centers in America. They have many hospitals in metropolitan Houston. In the 2017 session in the Texas Legislature, we got a resolution passed by both houses that authorized a study to be undertaken for a medical school at UH.

The problems of legislative authorization and funds has still not been solved, but we are getting closer. Two members of the Board of Regents, Durga Agrawal along with Welcome Wilson, Jr., are particularly keen on the UH Medical School.

Objective: Get UH into a BCS Conference. While I was chairman of the regents, we got a new football coach, a new basketball coach, golf coach, baseball coach, women's basketball coach, and women's softball coach. And, most importantly, a new athletic director. I take a small amount of credit for the AD selection, but certainly not for the others.

Art Briles was the head football coach when I became Chairman. Within a year, Baylor University in Waco had hired him away from us. We hired Kevin Sumlin as head football coach, who also succeeded.

Coach Sumlin was hired away from us to become the coach at Texas A&M. Kevin Sumlin was replaced by Tom Herman.

In 2015, our new head football coach, Tom Herman, won thirteen games and lost one. He also took us to the Peach Bowl for our first visit to a New Year's Day Bowl in almost thirty years. In 2016, Tom Herman had a successful year going, but in the middle of the football season, the University of Texas fired its coach, and Tom Herman started flirting with the idea of going to Texas. The team could sense it, and although it was a successful season overall, the team began to lose some games toward the end of the season. Tom was ultimately hired by Texas, and the president and athletic director replaced him with Major Applewhite as head football coach. Applewhite had been our offensive coordinator under Herman, and the players love him. We did just fine in 2017. Other teams like track, baseball, and basketball are also doing exceedingly well.

During the search for a men's basketball coach, President Khator asked our athletic director, "If you could choose any coach in all of America, who would it be?" The AD said it would be Kevlin Samson, but he had already turned down the job. President Renu Khator said, "Let me talk to him."

Samson came aboard, and he has made a major difference in basket- ball. In the 2015–2016 season, he won twenty-two out of thirty-two games. The expectations for the future are even brighter. The 2017 sea- son was even better.

Winning teams is the first criterion to get into a BCS conference.

We are getting there.

The natural conference would be the Big 12, which already has four Texas football teams. However, if UH became the fifth team, it might be considered a Texas conference and that needs to be overcome. Current Regent Chairman Tilman Fertitta (2017) has taken this as a high objective, and I expect major progress soon.

Objective: UH Enmeshment in the Art Community of Houston. As chairman, I made modest progress in this regard, but since then the art community's involvement with UH has increased tenfold. For ex- ample, when the Alley Theater downtown was being remodeled, they held their plays at the UH Wortham Theater in the Cynthia Mitchell Center on the campus of UH. The campus art committee includes representatives from major art organizations in Houston. The University of Houston Chorale has won the world championship in Vienna two years in a row.

Objective: Influence the Governor on the Appointments of Members of the Board of Regents of the UH System. When I was appointed, Governor Rick Perry's director of appointments was always slow in getting the appointments done. For example, although my term began September 1, 2005, I was not appointed until April of 2006 to the Board of Regents. That all changed when the director of appointments was replaced by Teresa Spears. Teresa had been a close personal assistant to Governor Rick Perry, and, as a result, was able to get the governor to approve the appointment to every board in the state of Texas in a timely way. My objective was to provide the governor and his director with a wide choice of candidates when selecting regents. I wanted them each to be either a Cougar or a major business figure in Houston. Instead of waiting until qualified people applied for appointment, the last few years I've been encouraging people to apply.

Today, eight out of nine regents are UH graduates. The only one who is not is my son Welcome Wilson Jr., who went to the University of Denver. But, because of me, Welcome has been involved with the University of Houston his entire life. He now serves as Vice Chairman of the Board of Regents (2016-2017).

Objective: UH Identification with KUHF and Channel 8. For sixty years, I have been a listener of KUHF radio. Beginning fifteen years ago and continuing until recently, I seldom heard the University of Houston mentioned. They identify the station as Houston Public Radio, and infrequently they would give the present temperature at the University of Houston campus. More frequently they gave the temperature "here at Houston Public Radio."

I was puzzled about why KUHF, as well as the UH television Channel 8, avoided identification with UH. After I became chairman

I was inducted into the Texas Business Hall of Fame at a ceremony in Dallas.

in 2007, there was substantial improvement for a few years. In 2015 and early 2016, however, those improvements were lost.

My request was simple. On the hour, KUHF and Channel 8 should simply identify themselves and say, "A service of the University of Houston." In mid-2016, our wonderful president Renu Khator got involved and handled the problem. The announcement is made on the hour, twenty-four hours a day.

Objective: Get UH Supporters Appointed to the Texas Higher Education Coordinating Board. When I became chairman, UH had no members on the board. I persuaded the governor to appoint Dennis Golden and Durga Agrawal, both Cougars, to the coordinating board. Recently, at my behest, Governor Greg Abbott has appointed attorney Ricky Raven, who is doing great. Presently he is the only Cougar, but I hope that will change over time.

Objective: Bring UH Alumni Association Back into the Fold. When I became the chairman of the Board of Regents in 2007, the UH Alumni Association (UHAA) had been estranged from the UH administration and the board of regents for six or seven years. The conflict went back to a previous UH president. In my first month as chairman, Cheryl Creuzot, the chairman of the UHAA, came to see me with Connie Fox, the interim president. They advised me that the alumni organization wanted to be an integral part of the University of Houston. That was the beginning of a major effort to align the UHAA objectives with that of UH.

In 2013, President Khator appointed me as chairman of a task force to merge the UHAA with the University of Houston. This was success- fully done, although there still remains an independent alumni board that supervises the expenditures of money from the alumni foundation. Now, the president of the alumni association has an executive role in the development department at UH. Mike Pede, the current president, is doing a great job.

Objective: Move the Board of Regents Office to the E. Cullen Building. When I was first appointed a regent by Governor Perry, I was shocked to find that the Board of Regents Office was located on the second floor at the back end of the alumni center. The offices were not only unimpressive but were also quite small. I complained bitterly to Leroy Hermes, chairman of the Regents, and he agreed. Leroy immediately started the initiative to move the office to the historic E. Cullen Building and appointed Regent Morgan O'Connor to supervise the enterprise. When I became chairman of the regents, plans were completed, but construction of the office in E. Cullen had not begun. I was pleased that I had the opportunity to make some major changes, to which Morgan agreed, to reorganize the space to provide a much larger board room and provide a regents' lounge to be used during graduation and others times when regents have downtime on campus. The E. Cullen Building is the building that houses President Khator and most of her vice presidents, and the regents now have prominent offices on the first floor.

Objective: Reinstate a Mass-Marketing Campaign for UH. Until the 1990s, UH had a very effective marking campaign, but for some reason it had been dropped. When I became chairman, I urged that we pump more funds into advertising. The UH billboard campaign has been extremely successful. Today UH is mentioned in the *Houston Chronicle* about three times a day, and its press around the world has been incredible. In 2015, Matthew McConaughey was selected to be the commencement speaker. It is estimated that the University of Houston generated many millions of dollars' worth of free advertising all over the country from the press as a result of his selection. Today UH is doing a masterful job of managing its public relations and advertising. Arnold Schwarzenegger spoke at the mass commencement in May of 2017. The publicity surrounding it was mammoth. A short statement of his speech went viral.

Objective: Strengthen the Ties between the University of Houston and the System Campus at Sugar Land. When I became chairman in 2007, a delegation from Sugar Land came to see me. It included several businessmen, as well as the mayor of Sugar Land, the county judge of Fort Bend County, and the county commissioner for the precinct in which our UH System campus is located. They had serious objection to most of the courses being taught by the University of Houston-Victoria. Degrees from Sugar Land were issued in the name

The cougar mascot kisses me on the cheek in the UH wagon in the Houston Rodeo Parade downtown Houston.

of UH-V. Their preference was that we have a separate University of Houston-Sugar Land. I did not think that was a good idea, but I was sympathetic to the fact that Sugar Land was part of metropolitan Houston and not Victoria.

After I left as chairman, a bill was introduced in the Texas Legislature to transfer the University of Houston-Victoria to the Texas A&M System. It was suddenly clear that the continuation of the connection of the Sugar Land campus to University of Houston-Victoria needed to be dealt with. Dr. Khator appointed me as head of a Sugar Land task force, and we held multiple hearings on the subject. In the end, the University of Houston Board of Regents approved our plan to transfer most Sugar Land programs to the University of Houston, and allow University of Houston-Victoria to expand at the Katy campus. The business community and elected officials from Fort Bend County were very pleased. (The Mayor of Sugar Land in 2017 and the county judge are both Cougars.)

For the first time in sixty years the University of Houston has a School of Nursing, thriving at the Sugar Land campus.

Objective: Beautify Scott Street. I must admit to total failure in getting this done. My plan was simply to get the city to provide a setback line for Scott Street so that, as redevelopment occurred, there would be room for landscaping. Additionally, I talked to then-mayor Bill White about using city money and METRO money to landscape Scott Street. He agreed completely. An objection to gentrification was raised when I discussed the matter with leaders of the Third Ward.

Because Scott Street is used by the public for all athletic events at UH, the public's view of UH is distorted by the appearance of Scott Street. Now, President Khator has initiated many programs in the Third Ward that are being very well received. It is my hope now that it may be feasible to get something done along Scott Street.

AT A UNIVERSITY, WINNING AT FOOTBALL FLOATS ALL BOATS

I often talk about how athletics "floats all boats." By that I mean that successful teams make everybody feel better about everything related to the university. A perfect example of this can be seen in a story about John O'Quinn.

One year during my chairmanship, the University of Houston was playing SMU in Robertson Stadium. As always, I was in the president's suite, and one of the invited guests was John O'Quinn. O'Quinn was a major benefactor to UH, and he had given us ten million dollars for the football field at Robertson Stadium. He also was a big supporter of the law school and other projects.

O'Quinn was on the other side of the suite talking to President Khator. After about fifteen minutes he walked over to me. "Welcome," he said, "I want you, as chairman of the Board of Regents, to tell John O'Quinn what he should do financially for the University of Houston. And, Welcome, whatever you tell me, that's exactly what I'll do."

O'Quinn, who was worth several hundred million dollars, seemed sincere. John continued, "Welcome, I mean it. Whatever you say I should do, I guarantee I will do exactly that." I told John that that was very generous, and I would give it serious consideration and meet with him in the next few days.

Fifteen minutes later, O'Quinn walked up to me and said, "Don't forget, Welcome. I mean it. Whatever you say, I will do."
At the end of the game, going down in the elevator, he said, "Don't forget, Welcome. I expect to hear from you soon."
That was Saturday at the football game, which we were winning. On Monday morning at about 9 a.m., John O'Quinn was killed in an automobile accident when he lost control of his vehicle on Allen Parkway. It was a tragic loss for his family and for the UH community.

When I think about his enthusiasm just a few nights before, I realize how important our winning the game was to his enthusiasm for the university. The fact that we were winning against SMU in a football game is what caused John O'Quinn to get carried away and offer anything we wanted. I've seen it happen many times.

Some of the most successful fundraisers I have had for the UH PAC was when our winning football coach came to speak. And the same generosity was present with our winning athletic director, Hunter Yurachek. Winning in athletics floats all boats.

TDECU STADIUM

When President Khator first came to UH, she explained to me clearly that we had to have a winning athletic program. She said it was the only way that a university ever got national recognition. You can have the best creative writing program in America, which I think we do, but few people outside of academia even know about it. The other thing she told me was that we had to have our own new stadium built on campus.

Many years before, in the 1960s, when the legendary UH coach Bill Yeoman was hired as football coach, he came to see me for lunch. Bill made the same point. He thought we needed a stadium on campus. At the time, UH was playing their football games in the Astrodome in the 1960s, and since I owned ten percent of the Houston Astros, I thought that was just fine. Robertson Stadium, then called Jeppesen Stadium and owned by HISD, had been built next to the campus in 1942, but football games were played at the Astrodome after it opened.

Two years ago, President Khator got her wish, and she opened TDECU Stadium on campus, replacing the demolished Robertson Stadium. It is a thing to behold. It seats 40,000 people and can easily be expanded to 60,000. In my view, that new stadium helped in our hiring Tom Herman to be head football coach. Tom was the very successful offensive coordinator at Ohio State University, the number one football team in America the previous year. In order to get him, we had to promise that we would raise the money for an indoor practice football field, which we did. But now Tom is at UT, having been replaced by the wonderful Coach Major Applewhite.

UT INVASION OF UH TERRITORY

Until about five years ago, any university that wanted to purchase land had to get approval from the Texas Higher Education Coordinating Board in Austin. But then the legislature quietly changed that requirement and removed that authority. I didn't object at the time, because I thought that we ought to have the ability to buy land anywhere we wanted to. But I didn't think it through.

In the fall of 2015, the University of Texas System announced that it was purchasing 332 acres five miles from the UH campus. They announced a purchase price of about $200 million. The UT system had just hired a new chancellor, former Admiral William McRaven, previously head of Special Forces in the Navy, the group who had captured and killed Osama Bin Laden.

McRaven insisted that he had no firm plan for the land, and that it was an open book, a "blank sheet of paper." I beg to differ. What executive would invest $200 million without knowing exactly what he or she had in mind?

We at UH were outraged. The University of Houston Board of Regents passed a resolution opposing this invasion. Chairman Tilman Fertitta called it asinine. I made a speech before the Board of Regents and made the point that if Texas A&M went to Austin and bought 332 acres five miles from UT's forty-acre campus, I thought UT would be justifiably concerned.

I appeared before the Texas Higher Education Coordinating Board and followed Admiral McRaven after he presented his plan for the Houston facility. I asked the Coordinating Board if we were going to have a coordinated higher-education system in Texas or would it be "dog-eat-dog."

The UH Alumni Association got rightfully involved and passed a resolution that has since been signed by thousands upon thousands of Cougars. Andrew Cobos, a former regent, and I organized a petition signed by thirty-five former members of the Board of Regents at UH.

I've talked to about fifty state representatives and state senators about this, and all but one agrees with us wholeheartedly. I've spoken to Lt. Governor Dan Patrick, and I think he shares our view. Governor Abbott certainly does. Two of the three new UT regents whom he appointed in January of 2017 told the Senate committee that they have grave reservations about UT coming to Houston.

I wrote an editorial for the *Houston Business Journal* and said, among other things, the following:

"Because the University of Texas is using money they are borrowing, secured by the Permanent University Fund, nothing can be done to stop them from making the purchase. No appropriated money is involved, and the legislature is powerless to do any more than threaten. My plan is to simply slow down their progress until the legislature meets and let the legislature deal with it. These are resources that could be available to UT San Antonio, or UT El Paso, or UT Dallas, all emerging Tier One universities. Instead, it is being used to simply dilute and dull the higher education institutions in Houston."

Texas Senator John Whitmire from Houston, the dean of the senate, took a major leadership role in objecting to the UT purchase.

Then, in March of 2017, Chancellor McRaven announced that the plan for Houston was canceled. He went on to say that the land would be put up for sale. In my opinion, this was the right thing for UT to do. We need to have a coordinated higher education system in Texas. In the eighteen months since the land was purchased, many Texas legislators and senators have complained bitterly about money being spent by UT in Houston. Many of them were from places like San Antonio, Dallas, and El Paso, where UT has separate universities. The point I kept making was that this money for a Houston campus was coming directly out of their pockets.

But I give most of the credit for this project's cancellation to Texas Senators John Whitmire of Houston, Senator Kel Seliger of Amarillo, and especially Governor Greg Abbott. Senators Whitmire and Seliger raised serious questions in committee meetings about the wisdom of the UT invasion of Houston. Greg Abbott appointed three members of the UT Board of Regents in January of 2017 and strongly suggested that they oppose the expansion into Houston. I have great respect for UT, and I have great respect for its chancellor, Admiral McRaven. I just want them to respect UH and limit their Houston presence to medical institutes.

After Admiral McRaven announced the withdrawal, I was called by the *Houston Business Journal* and asked for a quote. I told them his announcement of the withdrawal from Houston had given me a problem.

The reporter asked, "What problem is that?"

And I answered, "My problem is I can't stop smiling."

I was in attendance when Mayor Sylvester Turner of Houston proposed that multiple Texas Universities need to come together to develop a data center consortium. It would include UH, Rice, TSU, the University of Texas and Texas A&M. It would be a true consortium, not dominated by one university. In response, the 2017 Chairman of the UH System Board of Regents, Tilman Fertitta, issued a statement saying that it would be a great idea if it was a true collaboration. Tilman said "my door is always open."

Stay tuned.

UH KATY CAMPUS

The University of Houston has long planned a campus in Katy, Texas. We did it the right way. We went to the legislature and hearings were held in both the house and the senate. The coordinating board was consulted and approved the plan. Both houses authorized us to move forward. The appropriations committee provided tuition revenue bonds that would fund the acquisition and construction of the first building. I have served, along with Welcome Jr., vice chairman of the UH System Board of Regents, on a task force to locate the campus.

This is the way campus expansion should be handled—by getting concurrence from the legislature as well as the Texas Higher Education Coordinating Board instead of arbitrarily purchasing a tract of land in Houston in four parcels, which tract is eight times larger than the University of Texas in Austin.

I am pictured here with then-UH Board of Regents chair Nelda Blair and UH president Renu Khator.

CONCLUSION

Family, country, and Cougars: when people say these are my passions, they are correct. The University of Houston has been one of my main passions for most of my life. Welcome Jr. is now in a leadership role. I plan to continue to assist him to support our wonderful president in carrying the University of Houston forward. It is an institution that has given so much to me, and I would like to think I have given back to it, as well.

I would like to close this chapter by getting back to our wonderful President, Renu Khator. After she had been president for about six months, she came to the UH System of Regents board and said that she wanted to be judged every year on her progress. She made a list of about fifteen things that she thought she ought to be judged on. Most of them related to Tier One status. Each year since then at the Board retreat, she presents a report about how she's doing on each of the fifteen items. The progress has been phenomenal.

Let me make a partial list of what she has done from 2008 to 2017:

- Recently, UH was honored with the granting of a chapter of the Phi Beta Kappa Honor Society, a major accomplishment. Income from intellectual property owned by UH has gone from $800,000 when she became president to $27-million dollars a year. The SAT scores of entering freshman has gone up 100 points. There are more than seven applicants for every slot in the freshman class.

- The Princeton Review named UH as one of the seventy-five top "Best Value" colleges. The increase in STEM graduates has been 30%. UH has been recognized as one of the "fifteen most afford- able colleges."

- UH was recognized as one of the ten national universities for graduating students with the least amount of debt, as ranked by US news and World Report. UH College of Business Entrepreneurship program ranked #1 in the nation. Research expenditures in the UH system is up by 80%. Twenty-five percent of the student athletes made the Dean's list. The UH system has built buildings costing more than one billion dollars. Annual giving to the UH system grew by 70%. UH Alumni rate of giving increased by 130%.

- The UH Hilton Hotel College is ranked #1 in the nation. The UH Creative Writing Program has been ranked #2 in the nation for the last 10 years. The UH Law Center ranks #13 in the nation for the National Moot Court Competition. UH PhD's awarded each year are up 40%. Students living on UH campus up to 8,000 (second largest in the state).

- The UH Athletic Program ranked #6 in the nation for the best integration of academics. The UH Law Center has three programs ranked in the top ten nationally. The White House has since named UH #4 in the nation for "best bang for the buck" relating to the salaries of our graduates. Members of the National Academy of Science on the faculty up 75%. UH Chancellor Renu Khator served as Chairman of the Board of Directors of the American Council on Education; a major coordinating body for colleges and universities.

- The UH Bauer College of Business has more graduates who are CEOs of Fortune 500 companies than any university in America except Harvard. The UH Army ROTC was honored as best in the nation with the MacArthur Award. There are 700 applicants each year for 125 slots in the doctor of pharmacy program. This year, 100% of the pharmacy graduates passed the national and state test at their first examination. The UH College of Education Online Graduate Program ranks #2 in the nation.

- In my seventy-two-year involvement with UH, the Faculty Senate has been somewhat at odds with the administration. Not anymore. The faculty senate supports our president 100%.

Let me say it again: my proudest moment when I was Chairman of the UH Board of Regents was hiring Renu Khator.

In Conclusion

Faith And Family

It should be apparent by now that Joanne Guest Wilson has had a tremendous impact on me, not only at home, but also in my professional life. From the moment I saw her in that Daisy Mae blouse, brown-haired, beautiful, and quiet across the table at the Sadie Hawkins dance, I knew that she was the girl for me.

I believe partners and connections are what create opportunities, and Joanne has been my partner in our family, the heart of all my endeavors. Because she is more reserved than I am, when she says something is important, I know that it is important to listen. She has trusted me to be the deal-maker and breadwinner in our family, and I have trusted her to lead this generation of Wilsons in matters of faith and family. She has done an award-winning job. Without the solid foundation that Joanne provided for me and our five kids, it would have been easy for us to get caught up in the excitement of heady times and important people. Instead, she has done the seemingly impossible: she kept us all grounded and also allowed us to soar. I have talked a great deal about my experiences in these pages, but to provide you with a real understanding of what I have accomplished, you must understand the remarkable woman I married.

FAITH

Joanne was a devout Catholic and attended St. Anne Catholic School as well as St. Agnes Academy before attending public school. When we were engaged she prayed that I would become a Catholic, and it worked. I did. When we married we were not yet ready to have children, so we practiced the "rhythm system." Catholics were not to use contraceptives, but by planning sex at appropriate times, pregnancy

In Conclusion

Joanne and I with our five kids: Joanne Castleberry, Cindy Proler Ray, Welcome Wilson, Jr., Pam Wilson, and Craig Wilson.

could be avoided. In theory. After we had three children, all by surprise, Joanne decided the rhythm method didn't work.

Once we had the kids, we both felt it was important to get them to church. Especially with the three older kids, we never missed going to church on Sunday. On Sunday morning, I would go into the bedrooms of the three kids and pull off their covers. After going to Catechism and church, we'd go out to Sunday dinner. We would frequently go to either Brennan's on Smith Street in downtown Houston, or El Chico restaurant on South Main, where I owned the building and leased it to El Chico. The kids loved the desserts, especially the flaming strawberries at Brennan's!

After the first three kids, we started using contraceptives and carefully planned our last two children. As well as not following the church's dictates on family planning, Joanne also began to disagree with the church's teachings on abortion. She ultimately became an Episcopalian over the issue. We now belong to St. John the Divine Episcopal Church on River Oaks Boulevard in Houston.

She has also quarreled with the Republican Party about the abortion issue. She feels strongly that a woman should be able to get an abortion during the first trimester. She believes in family planning and is a big supporter of the day-after pill, as well as contraception. She took grave exception to the law passed in 2013 by the Texas Legislature that attempted to shut down ninety percent of the abortion clinics in Texas. She did not object to their ban after twenty weeks, although she preferred twelve weeks except for medical problems, but the bill purposely made access much more difficult for millions of Texans. In 2016 the US Supreme Court ruled the law unconstitutional. Joanne believes in easy access but feels strongly that the clinics should be absolutely safe. Her position is, "Let she who is pregnant make the choice."

I agree with her on all accounts.

My wife loves being a member of St. John the Divine. She likes it because she knows most of the congregation and "they are not being told what to do by a man in the Vatican." She likes the Episcopal denomination because it is peaceful and emphasizes forgiveness and God's love. She also enjoys the informal service conducted in the gymnasium where they have a string band and a lot of singing, but it still has Mass and Communion that remind her of the Catholic services that were so important to her as a girl.

Our most religious child was always our daughter Joanne. When the older children were young, we never missed church under any circumstance. By the time Joanne was a child we were less regular, but she is the one that ended up the most devout. She even influenced her husband, and he became an Episcopal priest at age forty-four. They now live in Nacogdoches, Texas, with their four children, where he is pastor of Christ Episcopal Church. She leads an extremely popular bible study class on Thursdays that is attended by churchgoers from all denominations. I thank her mother for making sure that our family had both a strong church background and the ability to question it when necessary.

HOME

From our first apartment, Joanne has always created a sense of home for our family. I have shared details of our wonderful thirty years on River Oaks Boulevard and the beautiful and inviting home she created for us there. After we moved from River Oaks Boulevard in the mid-90s, we bought a house in a gated community next to River Oaks from a prominent home-builder in Houston named Willie Carl. Willie built fine homes in the River Oaks, Memorial, and West University areas. During the process of buying the house, Joanne learned that Willie would frequently use outside partners to provide cash for the

Joanne and I at the Triple W Ranch in Waller Texas.

house construction. Because she had always considered herself a home designer, she quickly became a partner with Willie in building expensive spec houses inside the 610 Loop.

Together they built a number of houses in the one-million-dollar price range, all of which quickly sold. My wife's contribution, in addition to the money, was in the design and layout of the houses. She had a good eye as well as a good understanding of how families lived in a house. By the early 2000s, Willie was tired of building spec houses and became a sub-divider. His businesses have continued to thrive, and to this day Joanne knows just what details make a home work for a family.

MY TALENTED WIFE

Beyond her ability to create a wonderful home and a healthy faith practice, Joanne has numerous other talents. An accomplished and prolific artist of the impressionist school, a world-class chef, an able mother of five, grandmother to sixteen, and great-grandmother to sixteen, a ball chairman-type in her thirties and forties, a marathon athlete, an outstanding decorator, and a sky-diver—she impresses me daily.

Although we can now afford to have someone cook for us, after almost seven decades of marriage, Joanne still does all the cooking. We eat dinner at 7 p.m., and it's a sit-down affair with me in my coat and tie and my wife serving a gourmet meal. Until this year, she even did all the cooking for dinners at Christmas and Thanksgiving, usually hosting forty to fifty guests. Only recently did she finally agree to let caterers take over preparing everything for the large holiday dinner crowd.

She is also a talented impressionist painter. When I met her in college, she was in the School of Fine Arts, studying to be a painter. She had been artistic since childhood and was fascinated by abstract artists such as Picasso. A sophomore when we married, she continued to take courses part-time. That stopped a year later when she became pregnant with Welcome Jr. Her courses were few and far between for the next two decades as she raised two batches of children.

When the kids were bigger, she returned to UH part-time and over another two decades she completed her degree. In the meantime, she produced over 100 pieces of art. Her specialty was using a large canvas. In our home today, in the entry hall, two of her large modern paintings, eight feet wide and twelve feet high, are the first things to capture your eye.

In Conclusion

In 2013, the University of Houston approached me and proposed to name the largest gallery at the UH Blaffer Museum of Fine Arts "The Joanne Guest Wilson Gallery." Although a contribution was involved, the Wilson family thought it was a wonderful idea. The dedication of the gallery was held on December 15, 2013. Joanne knew nothing about the name until we arrived at the Blaffer Museum. She thought we were sim- ply attending an art exhibit for some famous artist. She seemed genuinely thrilled when she saw her name prominently displayed on the gallery wall. Shortly thereafter, the gallery held an exhibit of her artwork. The family and my assistant Kathryn Curtice gathered up at least 100 pieces of her art, and we hired a display expert to arrange the art and hang it on the walls in the gallery. About 200 people attended the exhibit, including many dignitaries such as Texas Lt. Governor David Dewhurst

A major showing of my wife Joanne's work was held in December of 2015 in the largest gallery of the UH Blaffer Museum. The gallery is named the Joanne Guest Wilson Gallery in her honor.

In Conclusion

Joanne chaired many charity balls over about twenty-five years. Here we are arriving at one of them in the early 1990s.

and his wife Tricia. It was a wonderful event, and on my office wall today, I have a photograph taken that night of almost our entire family.

After we moved out of the house on River Oaks Boulevard, Joanne's interest in painting diminished, and in 2015 I built her a studio on the back of our present house where I hope she'll take up painting again.

But it may be a while before she picks up the brushes again. In recent years, the artistic endeavor that Joanne has pursued most has been gardening. We bought the empty lot next door so she has a large area for her flowers. Her specialties are azaleas, impatiens, gerbera daisies, and hibiscus. She devotes many hours each week to tending them. Her arch-enemies are the possums and raccoons that occasionally come into the yard and dig up her flowers to eat the roots. She has an elaborate trap that catches the offenders unharmed, and then she takes them to Memorial Park and lets them out.

SOCIALITE

In the latter half of the 1960s, Joanne became interested in social activity. She became a ball-chairman-type. She was chairman for the St. Joseph Gala, the Houston Ballet Ambassadors, and many events for the Houston Grand Opera, Baylor College of Medicine, and Kinkaid School. Being president of the Ballet Ambassadors was one of her favorite roles. She served for several years and held many events that raised a great deal of money. Although we still attend the Museum of Fine Arts Ball and other special occasions, we are not as active these days. In 2015, Joanne was named a Houston Treasure by the Houston Social Book and honored at a luncheon at the River Oaks Country Club and a reception at the Citadel of Houston.

DECORATOR

Joanne's artistic sense makes her a talented decorator. After we bought the house on River Oaks Boulevard, she became a serious student of decorating. She hired Herbert Wells, the premier Houston decorator, and became a student of his.

She put her decorating skills to work on our second homes, too. At Jamaica Beach we spent the summers in five different houses. The first was on the beach, and was a joint house shared by all of the Jamaica Beach partners. All of the houses were built on pilings eight feet above the ground to accommodate hurricane-force winds pushing up the water. Although she did not supervise the building of several of the houses, she was always responsible for decorating them. Our last home was built on a big canal in Jamaica Beach, and she designed every part of it. It was a low- budget, three-bedroom house that did not even have air conditioning, but our family developed a million wonderful memories there.

READER

My wife is an avid reader. As I have explained, when Joanne became a mother, she determined to read every book that existed on how to do a good job at it. She sticks strictly to nonfiction now, especially history, and reads an hour or so every day. She always has a fountain pen so she can underline parts of the text that she finds particularly interesting. The more complicated the subject, the better she likes it. Recently she read The Grand Design by Stephen Hawking, which I found somewhat ponderous, and Great Scientific Ideas that Changed the World by Professor Steven L. Goldman. Each morning she reads a page from Jesus Calling by Sarah Young.

Joanne's reading, her interest in art, and her faith keep her mind alive, her ideas young, and her spirit healthy. She shares these qualities generously with me, with our kids, and with our grandchildren and great- grandchildren. Joanne is now the matriarch of a very large family (with spouses, fifty people), and she handles the role with grace and dignity.

Since I met her, she has always been a surprise and a delight to me. One day I learned that she jumped out of an airplane at 10,000 feet in a parachute. I have known her seventy years, sixty-nine of those have been as man and wife, and she still surprises me. She has always been, and always will be, the most important person in my life. I knew that she was the one for me the minute I saw her. And I was right.

THE RANCH AND THE SALT GRASS TRAIL RIDE

Joanne's most recent decorating project is our new seven-bedroom ranch house at the Triple W Ranch in Waller, Texas. The décor is

On my favorite horse, Freckless, in the Houston Rodeo Parade in 1967. I rode the Saltgrass trail ride (100 miles) for fifty-three years.

award-winning. It is fitting for a ranch setting but is still elegant. The great room is 3,600 square feet, and it includes everything from seating for forty-four people for dinner to a longhorn steer above the fireplace. The ranch is very special to me, and it is a place where our very large family can all gather.

In Conclusion

Being outdoors, and being on horseback, has been part of our family life since the beginning. I would frequently bring my older children on hunting and camping trips. It was a great opportunity for us to bond and for me to have quality time with each of them. We have had ranches in Rock Island, TX, Athens, TX, Columbus, TX and now Waller, TX. I have always enjoyed getting out in nature with my kids. Sometimes we would crawl up a tree and sit on a branch to hunt deer. Sometimes we would lie behind a log in the field to hunt turkey and deer. Whatever we were doing, we made it fun.

Additionally, with the kids, I have been involved in the Salt Grass Trail Ride for over half a century, and it's a tradition that I enjoy tremendously. I've often told rookie members of our trail-riding group, the Desperados, that the Salt Grass Trail Ride is a life-changing experience. Not only do you spend eight days on a horse, but you also develop fifty or sixty close friends.

My first trail ride was in 1967. I was watching the local newscast on Channel 2, and they talked about the fact that the Salt Grass Trail Ride had started the day before in Brenham, TX and was on its way to Houston. Pat Flaherty, a news anchor at Channel 2, was one of the four people who started the Salt Grass Trail Ride in 1952. It was started as a publicity to stunt to promote the Fat Stock Show and Rodeo. (The name was later changed from Fat Stock Show to Houston Livestock Show and Rodeo.)

I called my brother Jack and proposed that we grab a couple of kids and head to the trail ride. As always, Jack was supportive of whatever I wanted to do. He decided to take his daughter Kathy, and I took my daughter Cindi.

At the time, I only owned one horse, which we kept at Tri-Oaks Stables on Westheimer in Houston. I called the manager of the stables and he said he would lend me one of his horses so that two of us could ride at once. I drove to the stables, picked up the two horses in the horse

Beverly Wilson Smith, Jack Wilson, and I, the three children of Irene and E. E. Jack Wilson. My brother Jack was playing the piano here.

trailer I owned, and drove back to my home on River Oaks Boulevard where I picked up the others. We used a green Jeep that I owned to pull the horse trailer. It was the kind of Jeep that was used by drugstores for delivery and it was paneled. Jack and I were in front and the girls were in back with the saddles, clothes, and gear.

We arrived at Hempstead, TX, which was the first stop for the trail ride. It was almost 10 p.m. when we got there. We found a spot under a big tree, tied the horses to the trailer, and made camp. Early the next morning I decided to test the borrowed horse to be sure he was suitable for riding. I bridled and saddled him, and got aboard and rode a little after dawn. The horse did fine for about 300 yards until I turned him around to ride back to camp. The horse spotted the horse he came with, and, like all horses, began to run. I pulled on the bridle to stop him, and the bridle came off in my hands.

So, there I was on top of a strange horse running at full speed with absolutely no control because of the broken bridle. The horse headed straight for our campsite under the tree, and I quickly calculated that the low-hanging branches would knock me off the horse. I decided

In Conclusion

to slip off the side of the horse, hit the ground and then roll like cowboys did in the movies. Well, instead, I hit the ground like a sack of potatoes and slid for about forty feet, right into the fire. The horse stopped running and went over and stood next to the horse he came with. Over thirty years later, I had to have my hip replaced because of the impact of me hitting the ground. It jarred my hip joint, which later got arthritis and caused the need for a replacement.

About the time we got the bridle fixed, Stewart Morris, Sr., a friend from Houston, drove by. He was there with his daughter Lisa, who is a friend of my daughter, Cindi. Stewart suggested that we join the wagon he was on, which was owned by Jim Boroughs of Spring, TX. Cindi and I would ride the two horses for a couple hours and then we'd switch off and let Jack and Cathy ride. The non-riders would follow the trail ride in the Jeep, pulling an empty horse trailer. And thus, we became official trail riders.

In the early days of the trail ride, fifty percent of the riders were teenagers who drank Boone's Farm wine. Tickle Pink, Strawberry Hill, blueberry wine—along with Mad Dog 20/20. And the teenagers would ride up and down the line creating havoc. When they passed your horse, they would insist that you took a sip of wine. At first I would decline, but that got me into an argument with them, so then I began to just act like I was taking a sip of wine, but not taking any. They were perfectly satisfied. The trail ride organizers finally began to recognize that they needed some rules. With the restrictions, gradually, the teenagers stopped coming.

My brother Jack was responsible for one rule change. On the second year we rode the trail ride, Jack wore beach clothes thinking that he would promote Jamaica Beach, which we were developing in Galveston at the time. The next year, the Salt Grass Trail Ride passed a new rule: "No outrageous clothes. Only conventional western clothing will be permitted. No ball caps."

The second year of the trail ride, I showed up with a Dodge motor- home. Most people had never seen a motorhome, and I remember the air-conditioning going out after the first day on the ride. In the middle of the night, people would bang on the door and shout "you candy ass." The next year there were seven motor homes; the following year, twenty-five and today there must be 400.

Beginning that second year, I took all three of my older kids on the ride. When Craig turned seven and Joanne was six years old, they also rode. At that point, all the kids were enrolled at Kinkaid. At first the faculty resisted when I would take them out for the trail ride. Finally, John Cooper, the headmaster, said "We give up. We will not penalize your kids, as long as they make up the work they missed."

Mr. Boroughs believed that the working man should be able to ride the trail ride. Accordingly, his total cost for what was then a six-day ride was thirty-five dollars. That price included three meals a day, plus the feed for your horses. The meals were spartan, and lunch on the ride consisted of two pieces of bread and a half a slice of bologna in between.

After a couple of years, Mr. Boroughs dropped out of the trail ride and arranged for us to move to the wagon of J. T. Atkinson, a Houston fireman. It was a good group of riders, but their language was terrible. Profanity was rampant, and alcohol was everywhere. (J. T. did not use profanity, but everyone else did.) The profanity was a serious problem with me because of my three kids. I didn't want them to get the idea that such language was acceptable anywhere. By this time, my sister Beverly had joined the trail ride, along with my cousin Margaret Jo Johnson. We began to look for alternatives.

The wagon boss for the wagon in front of us died. We made a deal with his wife that she would be the wagon boss, and we would start a new group of riders, who we later named the Desperados. My daughter Pam designed the logo to go on the back of our Levi Jackets. Normally a new wagon group has to go the back end of the trail ride, but we liked being in the middle. The front of the trail ride is too quiet, and the end of the trail ride is frantic because you're either stopped or trotting. We were able to make a deal to continue in the same spot, and a year later, Beverly purchased the wagon from the lady and made her father-in-law, Archie Bennett, Sr., the new wagon boss.

The Desperados are the perfect trail ride group. We now have about seventy-five members, and normally about fifty of them show up for the trail ride. Ten or fifteen of them are non-riders and simply socialize and move camp.

In Conclusion

Joanne and I at a luncheon in Houston.

This year, I completed my fifty-third annual trail ride on the Salt Grass. In addition to the Salt Grass, there are about fifteen other trail rides that come in from various directions into Houston. All fifteen of the trail rides meet in downtown Houston and participate in a parade that has a hundred wagons and several thousand people. Thanks to Beverly, our wagon boss, and her perfectionist nature, the Desperados have won one of the two awards given each year for best wagon or best group eighteen times. The president of our group is Beverly's husband, Gary Smith.

Cindi, who was on the first trail ride fifty-three years ago and my daughter Joanne, are the only children I have still riding. Cindi comes with her wonderful husband Sam Ray, and two of her boys, Ryan Proler and Preston Proler. Cindi was president for three years a few years back. Now she is secretary. The Salt Grass Trail Ride has been a great experience for our family.

FAMILY

Joanne and I have been blessed in many ways, but the most important is our family. From the moment we found out that Welcome was coming, through Joanne's pregnancy ordeals, and to the joy of his healthy birth, we were excited to become parents. Then, so soon after we returned from the navy, we were excited to find out that our "Made in Japan" baby Cindi would be joining us. Then Pam came along, followed by

Craig and Joanne. The five of them, each with his or her own gifts, are their mother's and my absolute pride and joy.

We thought our happiness could not be more complete than when we had our last child, but we soon came to understand that love, like money, grows when you invest it well. Now, with five children, sixteen grandchildren and sixteen great-grandchildren, I would say our most important investment is thriving, and we are reaping the dividends. Joanne is my trusted partner, and we have made the best deal I could ever have imagined. It's a real Wilson deal, win-win for all involved and with terms completely in the family's favor

In Conclusion

Appendix

Things You May Not Know About Welcome W. Wilson, Sr.
By Cindi Wilson Proler Ray

- Witness to Hydrogen Bomb Test at Bikini Atoll in the Pacific – 1956
- Milked two Cows each Morning Before Hitchhiking to High School – 1943
- LBJ Special Ambassador to Nicaragua (President Somosa) – 1966
- Hired to Regularly Performed Live Singing Commercials on TV – 1949
- Five Children, 16 Grandchildren, 16 Great-Grandchildren & Only One Wife – 1949
- Served in the Executive Office of the President under Ike and JFK – 1956
- Three Year Chairman of the Board of Regents of the University of Houston – 2007
- Inducted into the Texas Business Hall of Fame – 2011
- Chairman of the Board, Homestead Bank of Houston – 1964
- Naval Officer in the Occupation Forces of Japan after WWII – 1951
- Invited & Spoke to a Joint Session of New Mexico Legislature – 1959
- Hitchhiked 720 miles Round Trip First 30 Weekends in College to see Girl – 1946
- Received Arthur Fleming Award as One of Ten Outstanding Young Men in US Federal Service (Award Later Given to Astronaut Neil Armstrong and Sec. Robert Gates) – 1958
- Married College Sweetheart, Joanne, on College Graduation Day – 1949

Appendix

- JFK Came to his Hotel Suite at Washington Hotel for Small Gathering – 1960
- Saved Best Friend's Life Using CPR – 1988
- At age 80, Traveled Half Mile on ZIP Line through Costa Rica Forrest – 2008
- Founding Member of the UH Phi Beta Kappa Society Chapter – 2016
- Given the Trailblazer Award by the American Advertising Federation- Houston – 2013
- Monday thru Friday Workout at Health Club for 55 years – 1963
- Worked for Hog Farm at age 13, Picked up Slop from Houston Hotels – 1941
- Developer of Jamaica Beach and Tiki Island in Galveston, TX – 1957
- Worked with Houston Mayor Lewis Cutrer to Integrate Lunch Counters – 1963
- Longshoreman on Brownsville, Texas Docks for Banana Boats – 1945
- Arrested for Touching Cop with his Car, Hired Racehorse Haynes, Acquitted – 1979
- In Front Page Houston Post Picture with LBJ at opening of Astrodome – 1965
- Distinguished Alumnus, UH Bauer College of Business – 1996
- Ten Percent Owner of Houston Astros Baseball Team – 1970
- Department Head at Houston City Hall at age 27 – 1956
- Age 30, Named by President Eisenhower to the Civilian Rank of 3-Star General – 1958
- Almost Lost at Sea While Swimming 100 miles off Texas Coast – 1989
- Member of Harris County Grand Jury Commission – 1970
- In College, Performed as Comedy Act Singer in Night Clubs – 1948
- Lifetime Achievement Award from the Houston Business Journal – 2012

- Back Stage with Willie Nelson during Houston Concert at the Summit – 1995
- Worked for the US National Security Agency in Japan during the Korean War – 1951
- President of the Student Body at Texas Southmost College in Brownsville, TX – 1945
- Talked with JFK and Jackie in Houston the Night Before He Was Assassinated – 1963

2. **MORE THINGS YOU MAY NOT KNOW ABOUT WWW, SR.**
   - Testified Twice Before a Federal Criminal Grand Jury (Sharpstown) – 1972
   - Led Drive to Raise Money to Install First Weather Radar in Texas – 1955
   - Watched Eisenhower Hit Golf Balls Daily from WWW Sr's DC Office – 1958
   - Conducted Hearing Which Changed Hurricane Reporting by the Weather Bureau – 1958
   - Shot Craps with Judge Roy Hofheinz in Las Vegas – 1954
   - His Signature is on 35,000 Diplomas from University of Houston System – 2007
   - Attended Democratic Convention in Atlantic City, NJ - LBJ was nominated – 1964
   - Performed Four Wedding Ceremonies under Texas Law – 2004
   - Developer and Owner of the Sixth Marriott Hotel in the World (Today 5,500) – 1967
   - Billy Gibbons & Dusty Hill played at Cindi's Debut Party before ZZ Top – 1971
   - Named a Texas Icon by Houston Local Magazine – 2016
   - President of the Student Body, Brownsville Jr College – 1945
   - Gets up Monday - Friday at 4:25 am, Picks up Welcome Jr at 5am to go to health Club – 1983
   - Lived in Army Surplus House Trailer on UH Campus. Bathroom a Block Away – 1946

- Had Lonesome Dove Author Larry McMurtry as House Guest – 1990
- Chairman of University of Houston Sugarland Campus Restructure Taskforce – 2015
- An Honorary Citizen of Galveston, New Orleans and Springdale, Arkansas – 1959
- Business Partner of Johnny Goyen, Mayor pro tem of Houston for 22 years – 1957
- Eats over 50 Red and Green Frozen Grapes Each Day – 2011
- Named Texas Business Icon by National Real Estate Forum Magazine – 2012
- Played Ping Pong Daily w/World Champion Chess Master Oswald Jacoby – 1952
- Friend of Original Seven Astronauts. Alan Shepherd was Neighbor – 1963
- Slopped Hogs & Fed Chickens Twice Daily During High School – 1941
- Met with LBJ at Jack Valenti's House about Civil Rights – 1963
- Chairman of the Board of an American Stock Exchange Company – 1969
- Went Nameless for 22 days When Parents Could Not Agree on Name – 1928
- Executive Assistant to Texas Oilman/Philanthropist Billionaire R.E.(Bob) Smith – 1953
- Texas President of the Pan American Student Forum – 1945
- Developer, Foxhall Apartments on I-10 at Chimney Rock in Houston – 1968
- Hunted Duck in Arkansas with Arkansas Governor Orville Faubus – 1958
- Snow Storm Flight to DC with Oklahoma Governor for JFK Inauguration – 1961
- His Birth Announcement had Pink Ribbon because Doctor said he would be a Girl – 1928
- Shot Pheasant in Scotland with Chairman/CEO of Sotheby's – 1980

- Investigated by the Los Angeles Times as being LBJ's Silent Partner – 1965
- Knew Eisenhower, Kennedy, Johnson, Reagan, Bush & Bush, Met Nixon & Trump – 1954
- Legendary US House Speaker Sam Rayburn Came to WWW's Texas Office – 1959
- Witness to Atom Bomb Test in Nevada – 1954

3. **EVEN MORE THINGS YOU MAY NOT KNOW ABOUT WWW, SR.**
   - Partner of Jack Valenti, President of the Motion Picture Association of America – 1957
   - Board Chairman of Colonial Savings Association of Houston – 1965
   - Named Distinguished Alumnus, University of Texas Rio Grande Valley – 2018
   - Ate Nothing but Free Bananas for 13 Days to Save Money in College – 1947
   - Rode the Annual Salt Grass Trail Ride 51 Times – 1967
   - Founding Chairman of UH Graduate Real Estate Program Board of Directors – 2010
   - Installed Houston Air Raid Sirens Heard every Friday noon for 30 years – 1955
   - Lived and Raised Five Kids on Houston's River Oaks Boulevard for 30 years – 1966
   - Special Assistant to Houston Mayor (Judge) Roy Hofheinz – 1954
   - Took $3 Airplane Ride in Ford Tri-motor Plane – 1935
   - Sat on Stage at Houston's Jones Hall when Tenor Luciano Pavarotti Sang – 1981
   - Visited with Secretary of Defense Robert McNamara in his Pentagon Office – 1962
   - Weighed Twelve Pounds When Born in San Angelo, Texas – 1928
   - Was Executive Director of the United Citizens Association of Houston, and Led a Slate of

Appendix

- Mayor and City Council Candidates to Abject Defeat – 1955
- Experienced Earthquake Tremors in Yokohama, Japan – 1951
- Ex-Texas Governor John Connelly Talked Him in to Becoming a Republican – 1973
- Designed and Built a Two Story Federal Office Building 50 feet Underground – 1960
- Rafted Through Rapids for Five Days on River of No Return in Idaho – 1980
- Named Distinguished Alumnus, University of Houston – 1970
- President of Mortgage Broker River Oaks Financial Group, Inc. – 1984
- Chairman of Desperado Horseback Riding Group for Forty Eight Years – 1970
- Given the Alice Graham Baker Crusader Award by Neighbor Centers, Inc. – 2013
- Developed Kingsbrook Apartment Complex on Katy Fwy in Houston – 1964
- Canoed Regularly Fifteen Miles down Buffalo Bayou with Best Friend – 1985
- Witness to Spacecraft Endeavor Liftoff from Cape Kennedy, Florida – 1990
- Selected One of Ten Outstanding Students at UH – 1949
- Shot Pheasant for 15 years in England, Scotland and Ireland – 1982
- With his wife, Joanne, Named a Houston Treasure by the Houston Social Book – 2015
- Hip Replaced 30 Years after Horseback Accident – 2000
- Graduated First in his Class at Naval Officers School – 1951
- Has Known Every Texas Governor Since Allen Shivers – 1953
- Trap Drummer for 17 Piece College Dance Band – 1945
- Was the Subject of Oval Office Conversation Between LBJ and J. Edgar Hoover – 1965
- Ran Three Miles Daily with Best Friend Jimmy Lyon for 20 years Until He Died – 1970
- Named Distinguished Alumnus for Texas Southmost College in Brownsville, TX – 2005

- Escorted Movie Star Gina Lolabrigida to Awards Dinner – 1982

4. **YET MORE THINGS YOU MAY NOT KNOW ABOUT WWW, SR.**
   - Eisenhower Administration Appointee, Five State Head of Civil Defense & FEMA – 1956
   - Had 38 Aunts and Uncles and 47 First Cousins – 1939
   - Received the Human Relations Award from the American Jewish Committee – 2015
   - Has been Alive for More Than 32,800 Days – 1928
   - Mother's Family Entered Texas before the Civil War – 1850
   - Quoted in Time Magazine about the Cold War and National Defense – 1959
   - Board Member of the Greater Houston Partnership, now Director Emeritus – 2008
   - At the Presidential Inaugurations of JFK, LBJ, GHWB, GWB and Donald Trump – 1961
   - Testified Before Five Texas Legislative Committees – 2009
   - Is a Fourth-generation Houstonian—Great-grandkids are Seventh – 1869
   - To Win a Bet, Ate 17 Pecan Balls at River Oaks Country Club – 1975
   - Chairman of University of Houston Drive for Tier One Status – 2010
   - At Age 5 Scared Witless By Boris Karloff in Bride of Frankenstein movie – 1933
   - He and his wife received the Community Service Award from the UH Tech College – 2015
   - Negotiated the Sale of Houston's Fifth Largest Bank – 1990
   - Beat Prostate Cancer after Year of Radiation & Hormone Therapy – 2007
   - Trapped 8 Days in Boston Hotel with 12 Feet of Snow at the Door – 1978
   - Higher Education Chairman of the Greater Houston Partnership – 2010

Appendix

- Drafted in World War II, Orders cancelled when Atom Bomb Ended the War – 1945
- Discovered High-rise Fire, Ran up 16 Floors to Evacuate Residents – 1975
- Attended Catholic Mass at Noon 7 Days a Week in Japan for 20 Months – 1951
- Spent a Night in a Tokyo Geisha House, Had to Pay Extra to Sleep Alone – 1951
- Board Member of A.A.White Dispute Resolution Institute – 1997
- Founding Chairman University of Houston Heritage Society – 1988
- Hitchhiked in Bombardier Seat of Air Force B-26s All Across America – 1951
- Early Board Member, Houston Convention Bureau – 1966
- With a One Tank of Gas and $40, Spent Three Weeks in Mexico with Brother – 1948
- Houston Chairman of March of Dimes Campaign – 1954
- Lived in Japan for Two Years, Wife and Son joined – 1951
- Bank Partner Bill Sherrill was later Member of US Federal Reserve Board – 1965
- Defense Battalion Commander in Yokosuka, Japan – 1951
- Developed Three Villa Marina Apartment Complexes in Galveston – 1966
- Stopped a 4 Engine Airline Plane as it Taxied from Gate by Arm-waving in front – 1956
- Had Kids or Grandkids at Kinkaid School Every Semester for 54Years – 1963
- Played Base Fiddle in 14 Piece Band in College – 1945
- Received the Real Estate Outstanding Service Award from Houston CoreNet – 2013
- Grand Marshal of Astronaut Gus Grisson's Houston Parade – 1963
- Business Partner with Charlie Wilson of Charlie Wilson's War – 1963

Appendix

Welcome's Rules Of Order
HOW TO SUCCEED IN BUSINESS AND LIFE
BY AVOIDING MY MISTAKES

1. **Don't take yourself too seriously. No one else does.** Don't ever act like a big-shot, the world loves humility. Never gloat. Big- shots create enemies, you don't need them.
2. **Schmooze people who can help you.** Be willing to approach important people and make a sincere pitch. Your success is a team effort, get important people on your team. To do so, you must add value to the Schmoozee.
3. **Never burn a bridge.** The person who hates you today is likely to be a good friend and supporter five years from now. Never overreact. Never burn a bridge. Forgive everyone, everything.
4. **Time heals almost everything.** Give time, time. Time is a great healer (but a lousy beautician).
5. **Never argue with a stranger.** Road rage is stupid. With strangers, always yield. Save your arguments for people you love. When someone insults you, do not insult them back. Say, "I am sorry you feel that way."
6. **Don't let success go to your head.** In a good economy, everything works. You are not invincible. There are things over which you have absolutely no control, especially the economy. Don't assume that "everything will work out."
7. **Don't ever go against your gut instincts.** Unless you agree with it, do not follow an expert's advice. Lawyers, engineers, architects, accountants, etc.
8. **Smile a lot.** It displays self-confidence, and everyone likes it. Learn how to smile. Always smile at strangers. Even if your smile looks forced, a forced smile is better than no smile. Teach yourself to smile. It is a great attribute, and it is free.

9. **Remember people's names.** Simply take the trouble to do so. Anybody can remember a face. A person's name is the world's sweetest sound to him.
10. **If you have five important things to do today, tackle the most difficult one first.**
11. **Dress like you are important.** If you want people to think you are important, you must dress as though you are.
12. **Know what you don't know.** Understand those things about which you don't have enough information.
13. **Whatever doesn't kill you, really does make you stronger.** Make peace with your past so it won't screw up the present. Don't dwell on a setback. When you foul up, don't take time to suck your thumb. Think about the failure, plan the solution and forget about the setback.
14. **Be on time.** Don't keep people waiting. It is easier than you think. Winston Churchill, the prime minister of England during World War II, was always ten minutes early for every meeting. You should do the same. It gives you time to organize your thoughts, it enhances your reputation, and it improves your self-image. And, it is a free way to help your brand.
15. **Always show enthusiasm.** People love to do business with people who are positive. To succeed, you must have pride and passion in what you do.
16. **My father always said, "Success takes guts, determination and kindness."** Some say "Work hard and be nice". Leadership is a privilege, not a right. You must earn it every day.
17. **Be willing to do things that others are unwilling to do.** You become a leader by helping other people, not by telling people what to do.
18. **Be self-reliant.** In any situation, be prepared and show up. No matter how you feel; get up, dress up and show up.
19. **Look people in the eye.** That is what successful people do. Avoid people who make you unhappy.
20. **Happiness can be a learned behavior**. Have a strong sense of love and belonging. All that truly matters in the end is that you loved. Believe you are worthy of happiness. Compassion makes you happier. Your happiness is most affected by your self-

image. Keep your self-esteem high. Always do the right thing, and be proud of it. Abraham Lincoln said, "Most people are as happy as they chose to be". No one is in charge of your happiness but yourself.

21. **When it comes to money, it is not what you make—it is what you keep.** Save something out of your next paycheck. Never spend your money before you have it. When you have money in the bank you are wise, you are handsome and you sing well, too.

22. **Don't hesitate to copy something that works.** In school, if you copy you are failed, in business you copy from someone successful and you succeed.

23. **You are lucky to live in the greatest country on earth.** Love and honor, it. Serving your country is the highest honor. You must stay informed about politics and vote in every single election. No exceptions.

24. **Don't let embarrassment keep you from straightening out a misunderstanding.** A friend from Monte Carlo used to say, "It is better to be red for a day than blue the rest of your life."

25. **Be curious, ask a zillion question.** The more questions you ask, the more you learn. You will have a reputation as a great conversationalist if you ask questions.

26. **If you are the boss, be willing to perform the lowest job of customer service.** Tony Vallone, Houston's premier restaurateur, will pick up your plate when you are through eating.

27. **Write at least 5 personal notes a week**. It shows you have class. It will help your self-image.

28. **If you're asked to do something that you don't want to do, say no fast.** Typically, you know instantly whether you want to do something, when asked, but you are reluctant to say no. The longer you wait to say no, the harder it is and the more explaining you have to do. A quick "no" is always received well.

29. **Practice your diction and grammar.** One mistake in diction or grammar with a new acquaintance will make his opinion of

you drop five points. Ask your friends to correct you when you say something wrong.
30. **Show genuine affection to your loved ones in public.** Your significant other will love it, and others will admire you for it. I have been married over 68 years and I frequently have my wife sit in my lap at receptions.
31. **Frame every so-called disaster with these words, "In five years will this matter?"**
32. **Motivation books work.** Read one at least once a year. You are never too old to be motivated.
33. **A change in your life is a good time to change a bad behavior.** A change in cities, a change in jobs, a change in colleges. Make a list of the improvements you want to make and start new in the new location.
34. **If you want something to happen, write it down.** The famous Chrysler executive, Lee Iacocca, said, "The discipline of writing something down is the first step towards making it happen."
35. **Do some exercise every day.** When you walk, walk swiftly. Not only will it help you to live until 90, instead of 70, but it will improve your self-image today. Get outside every day. Miracles are waiting everywhere.
36. **Believe in God.** Whether it is the God of Moses and Abraham, the God of John the Baptist or Spinoza's God, believe in Him. What do you have to lose? Research shows that belief in God makes you happier. And, it is okay to get angry with God. He can take it.
37. **Profanity is NEVER appropriate.** You might be used to hearing the "F" word, but most people are not, and it is not acceptable, ever. For people that are not used to it, it is a very offensive shock.
38. **Losing your temper is never acceptable under any circumstance**. Earlier I said road rage was stupid. Rage of any kind is stupid. Psychologist say that your IQ goes down 15% when you're angry. When angry, count to ten before you speak; if very angry count to 100.

39. **Meditation works and it's free.** Try it. It will make you more effective, more efficient and happier.
40. **Don't ever use an ultimatum.** It never works out well for you. This particularly applies to your spouse.
41. **Conflicts in marriage usually relate to money, in-laws or sex.** Couples who have similar spending patterns have fewer arguments. Avoid conflict. The level of difficulty in your marriage and how you cope with it will probably determine whether your marriage will survive. The idea that there is a perfect partner for you is delusional. Simply see life through your partner's eyes as well as your own. Sometimes you must agree to disagree.
42. **Except in spending money, live for today.** Burn the candles, use the nice sheets, wear the fancy lingerie, and always use the silver at meals. Don't save stuff for a special occasion. Today is special.
43. **Never regret for having eaten too little.** When I was 80, I bumped into my friend Dr. Michael DeBakey who was 99 ½. I asked him, "Michael, I am 80, you're 99 ½, how do I get from where I am to where you are?" He said, "Welcome, eat very little." At the inauguration of Governor Greg Abbott of Texas, Welcome and I met a 108-year-old veteran who lived in Austin. I asked him what his secret was and he said "eat one meal a day, and drink a lot of milk." You know what they say about women, you can never be too rich or too thin.
44. **Get a good night's sleep every single night.** Lack of sleep diminishes your ability to deal with stress. Get at least 7 hours sleep every night and try to average 8 hours sleep each day during a week. Do not take important phone calls or deal with big problems beginning two hours before bed time. Stop drinking alcohol at least an hour before bed time. Do not watch TV, your computer or your iPhone in the bedroom. The bedroom is for sleeping and sex. No late-night snacks. Finish eating at least three hours ahead of bed time. Pets have a different sleep cycle and can wake you up. Ban them from your bedroom. The National Sleep Foundation recommends that the thermostat should be 65 degrees Fahrenheit in your bedroom.

Begin dimming the lights around the house ahead of your bedtime to allow your body to produce melatonin, which makes you feel sleepy. Do these things and you will sleep like a baby. You may even wet the bed.

45. **Manage your time ruthlessly.** Focus on getting important things done. Have a sense of urgency.
46. **If you are nervous about something that you have to do, like making a speech, address it head on.** For the speech example, write out your entire speech including jokes and practice it 50 times. When I was 19 in college, a beautiful black headed girl invited me to the Sadie Hawkins Dance. I was a lousy dancer. But I accepted. I spent a miserable week worrying about me on the dance floor. When I got to the floor I was so nervous I was even worse than expected. On the other hand, if I had told her upfront that I was a lousy dancer, but a great kisser, the pressure would have been off and we would have had a great time. Address your fears head on.
47. **Don't let Nay-sayers slow you down.** Keep your eye on the ball and don't be distracted. There are always nay-sayers who create doubt. Arnold Schwarzenegger was in poverty in Austria as a teenager. All his peers said he could not possibly fulfill his dream of winning Mister Universe and becoming an American movie star. He refused to listen to them. Welcome Jr. introduced me to the Terminator in 2017. Their daughters were roommates at USC.
48. **There are other things you should do that are quicker to say:** Never lie to your doctor. When you have made your point, stop talking. Admit when you are wrong. Remember, all guns are load- ed. Give credit, take blame. When entrusted with a secret, keep it. Always keep your word. It is never too late for an apology. Don't litter. Don't ever ask a woman if she is pregnant.

The Values of the Greatest Generation:
a) Take Personal Responsibility for Your Life
b) Be Frugal
c) Be Humble

d) Love Loyally
e) Work hard
f) Embrace Challenge
g) Don't Make Life So Complicated.

Acknowledgements

Many people urged me to write this book, and many helped me do it. I would like to especially mention Mickey Herskowitz, who originally was going to be a co-author with me, but illness prevented him from continuing. Lindsay Scovil, student at the University of Houston, was of great assistance in editing. Lucy Chambers was also of great help in that regard. Chris Cookson was also in invaluable help.

I owe a special thanks to Joe Pratt, PhD, director of the Welcome Wilson Houston History Collaborative among many other roles at the University of Houston. Joe worked for months and made many important suggestions for the book, most of which were incorporated.

Lynn Morrow, an able attorney at Adams and Reese law firm, represented me.

I would also like to thank Courtney Stiles of my staff and Meredith Britt for transcribing the hours of dictation. My loyal assistant, Kathryn Curtice, was of great help in all aspects of the book, especially in selecting photographs.

Like all my achievements, I couldn't have done it without important partners.

www.ingramcontent.com/pod-product-compliance
Lightning Source LLC
Chambersburg PA
CBHW030610220526
45463CB00004B/1235